D0524204

I have had so many good teachers that to single out any of them seems ungrateful to the others. Still, two stand out. I dedicate this book to Mark Iutcovich of Edinboro University of Pennsylvania and Keystone University Research Corporation and to the late William H. Sewell, Sr. of the University of Wisconsin.

The Sociology of Education and Work

David B. Bills

Blackwell
Publishing

BLACKWELL PUBLISHING
350 Main Street, Malden, MA 02148-5020, USA
108 Cowley Road, Oxford OX4 1JF, UK
550 Swanston Street, Carlton, Victoria 3053, Australia

First published 2004 by Blackwell Publishing Ltd

Library of Congress Cataloging-in-Publication Data

Bills, David B., 1953–
    The sociology of education and work / David Bills.
        p.   cm.
    Includes bibliographical references and indexes.
        ISBN 0-631-22362-2 (hardback : alk. paper) – ISBN 0-631-22363-0
    (pbk. : alk. paper)
        1. Education–Social aspects–United States.   2. Work–Social aspects–
    United States.   3. Educational sociology–United States.   I. Title.

    LC191.4.B53 2004
    306.43–dc22

                                                            2003024828

A catalogue record for this title is available from the British Library.

Set in 10/12.5pt Sabon
by Graphicraft Limited, Hong Kong
Printed and bound in the United Kingdom
by MPG Books Ltd, Bodmin, Cornwall

The publisher's policy is to use permanent paper from mills that operate a sustainable
forestry policy, and which has been manufactured from pulp processed using acid-free
and elementary chlorine-free practices. Furthermore, the publisher ensures that the text
paper and cover board used have met acceptable environmental accreditation standards.

For further information on
Blackwell Publishing, visit our website:
http://www.blackwellpublishing.com

Contents

List of Tables, Figures, and Boxes

Tables

Figures

Boxes

Acknowledgments

Teaching a graduate course in the Summer at the University of Iowa requires that six students register for the course several weeks before the course is to begin. If fewer than six students register, the course is normally canceled. In the Summer of 2001, five students registered for a course that I had applied to teach. I would like to thank the anonymous sixth student for not registering, thus freeing up some dearly valued time to work on *The Sociology of Education and Work*.

I have been fortunate while writing this book to have two department chairs with the willingness and the skill to help me find ways to get it finished. Many thanks to my colleagues, friends, and sometimes bosses Chet Rzonca and Larry Bartlett for this great assistance.

I greatly appreciate the comments that I received, and, as important, the ongoing conversations about education and work that I have had, with my colleagues at The University of Iowa and elsewhere. They include Kevin Leicht, Dave Jepsen, Ernie Pascarella, Ken Brown, and Wonsup Chang. I owe a particular debt to colleagues who read all or part of this manuscript and who offered uniformly provocative and helpful comments. I offer many thanks for much good advice and no blame for the advice I failed to take full advantage of to David Brown, Claudia Buchmann, Bill Carbonaro, and Paul Kingston. I am also grateful for the assistance that Laura Lowe provided in constructing many of the tables and figures used in this book.

I have been fortunate to work with Susan Rabinowitz and Ken Provencher of Blackwell Publishing. I appreciate Susan's encouragement in helping me get this project off the ground and helping me focus on just what it was that I wanted to do, and Ken's sure, steady, and patient hand in seeing it through.

The motifs that appear on the first page of each chapter were designed by five remarkably talented students at the Senior High Alternative Center in

Iowa City, Iowa, under the guidance of their equally talented teacher, Hani Elkadi. I described to the students what I wanted to accomplish with each chapter, and was stunned with the creativity and insight with which they responded. They are Andrew Bennett, Kyle Bingham, Megan Bishop, Melissa Carlson, and Riley McCusker.

More than anything, I am deeply grateful for everything that I am provided by my wife Valerie and my three sons, Sam, Max, and Isaac. I cannot imagine being more blessed.

Education and Work: Establishing Some Terrain

The Ambiguous Relationships Between Education and Work

My goal in this book is to examine the relationship between two of the basic institutions in any society – education and work. I want to explore how the linkages between the vast number of social practices that we collectively call education (schooling, learning, training, and so on) on the one hand and those we refer to as work (the workplace, employment, labor, jobs) on the other have developed over time and what broad social trends are transforming them now. I also want to offer some empirically based, if speculative, projections about how these relationships are likely to develop in the future.

To characterize education and work as among a society's basic social *institutions* is to draw attention to their enduring and durable social characteristics. While there may be a sense in which every school building and every work setting is unique, I am more interested here in the features of schools and workplaces that transcend any particular setting. Richard Scott (1995, p. 33) has observed that institutions "consist of cognitive, normative, and regulative structures and activities that provide stability and meaning to social behavior." That is, schools and workplaces should be understood not only as places that educate students and elicit the productive behavior of workers, but also as social sites that help define the basic nature of a society and that provide a structure for how the members of that society live their lives.

Focusing on persistence and durability by no means, however, should be taken to mean that the relationships between education and work do not change greatly over time. This change can be abrupt, as with the GI Bill in the United States or the Cultural Revolution in China, or it may unfold only over the "long duree" of decades or centuries (Braudel 1992; Collins 2000). *How* schooling and work are related varies across time and space. Still, however tentative our knowledge sometimes may be about the relationship between education and work, we know enough to identify generalized patterns and processes with some confidence.

In this book I will discuss how the structures and activities in the realms of education and work are determined by social structure, and how they in turn help constitute that structure. I will ask, for example, how a society's broader beliefs and practices about the relationship between education and work influence (but never entirely determine) what that relationship will be, and how these relationships in turn affect such things as life chances, socioeconomic inequality, and personal development.

Institutions, as Scott and others understand them, often operate at fairly high levels of theoretical abstraction. While I will spend some time on that level, I am equally or more concerned with the level at which institutional life is actually experienced. The *institutions* of education and work are generally experienced in the *organizational* settings of schools and workplaces. Schooling and working in contemporary societies are for the most part activities carried out in organizations. This is not invariably true – think of home-schooling and telecommuting, and even these have their organizational dimensions – but educational and work *organizations* exert profound influences on the lives of virtually everyone.

Despite what many sociologists (functionalists and conflict theorists alike, as I will explain later) once thought, the relationships between school and work are far from seamless. Instead, they are often tense, ambiguous, and contradictory. Schools in the United States and elsewhere, for instance, value equality and the development of citizenship, norms that often clash with workplace norms of competition and hierarchy. At the same time, competitive and hierarchical schools may be in conflict with democratic and inclusive workplaces.

These inherently contested relationships raise issues that go to the heart of contemporary debates and concerns in American (or any) society. They quickly lead to difficult questions about such important and often conflicting social values as hierarchy, equality, privilege, merit, and fairness. By doing so, they speak to value-laden concerns of what constitutes a proper education, of who should control the educational system, of what constitutes a decent working life, and of what mutual obligations exist between educators and the world of work.

The answers to these questions are not obvious, nor is the simple fact of a linkage between education and work as clear as it may at first seem. Indeed, the strength of the connection between education and work currently found through much of the world would have at other times and seemed utterly confusing. Historian Barbara Finkelstein (1991, p. 464) raised the issue with exceptional clarity: "How has it come to pass that American politicians, academics, journalists, and labor leaders turn to schools to solve economic problems? What possible construction of thought about education and work could integrate economic problems and calls for school reform in this manner?" I will return to this theme repeatedly.

Education and Work: What Are We Talking About?

Both education and work cover enormously broad terrains. Researchers concerned with the workings of both schools and workplaces typically focus their attention on specific aspects of these two institutions. A given educational researcher, for instance, might confine her attention to elementary schools, or informal learning, or elite universities, or job training, or any number of other "parts" of the educational system. Likewise, a scholar of the workplace might concern himself with blue-collar workers, or occupational mobility, or marginalized workers, or other features of the experience of work. Those who examine the linkages between education and work need to make similar decisions of what to look at and what to defer for later.

Education and Work offers a chance to search for some of the breadth, hopefully without sacrificing too much of the detail and depth that is required for useful empirical research. In other words, offering this book as a synthesis and interpretation permits me the luxury of casting a broad net over "education and work." Thus, I adopt expansive (but not exhaustive) definitions of both education and work.

I take the "education" side of my title to encompass a broad array of activities and structures. These range from the socialization, instruction, and certification that occurs in elementary schools through high schools and postsecondary institutions, and then on through broader and less school-based avenues of "skill enhancement" as job training, adult education, and apprenticeships. That is, I will be considering learning that has been institutionalized in some form, but not necessarily in an institution that we ordinarily think of as a "school." As we will see, even this definition can become very fuzzy with the changing world of information technology and distance learning.

This understanding of what counts as education leaves out a great deal. Most importantly perhaps, it is not the same as "learning." People can and often do attend school without necessarily learning. Indeed, they can be credentialed, certified, and advanced to the next level of the educational system without demonstrable learning having taken place. I am, of course, interested in how much and what kind of learning takes places in educational settings, but also in the role played by education above and beyond that of passing on knowledge.

Similarly, people learn a great deal, including much of what they know that is pertinent to their work lives, from experiences that take place outside the boundaries of formal schooling or instruction. The foremost setting in which this takes place is the family, but peers, the media, religion, and neighborhoods, among others, are powerful teachers as well. This type of learning – some of it intentional and some of it incidental – is basic to any society, but is beyond the scope of what I can address here.

Many scholars make much of the distinction between education and training. By this, they typically mean that education is a long-term process of skill development, often with the claim that it also teaches people how to learn. Training, in contrast, is more short-term and tied to the demands of the here and now. The preference for one over the other is often based on its anticipated relationship to economic reward. That is, scholars favoring education point to its durability and transferability from one setting to another (Carnevale and Desrochers 1997), while supporters of training emphasize its more immediate value to mastering a specific skill or to meeting the needs of the rapidly changing workplace (Bishop 1998).

It may sometimes be useful to remember that education and training are different, but I do not insist on that distinction in this book and more often will avoid it. It may be clear to some that what goes on in second grade classrooms is education and what goes on in a contract training program is training, but there is a large gray area in between. The point at which general skills "morph" into specific skills is a hazy one, and my preference is to keep both education and training under the same broad umbrella.

Like education, "work" is an expansive concept. There is a rich and probing literature on the conceptual and empirical distinctions between such concepts as work versus labor, toil, employment, vocation, avocation, and calling (Bernstein 1997). Indeed, much of the legacy of the sociological tradition resides in this body of scholarship. Virtually all of classical sociology's founders, from Marx's stress on property relations to Durkheim's focus on the division of labor to Weber's delineation of the relationships between religious belief systems and economic enterprise, had an abiding interest in the world of work.

Many sociologists believe that the concept of "work" has grown too inclusive to let us understand the activities by which people gain their livelihood (Karlsson 1995). Some have sought ways to achieve greater precision in what should and should not count as work (Chajewski and Newman

1998). Precision is often a good thing, but for my purposes I am going to interpret the concept of work as broadly as I do that of education. Still, even such a wide concept as "work" needs some delimitations.

Most importantly, I consider only paid work, that is, activity that is done voluntarily in exchange for monetary remuneration. This definition follows longstanding sociological practice (e.g., Dubin 1965), albeit one that some (e.g., Daniels 1987) have criticized as too narrow. While reasonable enough, and certainly immense enough, this definition leaves out an enormous range of demanding, time-consuming, and economically productive activity. For instance, unpaid domestic labor is the primary activity of much of the world's population, and it is no great stretch to think of it as the world's most important productive activity. Likewise, voluntarism is fundamental to the maintenance of many social institutions and is a source of incalculable social benefit, but is beyond my scope here. Less positively, slavery and other systems of forced labor are historically of great importance, but are not the sort of "uncoerced exchange" on which I will focus.

Even with these delimitations, my definition of what counts as work takes in a vast range of human behavior (Terkel 1997). It includes self-employment, under-employment, work that brings its incumbent tens of millions of dollars in income every year and work that brings less than a formally sanctioned minimum wage, free agency and collective bargaining, work that demands a formal relationship to the educational system and work that is unconnected to the educational realm, and work that is regarded as dirty, demeaning, and despised and work that is seen as exalted, prestigious, and professional.

What do we mean by "skills"?

I need to say a few words about one additional concept before proceeding much further. There are few concepts in the social sciences that have been used as inconsistently as that of *skill* (Vallas 1990). Variations on this concept recur throughout this book, including worker skill, job skill, cognitive skill, non-cognitive skill, distributed skill, skill breadth versus skill depth, and more. "Skill" is a multidimensional and heterogenous concept. Being quiet, hitting a baseball, designing a circuit board, pouring coffee while maintaining a smile, and repairing organ damage are all skills, but share no obvious common denominator.

When social scientists wish to statistically examine the role of skills in the relationship between education and work, they need to define, operationalize, and measure skill in ways that permit it to be used in testing hypotheses, discarding some hypotheses as probably wrong and accepting others as provisionally right. The first step in this process is often the categorization of different kinds of skills. Dichotomous schemes are common – general versus specific skills, cognitive versus affective skills, basic versus advanced skills – but more elaborate categorizations are also available. Different research questions require different views of skills, and determining which of these many classificatory schemes is best is basically a function of how well it helps scholars answer these questions (see, among many others, Spenner 1983, 1985; Diprete 1988; Attewell 1987; Frenkel et al. 1999; Kerckhoff et al. 2001).

Sometimes I will speak of skills in this precise sense. More often, though, I will use skill in a broader sense (much as I will be using "education" and "work") to refer to a more encompassing if less precise idea. In the most inclusive sense, I will take skills to refer to any capacities to get things done. Some elaboration on this definition should help clarify what I mean.

First, "skill" is not the same thing as education. Treating one's level of schooling and one's level of skill as the same thing (or, in the language often used in the research literature, using schooling to "proxy" skill) is conventional in labor economics and common among sociologists (but see Handel 2000). Nonetheless, this practice cannot really be justified. Economists Ingram and Neumann (1999, p. 1) argue quite bluntly that "education per se does not measure skills adequately," while sociologist Alan Kerckhoff and his colleagues (2001) demonstrated that one's levels of skills and schooling are not only determined by different things, but also lead to different labor market outcomes (see also Carbonaro 2001). This point should become clearer throughout this book, but it needs to be established early that schooling and skills are related but distinct things.

Further, sometimes it is best to think of skills as characteristics of individuals, and other times to think of skills as characteristics of work tasks, jobs, or even of groups of workers. As Vallas (1990) observed, educational psychologists and human capital economists tend to see skills as something that workers have, while sociologists think about skills as inhering in jobs. A fuller understanding of skills would recognize that they are embedded in what Stinchcombe (1990) has called the "information processes" of organizations. Stinchcombe's (1990, p. 21) definition of skill deftly shows their multilayered nature:

> the capacity to routinize most of the activity that comes to a given work role in an uncertain environment . . . skill is a repertoire of routines which the workers can do accurately and fast, as well as a set of selection principles among routines, such that the complex of routines and selections among

them deals with most things that uncertainty brings to the worker. Thus, we will expect to find skill when a great many different things must be done to produce the product or service but when each of those things has to be done in several different ways depending on the situation.

This suggests that skills are elicited from specific workers or groups of workers in specific work settings. Certainly some individuals are more "skilled" than others, and some jobs demand more from their incumbents than do other jobs. Of most sociological interest, however, is how workers, jobs, and workplaces collaborate in the production, display, and rewarding of skills.

The Contested Nature of Sociological Concepts

Sociology, like any discipline, uses a set of foundational *concepts*. Phillips (1971, p. 47) sees concepts as the "building blocks" of sociological theory and research. He believes that concepts should be judged by how useful they are in helping us to understand important social processes. For Phillips, the value of a concept is largely determined by three criteria. These are clarity, scope, and systematic import. He notes that the clarity of a concept is often compromised when the term used to designate the concept is part of the lay vocabulary. This is true of many if not most sociological concepts. People may talk of coworkers as being "skilled," for example, without much worry about the precise empirical referents of what it means to be skilled. Sociologists lack that option.

By "scope," Phillips draws attention to the range of situations to which the concept applies. To continue the example, is "skill" the same thing in a software consulting firm as it is on a construction site, or on an athletic field? Can we talk about skills in the United States in the same way that we would talk about skills in Eastern Europe or South America? "Systematic import," then, is in large part a function of the clarity and scope of a concept. It refers to how successfully a concept can be used to develop propositions and theories.

To deepen their understanding of society, sociologists have to continuously rethink and recast core concepts. This has to be done carefully. Prematurely jettisoning concepts of long and proven standing can disrupt the cumulative nature of scientific research. Nonetheless, concepts need to be challenged. Indeed, many of the leading researchers in both education and work are calling for serious reappraisals of some of our bedrock concepts, such as occupational status (Hauser and Warren 2001), work (Tilly and Tilly 1998), learning (Resnick 1987), and occupation (Barley 1996). Quite simply, the conceptual apparatus used in the scholarship on education and work is generally sturdy and durable, but can never be taken for granted.

Thus, I make special efforts in this book to explain several core or foundational concepts that underlie the analysis. (A good example of this is my discussion of skills a few paragraphs ago.) I will frequently pause to offer a closer look at such concepts as meritocracy, credentialism, postindustrial society, technology, or occupation. All of these foundational concepts are in some measure socially constructed in that how they are conceptualized and measured determines in part what sociologists observe – what they see and what they don't see. Particularly because useful sociological understandings may differ from everyday ones, I will try to make as clear as possible things that are typically taken for granted.

Education, Work, and What Else?

Education and work are but two of many social institutions. At its best, "education and work" provides us with a lens to understand a host of interesting and pressing social phenomena. Taken too narrowly, though, it can leave other institutions out of the picture. Both schools and workplaces are influenced by and in turn influence other institutions – neighborhoods, legal structures, politics, culture, and many more.

A couple of examples can illustrate this point. Kerckhoff (2000, p. 454), in examining how young people make the transition from school to work, noted that this is not achieved in any socially isolated way, but rather involves many social actors. As he remarks, "the employment decision involves others besides the employer and the prospective worker. Not only family and friends, but also schools, labor unions, trade associations, and government agencies often provide access, evaluations and recommendations that assist in matching a worker's skills to the employers needs" (see also Rosenbaum and Jones 2000). For Kerckhoff, it is only by attending to the networks that link these various social institutions that we can understand the relationships between education and work.

We can also look outside of sociology for some insight. Geographer Meghan Cope (1998) cautions against ignoring the social context in which the relationships between education and work play out. Cope examined the experience of woolen mill workers in Lawrence, Massachusetts in the 1920s and 1930s. Her analysis documented the interdependence of the linkages between home and work and showed how these linkages influenced the social regulation of labor markets. That is, by understanding how these workers and their families conceived of the connections between their domestic lives and their economically productive lives, we can begin to see how "education" fits into these cultural and social patterns. Cope's work suggests that our current understandings of how education and work are related would have made little sense to people living in earlier eras, and that we need to think about historical and temporal *place* when we examine the relationship between education and work. How the education–work linkage "fits" with other institutions – how it is influenced by and in turn influences other institutional arrangements – is a critical part of the story.

Education and Work in the United States and Elsewhere

Most of the material on which I draw pertains to education and work in the United States. There are both benefits and costs to this strategy. On the one hand, it permits a focus on an already complex web of relationships, without being distracted by variations that arise from different cultures, histories, politics, and institutions. At the same time, it invites insularity and a temptation to view US practices as universal.

The fact is that US patterns are far from universal, and are not even particularly generalizable. The US educational system, and to a lesser degree the US "work" system, are not entirely unique among the world's societies, but are distinctive in some important ways. Still, the belief that the value of schooling lies primarily in its ability to help leverage the good life is not distinctly American, but is a belief that Americans share with most of the world. Further, while the specifics vary, every society uses education to allocate people into work roles.

This creates a real analytic and expository challenge. The evidence that school–work relationships vary greatly across the world's societies is compelling. Muller and Shavit (1998), in fact, see the cross-societal variations in this relationship as being far greater than any of the other relationships that characterize the "socioeconomic life cycle" (more on this in a later chapter). Many others have demonstrated cross-societal differences in how education and work are related (Kerckhoff 2000; Rosenbaum and Jones 2000). One cannot fully understand "the relationships between education and work" by studying only the United States (or even some small groups of nations), yet analyzing the full spectrum of the world's nations on all of the dimensions that I examine in this volume is impractical.

I search for a middle road as much as possible. Without making formal or systematic comparisons, I try at every opportunity to compare US practices and patterns with those elsewhere around the world. I do so more through a "naming" approach than a "variables" approach. That is, I am more likely to bring in illustrative materials from different nations to help develop an argument than I am to try to specify variables-based hypotheses that hold across societies. The latter tack of course is essential for theory and research on the relationship between education and work to advance, but seems unwieldy for this sort of book.

Education and Not-work

It is striking how much of the sociological literature fits under the tent of "education and work." More than once as I prepared this book it seemed as if sociologists could find virtually nothing else to write about. To a remarkable degree, societies organize themselves around school–work relationships, and this is reflected in the volume of attention that these arrangements attract not only from social scientists, but from those in the political and cultural realms as well.

But while the terrain of "education and work" is immense, it is a mistake to think of these two institutions solely in the context of the other. Both education and work are related to a greater or lesser extent to every other major social institution. We know, for instance, that more-educated people tend to be better integrated into their social environments, more likely to participate in cultural events, and are embedded in richer social networks. Schooling similarly enhances one's emotional and physical well-being and is positively related to one's family life, political participation, values, and use of leisure time.[1] I generally ignore these kinds of relationships here to avoid being distracted from the task at hand. Readers should remember, though, that learning that education is related to better dental hygiene, or more caring child-rearing, or more appreciation for theater, or more informed voting is of interest regardless of whether or not these things eventually lead to greater labor productivity.

Thus, while I hope this book proves to be of some practical use, I do not see it as a handbook for how to make education more relevant to the world of work. Enhancing this relevance is in many cases not even a particularly good idea, and my own preference (which I will try to keep distinct from my sociological judgment) is often to weaken the linkage between schools and workplaces. Studying ancient Greek literature is not a higher calling

---

1   In his article "The Effects of Schooling on Individual Lives," Pallas (2000) offers an invaluable review of this research.

than studying circuit board repair, but it is a different one. Analyzing the relationship between education and work and acknowledging its crucial location in society is not necessarily to endorse those arrangements as socially desirable ones.

Plan of the Book

After this introductory chapter, *The Sociology of Education and Work* proceeds as follows. In Chapter 2, I set the stage for the volume by asking "What *is* the relationship between schooling and socioeconomic success?" Clearly, unless this relationship can be shown to be a substantial one, there is little point in proceeding any further. This turns out to be a remarkably easy case to make – schooling and socioeconomic attainment are strongly related to one another. The extent to which this "social fact" is entrenched into American culture and social structure is a different question, and I spend some time in Chapter 2 discussing the "hold" that the relationship between education and work has in the United States.

Why this relationship should hold – why people with lots of schooling tend to have better jobs and make more money – is another question. In Chapter 3, I present two competing accounts of why educational attainment is associated with socioeconomic rewards. These are the Meritocracy model and the Credentialist model. These are broad umbrellas, and the adherents of each by no means agree on all of the specifics. Still, the contrasts between them are stark enough to illustrate the range of thinking about why schooling and work are so tightly enmeshed.

In Chapter 4, I use the model of the socioeconomic life cycle as a template to review evidence pertinent to the models of meritocracy and credentialism. My goal is not that of determining once and for all whether we can best characterize the United States as a meritocracy or a credential society. Such an adjudication seems unlikely and the question yields to no simple "either–or" answers. Rather, my goal is that of illustrating the range of ways in which scholars have attacked these questions, indicating along the way what questions are perhaps most worth asking in the future.

The Meritocracy and Credentialist models describe important features of a given society, but are perhaps less able to capture a broader understanding of social structure. In Chapter 5, I present the model of the Postindustrial Society. My goal here is to provide a means to understand the emerging social structure in which the relationship between school and work is embedded. Postindustrial theory emphasizes the centrality of "theoretical knowledge" as the United States (and other societies) continues its transformation out of the industrial era and into the "age of information." This model forces attention to such trends as the shift from goods to services and the changing nature of work.

The framework established in Chapters 2 to 5 provides a foundation for the book's later chapters. In Chapter 6, I describe the wide-ranging demographic changes that have characterized American society for the past few decades. I take as my point of departure the baby boom, the nearly two-decade surge in birth rates that transformed American society in ways that are in many cases only now becoming clear. Closely associated with the baby boom and the subsequent baby bust are three other demographic trends that continue to transform the education-work linkage. These are the aging of the American population, the ongoing trend towards cultural diversity, and the disruption in the normative American life course.

In Chapter 7, I examine recent transformations of American education and work and how these have affected the youth labor market. On the one hand, high school is both a place that competes (probably more than it once did) with the world of work for the commitments and time of teenagers. On the other hand, we can also think of the high school experience as comprising preparation for adult work. I describe in some detail the typically difficult transition from high school to work in the United States. I also discuss the often equally problematic transition from postsecondary education to work.

Chapter 8 discusses the possibilities of the "learning society." The idea that contemporary societies can only prosper by building institutions and structures that permit "lifelong learning" has attracted considerable global and national attention. I also use Chapter 8 to provide some historical and comparative perspective on "adult education." This is an area that has received surprisingly little attention from sociologists of education, but considerably more from historians (Kett 1994). This in turn leads to a careful look at worker training, one of the largest components of the education–work nexus.

Chapter 9 builds upon the analyses of the first eight chapters to pose a basic question about the emerging relationship between education and work. This is "Can the relationship between education and work tighten forever?" While both partly rhetorical and partly provocative, this question yields no simple or unambiguous answers. Like most good questions, it raises many new ones. I address these questions by asking how employers, job-seekers, and educational institutions are likely to respond to the social tensions and demands of a demographically and technologically transformed postindustrial era. My argument is that while the social impulses that have led to the ever-tightening linkages between schooling and work are unlikely to abate, the specific form of this linkage is going to look very different over the coming decades than it looks now.

When I was quite far along in writing this volume, I came across the following from Gosta Esping-Andersen's *Social Foundations of Post-industrial Economies* (1999, p. 184). "I therefore close this book inviting education experts to design a workable system of skilling entitlements, one that would befit an ideal post-industrial welfare regime." I think this exemplary sentiment could cut the other way as well, and that workplace experts could be invited to collaborate on designing a workable system of skilling entitlements that would befit an ideal system of open and inclusive education. Within some broad limits, we "get" the school–work relationships that we "want," but social goals have to be continuously informed by the sociological perspective. I turn to that task now.

2

Schooling and Socioeconomic Success: Establishing Their Relationship

Schooling and Socioeconomic Attainment

Americans expect many and often contradictory things from schools. They expect students to become cognitively, emotionally, and socially aware and mature adults who are prepared to make a living, establish a family, stay away from drugs, build a strong body, and succeed in higher education. They also expect schools to contribute to their communities, raise test scores, honor cultural sensibilities, and transmit a sense of *e pluribus unum*. Some of these goals are met through a formal curriculum of such broadly accepted subject matter as language and mathematics. Others are addressed less directly, but just as pervasively, through a "hidden curriculum" of everyday practices and structures that reflect unstated but still powerful norms and values (Jackson 1968).

None of these goals for and expectations of schools is more central than the belief that formal education is the path to socioeconomic success. Whatever the persistence of such deeply felt homilies as "education for education's sake," or "educating the whole child," the idea of schooling as an investment in the economic future is never far from the surface. Schools may be assigned different social and cultural roles at different times and places, but severing the linkage between schools and socioeconomic achievement is never a viable option.

We can illustrate this point with a few simple examples. The first involves the values and aspirations of America's entering class of college students. The second pertains to high-level, officially sanctioned endorsements of the economic purposes of education. The third refers to a range of cultural symbols and beliefs that illustrate the relationship between education and work.

The changing meaning of education for college freshmen

Every fall since 1966, Alexander Astin of the University of California at Los Angeles has surveyed the incoming freshman class throughout American colleges and universities (Astin 2000; also see Astin 1997). Among other things, Astin asks students what they want out of life – about their aspirations and goals beyond higher education. Because of the care and skill with which this survey is conducted, observers of American higher education have come to view Astin's findings as a trustworthy barometer of the state of mind of each new cohort of American college students.

Astin's survey for the academic year 2000/01 collected information from more than 250,000 students at 434 four-year colleges and universities. This survey allowed Astin to continue to chart trends, as he has for 35 years, in the attitudes and aspirations of college freshmen. Astin has found a student population that has grown more materialistic and with an increasingly instrumental view of schooling as the means to achieve that materialism. As a typical headline greeting Astin's most recent report read, "College Freshmen Rate Money as Chief Goal" (latimes.com Monday, January 22, 2001). Astin's findings indicate that if American students do not attend college only to enhance their ultimate earning power, that is certainly the chief reason that they go.

Box 2.1 shows Astin's findings from the Fall of 2000. To be fair, and despite the dramatic headlines describing greedy and acquisitive freshmen, their aspirations are more ambivalent and complex than commentators typically portray them to be. Students do, after all, rate "raising a family" (73.1 percent) about as highly as they rate "being very well off financially" (73.4 percent). Many are concerned with "helping others who are in difficulty (61.7 percent). Few, however, seem concerned with emerging in four years as active citizens or with developing artistic or expressive selves.

Most notable about the aspirations of college freshmen, though, is how they have changed over time. While never indifferent to the economic value of college, earlier generations of freshmen differed markedly in their willingness to endorse values of community, family, and personal development. In short, college freshmen increasingly see the linkage between education and work as the maximization of their prospects for social mobility.

Astin's findings are striking, but probably few people would consider them surprising. It is difficult (for reasons that will preoccupy much of my attention in this book) to understand why students would respond any differently, and certainly difficult to blame them for adopting such an instrumental approach to their education. After all, if everyone else is acquiring

Box 2.1   The values of America's entering-college class: Percentages of students who find these statements either "essential" or "very important"

Being very well off financially	73.4
Raising a family	73.1
Helping others who are in difficulty	61.7
Becoming an authority in my field	59.7
Obtain recognition from colleagues for contributions to my field	51.2
Integrating spirituality into my life	45.1
Developing a meaningful philosophy of life	42.4
Becoming successful in a business of my own	39.3
Influencing social values	37.6
Having administrative responsibility for the work of others	36.9
Helping to promote racial understanding	30.8
Keeping up to date with political affairs	28.1
Participating in a community action program	22.7
Influencing the political structure	17.6
Becoming involved in programs to clean up the environment	17.5
Making a theoretical contribution to science	16.0
Creating artistic work (painting, sculpture, decorating, etc.)	14.8
Writing original works (poems, novels, etc.)	14.7
Becoming accomplished in performing arts (acting, dancing, etc.)	14.5

Source: Astin (2000).

more schooling, one is in the position of also having to do so to maintain one's place in the "hiring queue" for good jobs. Schooling becomes the last line of defense against downward mobility as much as a basis for upward mobility (Thurow 1975).

A nation at risk (of tumbling down the economic ladder)

In 1983, the National Commission on Excellence in Education, created two years earlier by Secretary of Education Terrell H. Bell, presented its report, *A Nation at Risk: The Imperative for Educational Reform.* Bell gave the

Commission a broad charter, but there is little doubt that the preoccupations of both Bell and the Reagan Administration that instigated the effort were at bottom economic.

In language often as embarrassingly flowery as it was evocative, the Commission warned in its opening paragraph of the vulnerability of America's "once unchallenged preeminence in commerce, industry, science, and technological innovation" (p. 5). Despite occasional comments about the need for education to foster the "intellectual, moral, and spiritual strengths of our people" (p. 7), the tone of the report is almost reminiscent of the Cold War in its attention to international economic competition and the need for Americans to achieve a level and quality of schooling that will secure their mobility and prosperity in the workplace.

A Nation At Risk was in some ways a signal of a coming change in the institutional linkages between the US Department of Education and the US Department of Labor. While never entirely autonomous from the Department of Labor, the Department of Education became more reactive to (some might say subordinate to) the needs of labor (or, perhaps more accurately, management) as the 1980s progressed. Indeed, virtually every major piece of federal education legislation to appear since *A Nation At Risk* bears to some degree the imprint of the perceived needs of the workplace. While educational reform has perhaps always been to some degree responsive to the demands of the economy (Gaskell 1992), it is probably nowhere more apparent than in the educational policies of the Clinton Administration.

A Nation At Risk was a powerful, if empirically suspect, statement of a particular conception of how schools and work should be related to one another. It was, though, but one of many reports to bear a high-level imprimatur of legitimacy. Indeed, a mid-1980s assessment (Altbach et al. 1985) counted at least two dozen major reports. Some of these came from the federal or state level, while many more were the outcome of the efforts of private foundations. I will return to some of these later in this book, but highlight a couple of the most important here.

The reports with probably the most far-reaching impact were written by the Secretary's Commission on Achieving Necessary Skills (1991, 1992a, 1992b). Soon to be identified simply as SCANS, these reports provided a reasonably careful conceptual base for later federal and state initiatives for educational and training reform. If *A Nation at Risk* was the signal call to arms, the SCANS reports provided the ammunition.

The authors of the SCANS reports set themselves the goal of clarifying precisely what skills workers needed to succeed in the new economy, and how schools might go about teaching these. SCANS defined a "three-part foundations" of skills. These are basic skills (basically the three R's, which the report described as "reading, performing arithmetic and mathematical operations, listening, and speaking"), thinking skills (thinking creatively, making decisions, solving problems, visualizing, reasoning, and knowing how to learn), and personal qualities (e.g., taking responsibility, self-esteem, sociability, self-management, and integrity/honesty).

To these foundations skills, SCANS further defined five work competencies. These are:

1   the ability to identify, plan, and allocate such *resources* as time, money, materials, facilities, and human resources;
2   the ability to *work with others* as a team member, teacher, leader, negotiator; to negotiate agreements; to work with others from diverse backgrounds;
3   the ability to acquire, evaluate, organize, maintain, interpret, and use *information*, and to use computers to process information;
4   the ability to understand, monitor and correct, and improve *systems* and other complex inter-relationships; and
5   the ability to select, apply, and maintain a variety of *technologies*.

The authors of the reports were careful to point out that these skills and competencies are "generic." By this they mean that they are distinct from technical or "local" knowledge. The importance of this is that the inculcation of these skills cannot be left to employers, but rather devolves naturally to educational institutions. SCANS, no less than *A Nation at Risk*, was explicit about tightening the chain between schooling and the economy.

The SCANS conceptualization proved to be the foundation for much subsequent public debate about education and work. A particularly influential entry was *America's Choice: High Skills or Low Wages* (1990). Produced by The Commission on the Skills of the American Workforce, this report identified what it saw as a stark choice facing the United States (and, certainly by implication, other postindustrial nations). Put simply, the United States could choose between competing in international markets by, on the one hand, racing to the bottom position of low wages and an acceptance of a permanently lower standard of living, or, on the other, competing to provide the world's best products and services. The latter "high wage" option, which the Commission quite obviously preferred, was to rely on both restructured and more efficient workplaces, along with an investment in the "frontline" workers who would be staffing them. The Commission's most forceful recommendations involved a serious reappraisal and reorganization of education and training. Here again, education is straightforwardly advanced as the key to prosperity.

Yet another high-profile report was entitled *No One Left Behind: The Report of the Twentieth Century Fund Task Force on Retraining America's Workforce* (1996). Chaired by former New Jersey Governor Jim Florio and with a membership that included major figures throughout the public and private sectors, the task force continued the tradition of diagnosing America's economic problems as rooted in education. The report acknowledged low unemployment and inflation and high productivity, stock prices, and corporate profits, without attributing any of that to improved educational performance. It went on to point out that nonetheless, "these are not prosperous times for many American workers," and concluded that "improving living standards and relieving economic anxiety requires strengthening the education and training of Americans in the workforce as well as 'dislocated' workers who have lost jobs that will never return."

Even more than previous reports, *No One Left Behind* expanded the focus to lifelong learning. The authors targeted the less advantaged whom they believed had been left behind by economic growth, encouraged public–private partnerships to ameliorate their labor market disadvantages, and offered specific and generally sensible proposals for reform. The emphasis in this report on the less advantaged is welcome, and indeed, admirable. Still, the assumption that education *should* exist for economic purposes is never challenged. No less than earlier reports, the underlying assumption is basically "This is why we have an educational system."

The culmination, and perhaps the most direct statement of the American faith in the economic value of education, was a 1995 report produced by the Council of Economic Advisors and the US Department of Labor. Entitled *Educating America: An Investment for Our Future*, this document is virtually paradigmatic in its depiction of the proper role of education in a modern society. The report builds a powerful case, delineating not only the contribution of education to individual social mobility, but to the economic growth of nations as well.

These sorts of sentiments are not, of course, unique to the United States. Similar documents are available from probably every postindustrial nation on earth, and probably for those that are not postindustrial as well. One example can be offered from Great Britain. In 2001, The National Skills Task Force from the Secretary of State for Education and Employment released a report entitled *Opportunity and Skills in the Knowledge-Driven Economy*. The language of the report differs little from those we have been describing. The diagnosis is one in which prosperity depends on the widespread dissemination of high levels of skills, in which schooling and training systems need to be overhauled to meet these needs, and in which the linkage between education and work becomes ever tighter.

These statements of policy and preferences did not die quiet deaths, but were followed by considerable legislation aimed at strengthening and rationalizing the relationships between education and work. As a survey of state legislators about higher education (Ruppert 2001, p. 26) clearly showed, the faith of policy makers in the economic value of education is a strong one. The author of the report stated that, "When asked to identify their state's most important strategic needs and the role of higher education in addressing those needs, nearly all state legislators we interviewed framed their responses in terms of the state's economic development interests." Legislators saw this as involving both K–12 and higher education.

Perhaps the most important of these legislative initiatives was the *School to Work Opportunities Act* (STWOA) of 1994. Legislators intended this act to "include work experience, job training, workplace mentoring, and instruction in both general workplace competencies and all aspects of an industry" (Levine 1994, p. 34). In a like manner, the *New Workforce Investment Act* of 1998 reflects the tight correspondence between education and work. Pantazis (2000) describes this as "a major undertaking to streamline and improve public-sector employment and training services."

The policy expressed in such legislation as the School to Work Opportunities Act and the New Workforce Investment Act sends a powerful message about the role of schooling as a means to get ahead. Perhaps this is to be expected, since these laws were drafted at least in part with economic opportunity in mind. More broadly, though, the "schooling for success" perspective flows through all manner of federal policy initiatives. The passage of the GI Bill to provide World War II veterans with educational opportunities, the emphasis on education and training in President Lyndon Johnson's War on Poverty, and even the rejection of the "separate but equal" doctrine in Brown versus Board of Education are all based to some degree on the notion that schooling is the entrée to economic security. The direct recipients of this message may have been (in these examples) veterans, the poor, and children in segregated schools, but the purpose of education underlying these programs and decisions was more pervasive.

These are just a few of the many governmental and private foundation pronouncements on education and work, and there is little need to describe others in any detail (although I will return to some of them in later chapters). While the specific proposals and remedies may differ from one report to the next, the underlying rationale is the same. Drawing (as we will see) on a human capital model of economic behavior, all urge us to further rationalize and institutionalize the linkages between education and work. The point is not that these diagnoses are empirically wrong. Indeed, I will present considerable evidence below that the empirical case for education's relationship to socioeconomic success is quite strong, although not every-where and not always for the reasons given by the blue-ribbon panels. The point rather is to call attention to the assumption that education *should*, first and foremost, function as an engine of economic growth and personal social mobility.

The media, mass culture, and the public rhetoric of education and work

We can also think about America's faith in schooling as the key to a bet-ter life by looking at aspects of our cultural history. The cultural messages that Americans transmit and receive on a daily basis are certainly harder to quantify than legislative acts or federal dollars. Still, they again reinforce the sense that schooling is there primarily to advance one's economic pro-spects. We can demonstrate this with material from three of the great ex-emplars of American culture and education – Horace Mann, the McGuffey Readers, and Horatio Alger.

By virtually any account, Horace Mann is a towering figure in the history of American education, and indeed in American history more broadly. It may be too much to claim that Mann is single-handedly responsible for the Common School, but his influence on the course of American education – its mission as well as its structure – is undeniable.

Mann had an abiding interest in the proper relationship between educa-tion and work. Certainly there are risks in taking remarks from the early nineteenth century and wholesaling them into the early twenty-first. Still, Mann clearly saw the institutional interconnections. In his Twelfth Annual Report as Secretary of Massachusetts State Board of Education in 1848, he remarked, "for such a thing never did happen, and never can happen, as that an intelligent and practical body of men should be permanently poor." Elsewhere too, Mann articulated the connection between schooling and, if not a wealthy economic life, at least a secure one.

As culturally important as Mann were the McGuffey Readers. The Readers, inaugurated in the 1830s by Reverend William H. McGuffey, were central to the educational experience of thousands of American school children for decades. Between 1836 and 1850 alone, seven million copies of the McGuffey Readers were sold, even though the American population at the time was less than 23 million. The McGuffey Readers were unabashedly given to moralizing, story telling, and character building. The authors saw their mission as that of offering a vision of what the good society should be, and of the proper role of the individual in such as society.

Weiner (nd) has commented on how the Readers made the connection between education and the world of work: "There is another sense in which the Readers were practical. They taught the rules of capitalism – which were intimately linked to lessons about morality. Results of good and bad actions were usually material. Young scholars read: *Hugh Idle and Mr Toil, Consequences of Idleness, Advantages of Industry, The Miseries of Imprisonment, The Ambitious Youth, No Excellence Without Labor, Necessity of Education, The Good Reader.*"

Finally, the fiction of Horatio Alger stands as one of the major American cultural artifacts of the late nineteenth century. The son of a Unitarian church pastor, Alger published over 100 novels, equally concerned with social mobility and social uplift. Like Mann and McGuffey, Alger freely mixed morality with economic prosperity (if not wealth).

Alger's stories, featuring such characters as Ragged Dick and Frank Fowler, chronicled the theme of rags to riches through "hard work, education, a sponsor and maintenance of a high moral character." As this passage from *The Cash Boy* shows, schooling can yield a handsome economic return.

Frank opened the first book that came to hand – one of Irving's and read in a clear, unembarrassed voice about half a page.

"Very good indeed!" said Mr. Wharton. "You have been well taught. Where did you attend school?"

"Only in the town school, sir."

"You have, at any rate, made good use of your advantages."

"But will it do me any good, sir?" asked Frank. "People are not paid for reading, are they?"

"Not in general, but we will suppose the case of a person whose eyes are weak, and likely to be badly affected by evening use. Then suppose such a person could secure the services of a good, clear, distinct reader, don't you think he would be willing to pay something?"

"I suppose so. Do you know of any such person?" asked Frank.

"I am describing myself, Frank. A year since I strained my eyes very severely, and have never dared to use them much since by gaslight. Mrs. Bradley, my housekeeper, has read to me some, but she has other duties, and I don't think she enjoys it very much. Now, why shouldn't I get you to read to me in the evening when you are not otherwise employed?"

"I wish you would, Mr. Wharton," said Frank, eagerly. "I would do my best."

"I have no doubt of that, but there is another question – perhaps you might ask a higher salary than I could afford to pay."

"Would a dollar a week be too much?" asked Frank.

"I don't think I could complain of that," said Mr. Wharton, gravely. "Very well, I will engage you as my reader."

"Thank you, sir."

"But about the pay; I have made up my mind to pay you five dollars a week."

"Five dollars a week!" Frank repeated. "It is much more than my services will be worth sir."

"Let me judge of that, Frank."

"I don't know how to thank you, sir," said Frank, gratefully. "I never expected to be so rich. I shall have no trouble in paying for Grace's board and clothes now. When do you want me to begin reading to you?"

"You may as well begin to-night – that is, unless you have some other engagement."

Each of these three American benchmarks – Horace Mann, the McGuffey Readers, and Horatio Alger – anticipated much of what has become America's preoccupation with schooling as a route to prosperity. Each offered powerful visions of the proper role of education, which invariably spoke to its economic purposes. Like much of American culture, these messages are often accompanied by contradictory ones. Horace Mann's great concern was morality and democratic nation-building. The McGuffey Readers were more about character in the framework of Protestantism than they were about job training. Whatever Horatio Alger believed about preparation and perseverance, he believed as much in morality and pluck, always with a big role for luck. And for all three, the American Dream was more the province of boys than of girls, who were consistently assigned more domestic futures.

The point is not that American culture is consistent or unambiguous. (Mark Twain's devastating parodies of the Alger novels demonstrate this pretty clearly.) Americans are apparently quite able to believe both the American dream of schooling as the means to advance and the evidently opposite adage that "It's not what you know, it's who you know." The point, rather, is that the impulse of education as a means of social mobility has always been a part of American culture, an impulse that is by all accounts increasing even since the endorsement given it by Mann, McGuffey, and Alger.

Does the Myth of Schooling and Socioeconomic Success Hold?

If the idea that schooling is the key to the good economic life (at least, in these sources, for boys and cultural majorities) is an American cultural myth, this in itself does not make it wrong. Myths, after all, meet some sort of

Table 2.1   Labor force participation rate, 1999

	Less than high school diploma (%)	High school graduates, no degree (%)	Less than a Bachelor's degree (%)	College graduate (%)
Total	62.7	78.1	83.0	87.6
Men	74.4	86.6	89.4	93.0
Women	50.5	70.4	77.4	81.9
White	64.2	78.5	83.3	87.9
Black	55.1	76.5	82.9	88.6
Hispanic	67.0	79.0	84.0	85.0

Source: United States Census Bureau, Statistical Abstract of the United States, 2000.

social need, presumably rooted in some empirical reality. Before proceeding much further, we need to establish a few simple empirical facts about the relationship between education and work. The question is, quite simply, to what degree is education associated with socioeconomic success?

The answer turns out to be "quite a lot," and the evidence is convincing. Sociologists and economists have demonstrated for decades that educational attainment is consistently associated with occupational and economic status. Tables 2.1 to 2.5 present some evidence.

Two crucial things stand out in these tables. First, those with more schooling live better economic lives than do those with less schooling. The most basic indicator used by labor force analysts is the *civilian labor force participation rate* (Table 2.1). The Bureau of Labor Statistics (BLS) defines this as "the proportion of the civilian noninstitutional population that is in the labor force." This includes the unemployed, who are considered part of the labor force, but not non-working individuals who are not seeking work.

Clearly, labor force participation rates are closely related to educational attainment. Only a little more than three out of five individuals who have not completed high school are in the labor force. This number rises steadily as educational attainment rises, with nearly nine of ten college graduates participating in the labor force.

Similarly, as educational attainment goes up, unemployment rates unambiguously go down (Table 2.2). In 1999 (a generally good economic year), the failure to finish high school was associated with an unemployment rate of 7.7 percent. College graduates, in sharp contrast, were unemployed only 1.9 percent of the time. (Another way to think about this is that 49 of every 50 college graduates who wanted jobs were able to find them.)

Table 2.2 Unemployment rate, 1999

	Less than high school diploma (%)	High school graduates, no degree (%)	Less than a Bachelor's degree (%)	College graduate (%)
Total	7.7	4.0	3.1	1.9
Men	7.0	4.1	3.2	1.9
Women	8.8	3.9	3.0	1.9
White	7.0	3.4	2.8	1.7
Black	12.0	6.7	5.2	3.3
Hispanic	7.8	5.5	3.7	2.5

Source: United States Census Bureau, *Statistical Abstract of the United States, 2000*.

The relationships between education and unemployment merit a little more discussion. As I will discuss later, "undereducation" is a particular barrier to the employment chances of young workers. Osterman (1993) studied the barriers to working and holding a job during an economic boom period in the Boston area. He found that even after statistically controlling for a broad range of other factors, high school dropouts had less commitment and attachment to the labor force than did high school graduates. The simple lack of a high school diploma was a serious barrier to youths' prospects of getting out of poverty. Of course, this does not mean that providing high school dropouts with diplomas will suddenly provide adequate opportunities for them. It does mean that when jobs are scarce, the least educated have the least access to them.

National-level data show the same thing. A recent release from the Bureau of Labor Statistics (BLS) reported (2001) that:

> Between October 1999 and October 2000, slightly more than half a million youths dropped out of high school. Among these high school dropouts, more than two-thirds were in the labor force in October 2000. However, 28.1 percent of these young labor force participants were unemployed – a full 15 percentage points higher than the unemployment rate for recent high school graduates who were not enrolled in college.

The results for education and unemployment reported in Table 2.2 are from a *tight* labor market, that is, one in which jobs are relatively plentiful relative to job seekers. The disparities across educational levels tend to get even wider during cyclical downturns in the economy. This means that as unemployment rises, it hits the less educated the most. Using Dutch data, Van Ours and Ridder (1995) argued that this can result both from the lower likelihood that less-educated workers will be hired in a loose labor market (that is, one that favors employers) and from a higher likelihood that they will be laid off. The available evidence suggests that on balance, the less educated are more disadvantaged at the point of hire than at the point of layoff (at least in the 1980s recession; see Huang 2001). Either way, though, the lack of educational credentials stands as a serious barrier to job stability.

If higher levels of education buffer individuals from the risk of unemployment, they can also serve to buffer the economy more broadly from the harmful effects of extensive joblessness. Francesconi et al. (1999) have maintained that the educational composition of the labor force affects the overall level and behavior of unemployment rates. They illustrate this by noting how the educational composition of the American workforce has been upgraded over time. Even in the relatively brief period of 1971 to 1996 this educational upgrading was substantial. Francesconi et al. report BLS data that show that the share of high school dropouts in the labor force fell from 34.5 percent in 1971 to only 10.8 percent in 1996. At the same time, the share who had completed college doubled from 14.8 percent to 28.3 percent, while the share of the workforce with some college increased from 12.3 percent to 27.8 percent. Clearly, the American labor force was far more educated in 1996 than it was a quarter century earlier.

Why is this important? Francesconi et al. argue that because a greater share of American workers are now at educational levels that put them at lower risk of job loss, the overall rate of unemployment is considerably lower than it might otherwise be. They estimate this difference to be 2.5 percent, a substantial effect. One reason for this is that more educated workers are easier to train, making them less of a risk to employers during periods of economic bust. Francesconi et al. believe that the educational upgrading of the American workforce has permitted the United States to avoid the persistently higher unemployment rates that characterized most European nations during this time.

The relationship between education and socioeconomic success goes beyond whether or not people are working to the types of work they do and the rewards associated with that work. We look next at the question, "What are the occupational destinations of people with a given level of education?"

Once again, the broad trends are clear (Table 2.3). While high school dropouts make up about 11 percent of the male labor force, they comprise tiny fractions of managerial and professional (1.7 percent) and technical, sales, and administrative occupations (3.9 percent). They are far more likely

Table 2.3 Occupations, 2000

	Total employed	Managerial/ professional	Tech/sales/ admin	Service	Precision production	Operators/ fabricators	Farming/ forestry/fishing
Male total	58,770	18,641	11,124	4,782	11,581	10,693	1,949
Less than high school diploma (%)	11.0	1.7	3.9	17.1	16.1	22.5	32.1
High school graduate, no college (%)	31.5	11.7	26.8	37.6	46.4	50.9	37.1
Less than Bachelors degree (%)	26.1	19.9	34.8	32.5	30.4	21.4	19.9
College graduates (%)	31.4	66.7	34.5	12.8	7.1	5.1	10.9
White	50,125	16,451	9,493	3,558	10,295	8,551	1,776
Less than high school diploma (%)	11.0	1.7	3.9	16.8	16.3	23.6	31.6
High school graduate, no college (%)	31.1	11.8	26.9	35.7	47.0	50.9	36.6
Less than Bachelors degree (%)	25.8	20.0	34.2	33.8	29.9	20.6	20.3
College graduates (%)	32.1	66.4	35.0	13.8	6.9	5.0	11.5
Black	5,870	1,149	1,031	922	907	1,738	124
Less than high school diploma (%)	11.8	2.4	4.1	15.9	14.3	17.2	38.7
High school graduate, no college (%)	39.3	13.8	30.8	46.1	45.1	54.0	45.2
Less than Bachelors degree (%)	29.8	24.9	43.3	29.3	33.5	24.5	12.9
College graduates (%)	19.1	58.9	21.7	8.6	7.1	4.3	2.4
Female total	50,773	18,273	19,356	7,794	1,145	3,670	535
Less than high school diploma (%)	8.1	1.2	4.4	21.7	17.1	27.2	23.9
High school graduate, no college (%)	32.0	13.6	39.4	45.5	46.2	50.2	37.6
Less than Bachelors degree (%)	29.6	24.6	38.4	25.9	25.9	18.3	23.7
College graduates (%)	30.3	60.6	17.8	6.9	10.7	4.3	14.6

Table 2.3 (cont'd)

	Total employed	Managerial/ professional	Tech/sales/ admin	Service	Precision production	Operators/ fabricators	Farming/ forestry/fishing
White	41,700	15,571	16,202	5,726	918	2,780	503
Less than high school diploma (%)	7.5	1.2	4.3	21.0	16.6	27.7	22.9
High school graduate, no college (%)	32.2	14.0	40.7	45.5	47.8	50.5	38.2
Less than Bachelors degree (%)	29.4	24.5	37.6	26.4	25.4	17.6	24.3
College graduates (%)	30.9	60.3	17.5	7.2	10.1	4.2	14.7
Black	6,631	1,817	2,355	1,656	144	642	16
Less than high school diploma (%)	10.6	1.4	4.6	23.7	16.7	22.4	43.8
High school graduate, no college (%)	33.9	12.3	35.2	47.2	45.1	52.6	37.5
Less than Bachelors degree (%)	33.5	29.8	46.1	25.1	30.0	22.1	6.3
College graduates (%)	22.0	56.5	14.1	4.1	8.3	3.0	12.5

Source: Bureau of Labor Statistics.

to be found in operator and fabricator (22.5 percent) and farming, forestry, and fishing occupations (32.1 percent). The same general pattern holds for women who have not finished high school, except that they are also disproportionately found in service jobs.

The opposite pattern occurs for the college educated. Both male and female college graduates are very likely to end up as managers and professional workers, and unlikely to hold service or blue-collar jobs. For both men and women, those with terminal high school degrees or some education beyond high school but no postsecondary degree for the most part fall between these extremes.

A little thought will show that Table 2.3 hides as much as it reveals. Members of older generations, for example, are less likely to have completed high school than are younger generations. As another example, such categories as "service" are enormously heterogeneous. Nonetheless, Table 2.4 is perhaps the most telling. Earnings rise steadily and substantially with educational attainment. Workers at every level make considerably more money than do those at the previous level.

More educated workers also have more opportunity to further enhance their skills than do less educated workers (see Table 2.5). More educated workers are more likely to receive formal training than are less educated workers, and to receive more hours of it. The relationship of educational attainment with informal training is perhaps less direct, but this probably does not operate to the disadvantage of those with more schooling.

I noted above that the first important conclusion from Tables 2.1 to 2.5 was the clear overall relationship between education and socioeconomic success. The second thing that stands out in these tables is that the good life afforded by education is not equally accessible to everyone. For example, at all levels of education, African Americans and Hispanics are more likely to be unemployed than are Whites. The difference is especially great for African Americans. Further, women earn less than men at all levels of schooling. I will spend considerable time throughout this book discussing how race/ethnicity, gender, and other factors stratify the relationship between education and work. I merely point out here that everyone benefits from schooling, but some benefit more than others.

The figures in the tables seem straightforward enough, but a couple of things about them should be kept in mind. First, they pertain to people who have already achieved a given level of education. They might, for instance, compare African Americans and Whites who have completed college. Obviously, though, not everyone has the same likelihood of achieving a level of schooling that will provide them access to socioeconomic rewards. In particular, racial and ethnic minorities in the United States are less likely than

Table 2.4 Median annual earnings of full-time wage and salary workers 25 years and older, 2000 (US$)

	All races		White		Black		Hispanic	
	Men	Women	Men	Women	Men	Women	Men	Women
No high school diploma	24,279	16,330	27,611	17,819	21,499	15,396	20,225	14,555
High school graduate	32,098	21,970	34,839	22,469	27,408	20,609	25,291	19,923
Some college	37,245	26,456	39,817	27,136	31,961	25,209	31,446	24,236
Associate's degree	40,474	30,129	41,186	30,547	31,206	27,198	36,212	24,744
Bachelor's degree	51,005	36,340	51,884	36,909	40,805	34,692	41,467	31,996
Master's degree	61,776	45,345	61,904	45,914	52,308	41,780	50,410	43,718
Doctorate	76,858	56,345	80,697	59,010	55,700	41,593	60,690	55,425
Professional degree	96,275	56,726	100,000	59,098	67,449	39,371	60,432	56,666

Table 2.5 Received employer-provided training, 1995

	High school graduate (%)	Some college or less (%)	BA degree or more (%)
Employees receiving formal training	60.1	67.8	89.7
Hours of formal training per employee	10.9	14.3	16.1
Hours of informal training per employee	24.8	37.0	31.8

Source: Survey of Employer Provided Training.

are Whites to attain postsecondary degrees. This suggests a sort of "double disadvantage," in which some groups get less schooling than do other groups, and then get a lower payoff from the schooling they do get.

The second point is that these figures pertain either to years of schooling or the degrees that people earned. That is, they indicate the quantity of education, and not its quality or its type. More qualitative indicators of this sort would provide a more fine-grained portrayal of how education is related to work. Some college majors yield higher incomes than do others (Horn and Zahn 2001), and there are some (though small) effects of attending a "higher quality" college. The effects of the qualitative aspects of elementary and secondary schools (e.g., resources, curriculum, grades, and so on) are, if less clear, consequential as well. If what counts the most at the end of the day is years of schooling and degrees, there are many other features of schooling that lead to differential life chances as well.

Third, none of this statistical information suggests that the association between schooling and success is perfect. Education is neither a foolproof inoculation against economic hardship nor an ironclad guarantee of the good life. Nor is the lack of schooling an automatic consignment to low wages and dead-end work. Some highly educated individuals live lives of poverty, and some individuals with little formal education climb well up the socioeconomic ladder. Within any given level of socioeconomic reward (that is, prestigious occupations, rewarding work, high income), one will find individuals of all educational levels.

Mariani (1999) showed that in 1998, 15 percent of full-time workers over age 25 who lacked a Bachelors degree earned more than the median salary of college graduates. (Another way of seeing this is that half of college graduates earned less than 15 percent of non-college graduates.) Clearly, significant numbers of workers are able to achieve relative economic success without the benefit of advanced degrees.

But while not perfect, the empirical associations are high, persistent, and according to many accounts, increasing. Schooling may not guarantee its holder a bright socioeconomic future, but if one had to bet on a secure investment in one's future (which of course is precisely what people do all the time), investing in educational credentials is generally a sound policy.

How Do We Explain the Grip of the "School for Success" Model Among Americans: Schooling as Panacea

Americans' belief in the economic power of schooling is rooted deeply in their cultural and institutional history. It is unlikely, however, that Horace Mann would have forseen (let alone endorsed) the vast array of institutions, credentials, programs, degrees, bureaucracies, and regulations that has come to define American education. Nor would he have envisioned a postindustrial economy creating an insatiable demand for a skilled and certified labor force. It is time to look in more detail at the persistence of the "school for success" model.

Historian Henry Perkinson (1991) has argued that Americans typically look to the schools to solve all sorts of social problems. Americans' belief in the power of education to solve social problems is a strong one (Levin 1991, Tyack and Cuban 1995). It is not surprising that Americans look to education as a solution to the "problem" of economic mobility. In this sense, education is in Perkinson's terms, America's "Great Panacea."

Sociologist Jane Gaskell (1992, p. 16) has argued that the belief that the purpose of schooling is to prepare people for work "accounts for most of the funding that has gone into education since the Second World War." This implies an enormous faith in the ability of teachers, curricula, and educational administrators to solve labor market problems. Why, though, should this task be assigned to educators?

But if schooling as preparation for work has taken on the status of a "social given," and if hints of this relationship can be found in Mann, McGuffey, and Alger, the sheer weight of this belief has not always been as powerful as it is today. As historians have reminded us, the linkage between education and work that we now take for granted would never have occurred to Americans in the Colonial Era. How did this transformation of both ideology and practice come about?

Finkelstein (1991) has offered a penetrating treatment of this question. She begins by identifying three historical stages of "labor–learning relationships" in the United States. Finkelstein refers to these as "dreamers of an educated republic" (1790–1840), "architects of public education" (1840–70), and "schools as laboring communities" (roughly, post-1870).

For Finkelstein, the 1790 to 1840 period was characterized by diffuse and uncertain relationships between education and work. The major fault line in this period was between the traditional and still predominant rural setting in which most Americans lived and worked and the emerging but still secondary urban one. Finkelstein distinguished "a rural [pattern] in which schooling and work were disjointed, and an urban one where schooling penetrated the workplace, or alternatively the culture of the workplace resonated within the schools" (1991, p. 466).

Why should this have been the case? Finkelstein argues that in rural areas, neither farmers nor small business owners and crafts workers had any need to build either formal or informal linkages between school and work. As she states, "The skills of the classroom and of the farm were distinct. . . . The work environment and the school environment were distinct" (p. 468). Simply, the social relations of the school and the workplace were more attuned to one another in the industrial city than in the preindustrial countryside. Essentially, urbanization and industrialization brought tighter connections between schools and work.

Finkelstein is careful to recognize the ambiguous and contradictory nature of these broad social transitions. Even with the tighter linkage in urban areas, she points out that "The apparent resonance between schooling and work in these irregularly constituted environments in early nineteenth-century cities should not obscure the fact that group learning for children in cities and factory towns, like schooling for children in rural areas, did little to constitute or regulate relations between schooling and work" (1991, p. 471). In short, as late as 1840, education and work were still in many ways autonomous institutions operating on their own logics. Only later were these logics to become more enmeshed.

This leads Finkelstein to her second period, the "architects of public education" era of 1840 to 1870. In this period, the relationships between schooling and work became regularized and institutionalized as "broad coalitions of social reformers and community leaders throughout the United States reorganized the relationship of children to the workplace, and rearranged the networks of association within which children would, among other things, learn about labor" (1991, pp. 471–2). In large part a response to an enormous growth in immigration and the great influx of working class children into the schools, school and social reformers in both rural and urban areas strove to both bureaucratize and standardize schools.

All of this contributed to the "vocationalization" of public schooling in the United States. American schools gradually but inexorably were transformed into bureaucratic structures governed by norms and expectations consonant with those of the emerging urban industrial landscape. In short, Finkelstein provides an account of the ever-tightening relationship between education and work, which may not have been historically inevitable, but which once begun was driven by a powerful logic. While occasionally differing in the specifics, other historians concur that schools and work have grown closer over time (Hogan 1996).

The result of these historical trends is that Americans have come to see little alternative to the idea that schooling should lead to socioeconomic attainment. This cultural belief is not limited to some broadly defined public. With important exceptions, many social scientists accept the idea that education *should* lead to socioeconomic success as readily as do politicians and the public. A recent publication from the Brookings Institute, a respected and nominally bipartisan organization, carried the message that "The question is, What would be best for our children? This volume of essays seeks to restore the notion that public education should be an engine for social mobility, a concern that animated Brown v. Board of Education and the 1965 Elementary and Secondary Education Act." Social scientists, no less than the public, generally accept the claim that in a good society, a fundamental purpose of schooling should be to help people move up the socioeconomic ladder. It is probably fair to say that most people most of the time take the economic linkage between school and work for granted, as one that has always existed and to which there is no viable or even desirable social alternative.

Some Dissenting Views

There are some dissenting voices. While not doubting the empirical association between education and work (a level of doubt that would entail an extraordinary disregard of evidence), some sociologists have attacked the idea that society is best served by a close correspondence between these institutions. Among the most forceful of these is David Labaree (1997). Labaree has stated that "we need to back away from the whole idea that getting ahead should be the central goal of education" (1997, p. 1). Labaree has argued that schooling for individual upward mobility is but one of three defining goals of American education, and one that has only recently achieved prominence. For Labaree, throughout American history schools have also served the goals of democratic equality and social efficiency. That is, Americans have built schools not only to provide people with a means to compete more effectively for valued social positions, but also to prepare citizens to participate in their own governance and to train workers to contribute to the broader social purpose of economic productivity and growth.

Labaree sees this third "social mobility" goal as having the harmful consequence of recasting education from a public good to a private good, primarily for the benefit of educational consumers. By doing so, the public perspectives of citizens, taxpayers, the state, and even employers are, if not entirely edged out, at least undermined. The result, says Labaree, "has reshaped education into a commodity for the purposes of status attainment and has elevated the pursuit of credentials over the acquisition of knowledge" (1997, p. 39). Americans have become unable to talk about schooling without reference to its link to personal gain.

Another important sociological doubter is Randall Collins. In Chapter 3, I discuss his important book *The Credential Society: An Historical Sociology of Education and Stratification* (1979). Too often ignored about that volume, however, is its provocative final chapter – "The Politics of a Sinecure Society." Collins responds to what he sees as rampant credential inflation in American society (as Dore 1976a, 1976b and others have documented for other societies). Credential inflation means that the demands for educational credentials by employers when filling jobs has become radically out of correspondence with the skill needs of those jobs. For Collins, few job skills are learned in school, and most people have too much education for the jobs that they do. The result is an expensive and exclusionary system of occupational placement that teeters on the verge of collapse.

Collins's preferred solution for this is what he calls "credential abolitionism" (1979, p. 197). Such a policy would sever the linkages between education and work by "returning [schools] to a situation where they must support themselves by their own intrinsic products rather than by the currency value of their degrees" (p. 198). Collins observes that "Legally, this would mean abolishing compulsory school requirements and making formal education requirements for employment illegal." Such decredentialing would both "improve the level of culture within those schools that continue to exist, and . . . provide the opening wedge of a serious effort to overcome economic inequality" (p. 198). Collins concedes that this proposal has little chance to overcome "an expansion of current credentialism" (p. 203). Nonetheless, his perhaps-utopian proposal does at least help us question the inevitability of the school–work linkage.[1]

1 Labaree and Collins have offered probably the most sustained critiques of Americans' preoccupation with education for social mobility, but others also are critical of this relationship. Some of the most compelling of these are Hogan (1996); Katznelson and Weir (1985); Livingstone (1998); and Powell et al. (1985).

Where does all of this leave us? First, Americans believe that education and work are intimately related, and that this is how it should be. The first belief is staunchly supported by the evidence. Whether or not people *want* schooling and work to be closely enmeshed with each other (and this would be a welcomed debate), the fact is that they are. I will spend considerable time in the coming chapters analyzing the finer points of this relationship – the institutions, practices, regularities, and behaviors that make up the system of schooling and work.

The second belief – that this is how things ought to be – is up for grabs. The question remains, why do those with more schooling get better jobs and higher incomes? I turn to this question in the next chapter.

3

Two Models
of the
Relationships
Between
Education
and Work

Meritocrats and Credentialists

The relationship that we now take for granted between schooling and the world of work is not historically inevitable. The strength and persistence of this linkage has varied across time and across societies, and one can imagine alternatives to it. However, the relationship guides much of the behavior of individuals, institutions, and policy making in the United States. Americans attend school and send their children there largely because of the economic benefits they see emerging from this activity. They have constructed (if not exactly designed) an elaborate postsecondary system of educational institutions, encompassing informal community-based education, community colleges, job training, research universities, accreditation agencies, and unaccredited web-based instruction. Generations of social policy makers have assumed and acted as if the key to escaping poverty, achieving social mobility, and even enhancing international competitiveness is ever-expanding education. This assumption has not waned over successive presidential administrations.

My goal in this chapter is to dig deeper beneath the surface of these assumptions by asking why we would even expect schooling to be so intimately related to the world of work. What is it about schooling that causes those with more of it to hold better jobs and earn higher incomes than those with less? Why should more-schooled nations also be wealthier nations? It turns out that the answers to questions like these are far from self-evident.

Making some progress on answering these questions requires developing a set of concepts. I establish a framework for the rest of the book by presenting two competing models of the relationship between schools and work. These are the meritocracy model and the credentialist model. The meritocracy model holds that the associations between school and work developed for rational, socially productive, and beneficial reasons. It maintains that socioeconomic success goes to those who deserve it, rather than those who are privileged by having been born into the right class, gender, or race.

Credentialist theory, in contrast, sees the relationships between education and work as contributing to the reproduction of persistent social inequality and conflicts of economic and cultural interest. What is learned in school, in this model, bears little relationship with what is needed to perform a job. This perspective asserts that educational credentials operate as a means by which the "haves" can restrict access to privileged positions and higher incomes.

These two models are perhaps most easily understood at the level of individuals. That is, scholars typically ask how people with more or less schooling attain or fail to attain given levels of economic rewards. These are important questions. They direct attention to how schooling helps to sort people throughout a hierarchical structure of jobs, workplaces, and careers. In the end, however, they leave open questions about the social forces that underlie that hierarchical structure, or about the nature and origins of the hierarchy itself (Mare 2001).

The two models need to be understood not only as explanations for the behavior of individuals, but also on the level of societies, organizations, and institutions – as "structural" models. Meritocracy and credentialism operate not only at the micro-level of people and positions, but also serve as ways to understand how the social relations of the workplace (e.g., authority, hierarchy, and the division of labor) influence those of the educational enterprise (e.g., curriculum, pedagogy, and assessment), and how they are in turn influenced by the social organization of schooling. Moreover, they provide models for understanding the "organizational fields" of schooling and work (Scott 1995; Arum 2000), those often loosely related but intricately connected assemblages of schools, employers, government, and other social actors. Scott has characterized the organizational field as a "community of organizations." Both meritocracy and credentialism provide ways to think about the community of organizations of which education and work are a part.

Casting meritocracy and credentialism as social as well as individual models provides a strong perspective for thinking about the linkages between education and work. Moving to this sociological level reminds us that "education" is not simply something people "have," and that "work" is not just something that people do. Education and work are *institutions*. Scott (1995, p. 33) has said that "Institutions are transported by various carriers – cultures, structures, and routines – and they operate at multiple levels of jurisdiction." These cultures, structures, and routines are important parts of the stage on which is played out the relationship between education and work.

Nowhere in the world is there a pure model of either meritocracy or credentialism, just as there are no pure instances of democracy, capitalism, caste systems, socialism, or any other social arrangement. I present meritocracy and credentialism here as *ideal types*, not as empirical descriptions of the way things really are. In other words, I present ideal types of meritocracy and credentialism fully aware that they nowhere exist in anything like a pure form. Emphasizing their ideal, almost utopian, features should allow a clear distinction of what is at stake when one adopts one model or the other to help understand school and work.

The Meritocracy

Whether portrayed as a cultural myth, an empirical description, or a goal to be pursued, meritocracy is an important organizing principle of American society. At its simplest, it describes a society in which contributions and rewards are commensurate. In a meritocracy, individuals are rewarded, and systems are structured to permit this to occur, based on the merit they bring to bear to a given economic exchange. This means that such "traditional" bases of privilege as inheritance, property, connections, or a variety of inherited markers such as race, ethnicity, or gender are of little importance in the race for economic advantage.

The idea of meritocracy rests on some fundamental sociological concepts. Many of these grow out of the sociological tradition of *functionalism*. This theory, most closely associated in American sociology with Talcott Parsons (1967) and Robert Merton (1963), takes different forms, but most forms share the tenet that the way to understand social institutions is to examine the function that they fill in maintaining a society. Functionalists contend that each aspect of a society renders a positive contribution to that society's persistence and stability over time.

For the purposes of understanding how the functionalist theory might be applied to the relationship of education and work, the paradigmatic argument was offered some time ago by Kingsley Davis and Wilbert Moore (1945) in their article "Some principles of stratification."[1] Davis

---

1 Without following through all of the connections here, the gist of what became known as the Davis–Moore theory was almost completely anticipated much earlier in Pitirim Sorokin's *Social and Cultural Mobility* (1927).

and Moore argued that all societies are faced with seeing that activities that are functionally important to the maintenance of the social order are carried out. All societies need to find ways to ensure that the most important and difficult positions are filled by the most capable and skilled people. Such people will be scarce, so societies need to provide incentives to match skills and needs. Societies thus develop ways to provide both economic rewards and enhanced social status or prestige to those willing and able to develop their skills. The chief institution in which this takes place is the school.

This is hardly an overly complicated theory, and on first consideration may seem plausible and even elegant enough. Sociologists have over time grown wary of it, however, both because of its inattention to structural bases of inequality and its ultimately tautological nature (Gaskell 1992). That is, the theory identifies functionally important positions by their level of reward, which is presumably the outcome of their functional importance. By doing so, functionalism assumes what it needs to demonstrate. The theory is helpful, however, in directing attention to the degree to which rewards are based on the merit displayed by their recipients, or whether the basis for rewards lies elsewhere.

This leads to an important distinction between *ascription* and *achievement*. This can also be identified as the distinction between ascribed statuses and achieved statuses, and as the distinction between particularism and universalism. Ascribed statuses are those to which one is assigned at birth and which are essentially immutable through one's lifetime. People are born into given genders, residential areas, social class backgrounds, race and ethnic categories, and any number of other statuses. These are neither sought nor earned. In a meritocratic society, the allocation of rewards on the direct basis of an ascribed status is considered illegitimate. A social system in which rewards are based on ascription is said to be particularistic.

Achieved statuses, in contrast, are those that the individual has in some way earned. Within the framework being presented here, the crucial achieved statuses are education, occupation, and earnings, but there are many others. One's marital status, membership in voluntary organizations, and political affiliations are all achieved statuses. Societies that assign rewards based on achievement are considered universalistic.

As always, there are grey areas. In some cultures, for instance, age is considered to be a meritocratic marker of achievement and esteem. In others it signals an illegitimate basis of discrimination and bias, and is often even an illegal basis for the allocation of rewards. Good health, as another example, can be achieved through diet and exercise, or ascribed through an accidental combination of genes. An interesting analysis of social stratification in China by Li and Walder (2001) shows how political party membership does not reside easily in conceptualizations based on such simple pairings as ascription and achievement or particularism and universalism. They maintain (2001, p. 1375) that party membership "represents neither a quality given by birth nor an achievement-based indicator of ability."

Further, evidence that socioeconomic rewards are empirically associated with ascribed statuses is not in and of itself sufficient evidence for the failure of the meritocracy. One can imagine ascribed statuses being correlated with achieved statuses in ways that produce an association with rewards. Children of entrepreneurs, for example, are quite likely to become entrepreneurs themselves. Whether they do so because of the accident of birth (ascription) or because they have mastered values and skills important to entrepreneurial success (achievement) is an open empirical question.

Following through this line of thinking, we can conceptualize the realization of a meritocracy as the triumph (or at least prevalence) of achievement over ascription, or of universalism over particularism. Again, we are referring here to the ideal typical meritocracy, and have no illusions about ever actually seeing one in its pure form.

What counts as merit?

All of this seems quite simple and direct. It is not, and in fact several problems arise when one examines the meritocracy more closely. First, meritocracy has conflicting meanings, both for scholars who study the meritocracy and in the broader public perceptions of what counts as merit. Olneck and Crouse (1979) cited survey evidence that Americans tend to see meritocracy more as what people *do* than as the characteristics that people *have*. That is, people would rather see socioeconomic success go to "deserving" people who work hard, behave virtuously, and display talent, rather than to those with exceptional intelligence or "IQ" (more on IQ shortly). Olneck and Crouse add that there is a second understanding of meritocracy that does emphasize technical and cognitive ability, and that this may even reflect inherited or genetic traits. They observe that in the United States this understanding of merit tends to devolve to the scores that people achieve (or perhaps those that are ascribed to them) on various kinds of standardized tests (see also Lemann 2000).

A second difficulty with the concept of meritocracy is that it carries the risk of descending into tautology. That is, one can fall into the trap of identifying the meritorious as those who are the most handsomely rewarded. As we saw above, this was the underlying problem with the functionalist theory of stratification.

But the question remains, how are we to recognize "merit?" What counts as merit? The answer to this is far from clear. Even such promising candidates for merit as educational credentials and cognitive ability turn out on closer inspection to be ambiguous. Is Grade point Average (GPA), which would seem to be something that is earned, more meritocratic than Scholastic Aptitude Test (SAT) scores, which are in some measure assigned? Or is seniority on the job more or less meritocratic than the ratings that one receives from a work supervisor? Or what can we make of Petersen et al.'s (2001) casting of age as a measure of meritocracy in the workplace, when the explicit selection on age in the workplace is usually illegal?

Any discussion of the meritocracy must eventually deal with Michael Young's classic dystopian novel *The Rise of the Meritocracy* (1994 [1958]). Set in Britain in the year 2034, *The Rise of the Meritocracy* describes the unintended and eventually catastrophic consequences of a society based rigidly on the principle of merit. *The Rise of the Meritocracy* is a rare book in the sociological canon, a work of fiction that is almost routinely cited as an authoritative source by even the most rigorous and sophisticated empirical researchers. It is a classic in both the sense of its broad influence on how people think about meritocracy, and in the sense of being probably more often cited than read.

For Young, merit was "IQ + Effort." By this, Young meant that those who most deserved positions of responsibility and authority (not only positions of wealth and status, as the meritocracy has come to represent, at least in the United States) were not those who simply possessed innate ability. Rather, the meritorious were those who coupled this capacity with effort. Neither of these factors alone was sufficient to indicate merit. As Young (p. 84) said, "The lazy genius is not one."

The mere fact that Young wrote a highly effective, even brilliant, novel, does not of course entitle him to any monopoly on how the word meritocracy is to be applied. In fact, the gradual transformation of a cautionary novel into a broad program of empirical research has taken some unexpected turns. For one thing, Young was as concerned with who achieved high ranking positions of public service as he was with who made the highest incomes or who attained the best jobs in the private labor market. British traditions and understandings of meritocracy were from the beginning very different than American ones.

Processes of socioeconomic inequality are important to any society, and *The Rise of the Meritocracy* both devoted a great deal of attention to them and provided some concepts to help think about them. Unfortunately, though, Young's meritocracy of "IQ + effort" has too often been cast strictly as IQ. The effect of this has been a poorer understanding of meritocracy than we might have achieved had Young been taken more seriously.

The idea of conceptualizing and measuring something called an "Intelligence Quotient," or IQ, comes from various strands of psychology. The story of the development of IQ has been capably told from a variety of perspectives (Gould 1996), both as a tale of triumph and as one of failure. Recounting that history is more than I can do here, but the idea that the range of human intellectual and cognitive aptitude or ability can be captured with a single score is one that has a powerful grip on American culture. To a surprising degree, Americans have invested standardized test scores with the legitimacy of the meritocracy. Writer Nicholas Lemann (2000) believes that high IQs justify high incomes because America's elite have tacitly conspired to design a stratification system that permits this.

While Lemann's case may be overstated, there is little doubt that people with more cognitive ability than others do better in school, and ultimately are more likely to do better in the workplace (Brody 1997). Schools are places in which cognitive skills are developed, valued, and rewarded. The preoccupation of social scientists with the notion of IQ as an indicator of merit, however, is surprising, and it is not obvious why such a narrow understanding of IQ has come to be associated with merit. Robert Hauser and his colleagues (2000, p. 203) have offered a particularly insightful observation about this:

> It is not clear to us why the term *merit* should be identified so closely with mental ability as distinct from many other considerations and traits that improve the chances of social and economic success. Among these, for example, one might list ambition or drive, perseverance, responsibility, personal attractiveness, and physical or artistic skills or talents, along with access to favorable social and economic networks and resources. To be sure, cognitive functioning plays an important role in the occupational structure of complex societies, but it is surely not the only identifiable factor in achievement beyond the initial conditions of race, sex, and socioeconomic origin.

Hauser et al. go on to charge psychologists and economists with oversimplifying a complex array of skills and abilities when they limit their conceptions of them to a single indicator of IQ. Such a limitation indicates confusion between test scores per se and the underlying abilities that the scores presumably index, and Hauser et al. urge sociologists to do better. The point is that while Young could afford to make an important satirical and dramatic point by conceiving of a single measure of ability, empirical sociologists need to recognize the assortment of factors that collectively make up a meritocracy. We need to understand not only Young's idea of effort (which, with such important exceptions as Schuman et al. 1985, and DeLuca and Rosenbaum 2001 has been generally overlooked), but also a range of other cognitive, affective, and behavioral factors.

There is a pretty solid body of research in this area, and we do know quite a lot about how such factors as ambition, aspirations, and various forms of self-perceptions influence educational and economic achievements (Jencks et al. 1979; Olneck and Bills 1979). We are also developing more powerful ways of conceptualizing these factors. Economists Samuel Bowles and Herbert Gintis (2000), for instance, characterize the worker orientations and traits that employers are willing to reward as "incentive-enhancing preferences." For example, a worker with the ability to think ahead and plan for future contingencies is more valuable to an employer, but this is not something that would be readily detected with an IQ score. The point is not that mental ability is unimportant in the relationship between education and work, but rather that it makes little sense to conceptualize a meritocratic society solely in terms of a narrow understanding of mental ability.

But if mental ability (or IQ) is a flawed indicator of merit, what of educational attainment? Certainly this must be an achieved status. As Turner (1960) argued long ago in his classic discussion of how societies organize themselves around norms of success and mobility, schooling is a status that cannot be granted, but which must be taken by an aspirant's own efforts. Surely this counts as merit?

Again, though, the answer is not self-evident. Not everyone has the same access to educational opportunities. Structured social inequalities hamper the ability of less privileged members of society to either demonstrate or enhance their skills and talents through the educational system. Further, such theorists as Bourdieu (Bourdieu and Passeron 1974) maintain that the more privileged members of society, while having lost the ability to transfer their advantages across generations in any direct way, can now do so by securing access to schooling for their sons and daughters. Schooling, for Bourdieu, is thus a "strategy of reproduction" that works against the meritocratic principle. To the extent that schooling reflects social reproduction, is this really meritocratic?

Of course, educational attainment is not only a strategy of reproduction, just as mental ability is not solely a cultural invention. Both to some degree index merit. Both, however, do so in ways that can be ambiguous and problematic.

The meritocracy and human capital theory

While rarely using the language of the meritocracy, many economists have embraced its central ideas. In particular, the human capital school of economics, associated with the pioneering work of Gary Becker (1964) and

Jacob Mincer (1958, 1974, 1989), and ultimately with the mainstream of economists interested in labor, human resources, and wages, has insisted that schooling imparts the sorts of skills that employers value.

At its core, the human capital theory of the role of education in socio-economic achievement (by which human capital economists typically mean wages) is remarkably simple. Schooling provides marketable skills and abilities relevant to job performance. This makes the more-schooled more valuable to employers, thus raising their incomes and their opportunities for securing jobs (Becker, 1964; Mincer 1958, 1989; Schultz, 1962). Schooling-acquired skills are typically seen as "general," that is, transferable across employers, while "specific" skills are acquired in the workplace. In this view, employers act rationally by selecting on educational credentials (although this need not be the only hiring criteria) because schooling has prepared the more educated to be better workers. Similarly, job seekers (in their prior role as students) act rationally by investing in their own human capital.

"Human capital" need not be reducible to IQ or cognitive skills and ability. Even such mainstream human capital economists as Heckman and Rubenstein (2001) have acknowledged the importance of noncognitive skills. Still, the bulk of human capital research relies on generally simple measures of educational attainment to index human capital. To the human capital way of thinking, the meritorious are those with the most human capital, and educational institutions are one of the primary locations at which this is acquired. Claudia Goldin (1998b, p. 49) has succinctly argued this position.

> The progress of labor across the twentieth century is closely associated with educational advances. The virtual elimination of child labor, the rise of the female labor force, the increase in the ratio of women's to men's earnings, the narrowing of the gap between black and white incomes, the compression of the wage structure in general, and the evolution of various modern educational institutions can all be related to educational progress.

As with the functional theory of stratification, human capital theory is subject to the danger of tautology. That is, the attainment of high wages is often taken to indicate the presence of high rates of human capital. As both sociologists (Bills 2004) and economists (Blaug 1976) have observed, human capital theory often assumes away what it needs to demonstrate – that schooling provides or enhances the capacities and skills that make workers more productive.

The idea of "human" capital as something analogous to more traditional forms of capital merits a closer look. Despite some ambiguities, such paradigmatic concepts as physical, natural, and financial capital have relatively clear meanings. Physical capital (or produced assets) is typically taken to mean the machinery, tools, buildings and other resources that are brought to bear to produce goods and services and ultimately wealth. Natural capital refers to renewable and nonrenewable factors that are used in economic production, such as land, water, and minerals. Financial or monetary capital is comprised of a variety of paper and nonpaper forms of investments and purchases that are eventually converted into physical capital.

As clear as these examples may appear to be, they often become less so when one shifts toward the real world and away from the world of economic theory. Sociologist Fred Block (1990, p. 152), in an excellent discussion of "The problem of conceptualizing capital," concluded that "it is increasingly problematic to view capital as a thing that can be accurately measured in dollar terms." Analyzing Block's reasoning would take us far afield here, but the problems with conceptualizing and measuring human capital are at least as great, and probably greater, than is the case for these forms of capital.

The ideas that individuals can invest in themselves in ways that resemble investments in physical capital, and that they therefore carry around with them a "stock" of human capital, are not entirely self-evident. In fact, the core concept of human capital theory – human capital – is plagued with the basic measurement problem of determining what exactly it is, and how one knows when it has been observed. Human capital has been proxied – that is, its presence has been inferred – in two ways. First, analysts often estimate human capital with indicators that are thought to enhance it. These include such activities as education, work experience, health care, nutrition, or training. Others infer the level of human capital from its presumed outcomes, most commonly wages. The fact is that human capital is very rarely actually measured directly.

Human capital theorists have to their credit been assiduous about responding to such criticisms, leading to both efforts at better measurement and to more realistic variations on human capital theory. These include theories of screening, signaling, and filtering (Bills 2004). The point for now is that in its basic logic, a meritocratic society would be one in which human capital theory provided a pretty complete explanation of processes of status attainment and socioeconomic mobility.

Is the meritocracy a utopia or a dystopia?

Advocates of both liberal and conservative social policies have appealed to the ideal of the meritocracy (Breen and Goldthorpe 2001). While political motives and platforms may vary, social critics and social engineers of all stripes typically portray the meritocracy as a desired, rational, and progressive state of affairs.

Of course, in its ideal typical form the meritocratic society is relentlessly fair and efficient. It is not difficult to build a case that those who make the most contributions should reap the most substantial rewards. The norm of a correspondence between ability and effort, fair play, and just reward is a potent one.

Still, as both the fiction of Michael Young and volumes of social research and commentary show, the efficiency and rationality brought about by meritocracy can mask some of its other characteristics. In an unrestrained meritocracy, the ability to rise as far as one's abilities allow can only be matched by the ability to fall as far as one's lack of ambition or talent might merit. A meritocracy might bring great reward, but at the cost of social harshness and rampant competitiveness. No one should expect a meritocratic society to be an egalitarian one.

None of this means that we should launch a full-scale retreat from the meritocracy. If a pure meritocracy is unacceptable in its relentless striving and competition, the pure form of an alternative is inherited privilege and blocked life chances. Moreover, increasing merit competition brings with it decreasing non-merit competition, attenuating many of the more blatant forms of social inequality (Lerman 1997). In some ways an unintended counterpart to Young's dystopian meritocracy is Kurt Vonnegut's (1961) dystopian anti-meritocracy. In his short story *Harrison Bergeron*, Vonnegut describes a society in which merit – creativity, effort, skill – is as aggressively abolished as it is rewarded in Young's future society. The social consequences are no less self-defeating.

Credentialism

> "Why, anybody can have a brain. That's a very mediocre commodity. Every pusillanimous creature that crawls on the Earth or slinks through slimy seas has a brain. Back where I come from, we have universities, seats of great learning, where men go to become great thinkers. And when they come out, they think deep thoughts and with no more brains than you have. But they have one thing you haven't got: a diploma." (*The Wizard of Oz* (1939))

Credentialism offers a very different vision of the association between education and work. Just as there are many versions of meritocracy, there is no single credentialist thesis. In fact, those who adopt the language of credentialism often differ sharply from each other. At bottom, credentialism holds that educational credentials, which are virtually incontrovertible markers of merit in the meritocracy model, are little more than arbitrary and exclusionary means of preserving socioeconomic advantage across generations and socioeconomic groups.

Probably the two most well-known sociological statements on credentialism are Ivar Berg's *Education and Jobs: The Great Training Robbery* (1971) and Randall Collins' *The Credential Society: An Historical Sociology of Education and Stratification* (1979). Neither is in any sense the last word on credentialism, but each has had a deep influence on how sociologists conceive of the role of educational credentials in labor markets.

Berg's *Education and Jobs* appeared at a time in which there was little doubt about the policy role of education and training as a solution to poverty and labor market marginalization. The "War on Poverty" of the Lyndon Johnson administration seemed almost self-consciously modeled on the proverb "Give a man a fish and you feed him for a day. Teach a man how to fish and you feed him for a lifetime." Less proverbially if more academically, Berg inserted his volume into a scholarly and policy community almost completely dominated by a human capital approach to labor market processes.

Berg's critique was sometimes as polemical and provocative as it was detached and scholarly. It did though provide a powerful corrective to the idea that ever-increasing amounts of education and training were the key to either economic growth and prosperity on the one hand, or to escaping poverty among the "unemployable" on the other. Berg argued that the American labor market was characterized by excessive and unreflective preoccupation with educational credentials. He saw the relevance of these credentials to work performance as dubious at best, and at worst, a hoax perpetrated by the educational elite on the less-educated. For Berg, employers' decisions to use educational credentials as selection devices had no basis in any evidence that these credentials were associated in any meaningful way with actual skill demands, worker productivity, turnover, or anything else. Economists and sociologists were as guilty as employers in their failure to examine the contribution of schooling to productivity.

In his influential *The Credential Society: An Historical Sociology of Education and Stratification* (1979), Collins used the concept of credentialism to explain the role of formal schooling in the system of social stratification of contemporary societies (see also Collins, 1971, 1974). Collins claimed that "education is an artificial device for monopolizing access to lucrative occupations" (1979, p. 9). He added that "the demands of any occupational position are not fixed, but represent whatever behavior is settled upon in bargaining between the persons who fill positions and those who attempt to control them" (p. 27). While for Berg credentialism grew out of employer and societal inattention to rationality, for Collins power and access to elite positions were at the forefront. For both, there was no reason to believe that schools taught skills that had much to do with how well or how poorly workers performed on the job.

Key to Collins' analysis is his focus on the history of ethnic and cultural conflict, rooted in turn of the twentieth century immigration. This aspect of Collins' theory is often overlooked, and D.K. Brown (1995) in particular has challenged the empirical adequacy of his account of ethnicity. Still, Collins' emphasis on ethnic conflict is crucial in that it provides him with a non-technocratic causal mechanism for rising educational requirements beyond the broader and more empirically elusive "education craze" that drives Berg's model.

Collins is highly critical of what he characterizes as the "myth of technocracy." He sees little linkage between the form and content of school-acquired skills, productivity, and the demands of the workplace. Thus, for Collins (as for Berg), schooling no more indicates merit than does the accident of racial, ethnic, or social class origins.

What are credentials?

Before we assess the credentialist position in greater depth, it may be worth-while to spend some time on more descriptive matters. If we need to ask what exactly it is that we mean by merit, we need to do the same with credentials. As is commonly the case, the answer is not as direct as it may first appear. What do we talk about when we talk about credentials?

At least in the United States, the credentialist thesis is most commonly applied to postsecondary education. This is because in a society in which high school completion is nearly universal, educational distinctions below the postsecondary level do little to differentiate the productive capabilities of individuals (whether or not these capabilities were actually acquired in school). The American system of postsecondary credentials is, however, a complicated and elaborate one. Unlike the case in much of the world, there is no central national bureaucracy (i.e., a Ministry of Education) governing American postsecondary education. One consequence of this is that post-secondary credentials in the United States often have ambiguous meanings.

One implication of this is that the *degrees* granted by postsecondary institutions take on a bewildering range of forms. The basic distinctions are not difficult. One is a hierarchy running from Associate, Bachelors, Masters, through Doctoral and Professional. The other distinction is between academic and vocational degrees. These distinctions often overlap. For example,

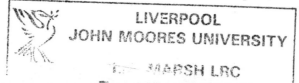

75 percent of Associates degrees are vocational (Leigh and Gill 1997). Partly because of the lack of a central authority or a unified system of accreditation, the content of degrees – what learning is signified – can vary widely (Kerckhoff and Bell 1998; Carnevale and Desrochers 2001).

In part as a response to the fact that the "same" degree can signify very different things, American postsecondary institutions are subject to an elaborate but generally loose system of *accreditation*. Under this system, both regional and national level professional educational associations evaluate institutions and programs using criteria meant to insure basic levels of quality. According to its proponents, the purpose of accreditation is to provide non-governmental and peer evaluation. From 1974 to 1993, The Council on Postsecondary Accreditation (COPA) existed as a non-governmental agency whose function was to coordinate the work of various accreditation agencies. This function was filled from 1993 to 1997 by The Commission on Recognition of Postsecondary Accreditation (CORPA). Currently, the Council on Higher Education Accreditation (CHEA) fulfills the role of a private, nongovernmental agency that carries out the recognition function.

In contrast to accreditation, *certification* is an occupational designation. It provides a means by which a governmental or non-governmental body can confirm that an individual possesses the skill or knowledge required in a given occupation. Unlike licensing, which I describe below, certification is not always required in order for an individual to practice a specific occupation. (This distinction is sometimes unclear in practice.) There are two broad types of occupational certification: those granted by organizations or professional associations and those granted by industry or product-related certifications.

Finally, *licensing* is the most restrictive form of occupational or professional regulation. Non-licensed individuals are not permitted to practice in professions designated by the state as subject to "right-to-practice" regulations (Bradley 1995). The Council on Licensure, Enforcement and Regulation (CLEAR) is the umbrella organization for issues of occupational and professional licensure. The massive *Professional and Occupational Licensing Directory* (Bianco et al. 1996) contains detailed information describing issues pertaining to licensing, certification, and registration.

All of this seems straightforward, if complex, enough, but in fact this system of postsecondary credentials is in considerable flux. Policy analyst Clifford Adelman (2000) of the US Department of Education has described what he sees as a vast new emerging system of credentialing in the technology and telecommunications industries throughout the 1990s. This is a global system centered around students rather than around institutions. In this system, both corporate vendors and industry or professional associations offer certifications of competence. Adelman claimed that over 300 of these certifications had been earned by over 1.6 million people as of 2000. He sees this emerging system as, if not a direct threat to current arrangements, at least a potent alternative to them.

Lowe (2000) provides a tentative but intriguing illustration of the sorts of institutional realignments that Adelman is talking about. Lowe is concerned with what he sees as a growth in the demand for school-level international examinations and credentials. He notes that it is still unclear whether these represent merely more credential inflation, of if they signify a qualitative shift in the relationship between education and the economy.

Lowe defines international examinations as "those that originate in and are recognised for access to university or the labour market in countries outside that in which they are taken" (p. 363). While his analysis is admittedly speculative, Lowe hypothesizes that there is a growing convergence of cultural identity among the elites of different nations, partly because of common educational experiences as certified by these international credentials.

Credentials and the organization of labor markets: Credentialism as credential inflation and as sheepskin effects

One difficulty in getting a grasp on the credentialist thesis is that it can refer to two very different processes that may or may not be directly related. For some, credentialism describes *credential inflation*. This position, favored by Berg, describes a system of job assignment in which employers demand more and more education for the same work. As evidence, analysts point to a rate of expansion in educational enrollments that is much more rapid than technologically induced growth in the demand for skills. As the Red Queen said to Alice, "It takes all the running you can do, to keep in the same place. If you want to get somewhere else, you must run at least twice as fast as that."

Batenberg and Witte (2001) provide an example of the idea of credentialism as credential inflation. They maintain that the idea of a general skill shortage in the labor market is mistaken, and that in fact many workers are underemployed, that is, they have more schooling than they need to effectively perform their jobs (see also Livingstone 1998). Batenberg and Witte claim that it is well-established in US and Canadian labor markets that the true shortage is one of good jobs, rather than one of worker skills. Using data from the Netherlands, they conclude that for the period 1977 to 1995, "the average skill increase involved appears to have been exceeded by rapid increases in the educational level of the workforce" (p. 79).

Batenberg and Witte's analysis is often, by their own admission, provisional, and beset by several problems of measurement that often accompany longitudinal research.[2] Still, they claim to see substantial credential inflation in the Dutch labor market. They also, however, see quite a lot of overemployment, in which people presumably have too little education for the jobs they hold. While they do not develop the point in depth, this does indicate that economies can and do experience skill shortages and skill surpluses at the same time. Credential inflation may well operate in some sectors and not in others.

A second way to think about credentialism is as "sheepskin effects."[3] Park (1999, p. 238) articulates this position quite clearly: "Sheepskin effects are usually defined as disproportionately large increases in returns to schooling after the completion of certain years that usually entail a degree." In other words, people are economically rewarded simply for holding a given degree. (One could as easily say that they are economically penalized for not completing a degree.) The difference in earnings between, for example, someone with four years of postsecondary education but no degree and someone with the degree (the sheepskin) is in effect the "rent" one collects for being credentialed.

Until fairly recently, it was difficult to empirically test for sheepskin effects because few data sets had information on both years of schooling and degrees. Such data are now more available, and several analysts have reported empirical support for these effects (e.g., Belman and Heywood 1991; Hungerford and Solon 1987; Park 1999; Ferrer and Riddell 2000). The best evidence at this point indicates that there are nonlinear patterns in the returns to schooling that can justifiably be interpreted as credentialism.

Once again, though, the resolution of the issue is not that simple. Both of these understandings of credentialism – credential inflation and sheepskin effects – pose strong challenges to human capital theory. Neither, however, necessarily discredits the theory. College graduates may really be different from those who finished four years but failed to earn a degree. They may,

---

2 For instance, they recognize the difficulties in both subjective (i.e., self-assessed) and objective (i.e., some ratio between one's schooling and the demands of one's job) measures of underemployment.

3 The term "sheepskin" refers to the fact that diplomas were once printed on parchment made from actual sheepskin. Sloane (2002) traces this practice to second century Asia, while the Online Etymology Dictionary (http://www.etymonline.com) locates the first use of the term in this context to only 1804. The persistence of the sheepskin has recently led to some protests from students and faculty concerned with the well-being of animals. This took place at Amherst College at about the same time that students at Georgia State University were protesting the university's decision to switch from sheepskin to laser-printed diplomas.

for instance, be more persistent, or more goal-oriented, or more ambitious. If this is the case, employers may be acting wisely by rewarding degrees. As Ferrer and Riddell (2000) note, we need more fine-grained data to make these judgments.

Overeducation

Both the inflationist and the sheepskin accounts lead to the idea of *over-education*, at once one of the most curious and most enduring concepts used by scholars of the relationships between schooling and work. There are different terms for overeducation that are (at least to the uninitiated) more or less synonomous. From one side of the equation, we hear of *overquali-fication*, *surplus education*, or *educational mismatch* (but rarely, strangely enough, *overskilled*). From the other side, scholars often speak of *underutil-ization*. From either side, overeducation has proven to be a remarkably expansive concept.

The idea behind overeducation is that some workers, usually con-sidered to be a growing number, have more education than is "needed" for the jobs they hold (Duncan and Hoffman 1981; Rumberger 1981, 1987; Halaby 1994). Determining the criteria for how much education is "needed" is far from self-evident, and there is no uniform definition about what counts as overeducation. Some see overeducation subjectively, as workers' own assessments of the adequacy of their educational backgrounds for the demands of the jobs they hold. Those who see their own credentials as significantly higher than those needed to either secure or perform a job are held to be overeducated. Others measure overeducation more in terms of the objective characteristics of jobs. One might, for example, com-pare the educational level of a given worker to the educational level of the typical worker in that occupation or to some "job-level requirements" of the occupation. In objective conceptualizations, workers who are sig-nificantly more highly educated than other workers in the same occupa-tional category (regardless of their self-assessments) are considered to be overeducated (Groot and van den Brink 2000; Hartog 2000; Green et al. 1999).

If workers can be overeducated on any of these measures, they can as easily be undereducated. Indeed, undereducation has received considerable attention, if less than overeducation. This imbalance in research commit-ment in itself is curious, given the broad preoccupation with the supposedly inadequate skill level of the workforce and the search for a "learning solu-tion" to the difficulties that such deficiencies presumably produce.

Any conceptualization of overeducation has shortcomings (Groot and van den Brink 2000). For instance, workers may or may not provide accurate assessments of how their own skill levels "fit in" across a broad array of jobs and employers. Further, the standard to assess whether a particular worker is significantly more or less highly educated than the typical worker is inevitably somewhat arbitrary. There is also great variation in work tasks and responsibilities within any given occupational category – it certainly takes more educational preparation to be an engineer in some firms than in others.

One way to think about overeducation is that it is what results when the supply of skills in the labor force increases faster than the demand for those skills. That is, when educational expansion outpaces changes in the workplace, an increasing number of people find that they have more schooling than is in some sense "needed" for the job. (Recall that this was central to Collins' argument.) One might object that this proposition assumes that the match between worker skills and job demands was somehow closer to being in proper alignment before educational expansion threw it out of kilter – that is, perhaps the growth in educational attainment led to a societal shift from being undereducated to being appropriately educated – although this possibility is rarely considered.

It was this hypothesis of the pace of educational expansion outstripping the demand for skills that led to the first sustained treatment of overeducation in the United States. This was economist Richard Freeman's *The Overeducated American* (1976). Freeman was concerned that the tremendous postwar expansion in American higher education had devalued the economic returns to a college degree in the 1970s. In other words, Freeman contended that as a society, we had over-invested in higher education. On his reasoning, too many highly skilled workers were chasing too few high-skill jobs.

Of course, such reasoning implies that potential college-goers would catch on pretty quickly and make other sorts of educational plans. That is, supply should eventually come in to equilibrium with demand as young people opt out of college. This, of course, did not happen. While Freeman's analysis predicted that the supply of college-educated workers should have fallen in the 1980s, in fact it kept right on growing. This continuing expansion in the face of an apparently declining payoff indicated two things. First, the demand by employers for college-educated labor was in fact robust. Second, potential college students did not respond to a less rosy economic future by opting out, but rather by recognizing that the true cost to them would come in *not* pursuing higher education. Individuals chose to invest in their schooling to preserve their relative place in the hiring queue (Thurow 1975).

While it might appear that the concept of overeducation assumes an exceptionally narrow vision of the purpose of schooling, this is not necessarily the case. Green et al. (1999) say that the term is only intended to apply to the human capital component of education, and thus still leaves room for nonpecuniary benefits of schooling (see also Vignoles et al. 2002; Brynin 2002). Still, the term "overeducation" carries considerable emotional freight, suggesting as it does that people have spent more time in classrooms than is justified by what they can anticipate in return. The presumption seems to be that the overeducated show up for work (if in fact they can find work) with cognitive or perhaps manual skills that their jobs never elicit from them, and spend the day doing tasks of a lower level than they could do if given the opportunity. As folk singer Steve Goodman saw it (at about the same time that Freeman's book appeared), "It's a sorry situation that you can't avoid/When you're overeducated and you're unemployed."

The evidence on the consequences of overeducation turns out to be less than definitive. Empirical findings differ quite substantially across societies, and different conceptualizations of overeducation often produce different results. Most analysts believe that overeducation is both fairly common (sometimes held to be nearly one-third of the workforce) and increasing (Green et al. 1999). Others believe there may have been some decline in the incidence of overeducation (Groot and van den Brink 2000). Some data suggests that women more likely to be overeducated, and men more likely to be undereducated.

In general, the returns to overeducation (typically taken as "years of surplus schooling") are lower than the returns to "matched" schooling, but are positive nonetheless. American and British data often indicate that overeducated workers do much less well than more "appropriately" qualified workers. This, however, may not hold in Germany, where overqualified employees do relatively well economically (suggesting that employers make generally sound decisions by hiring them) (Buchel 2002). The "career mobility" reasoning here is that even if formally overeducated workers are not currently in positions that draw on their full range of skills, they may be on a trajectory that will eventually allow those skills to be expressed and rewarded (Rosenbaum and Binder 1997; Buhlmann and Krakel 2000). Others, however, see little evidence that overeducation is a short-term "life course" condition for those experiencing it (Brynin 2002). At least for Britain, in contrast, it appears that overeducated workers are disadvantaged in the job market precisely because they are less able than appropriately matched workers. That is, those with "surplus schooling" tend to be those without such other bases of human capital as training, tenure, and work experience (Green et al. 1999).

What motivates credentialist behavior?

It is fairly obvious how people would behave under a human capital or meritocratic regime. Job seekers would be doing all they could to enhance their skills, and employers would be doing what they could to identify and reward those skills. Credentialist theory suggests more complex social actors. If credentialist theory is correct, labor market participants "use" educational resources (degrees, licenses, and so on) in order to control access to good jobs and high incomes. This, as far as it goes, is not terribly different from the meritocracy model. The difference comes with credentialist theorists' claim that the monopolization of the best positions by the highly schooled does not represent their greater merit so much as it does processes of social exclusion by which the less schooled (who are not necessarily the less deserving, in the sense of having less productive potential) are systematically barred from upward mobility by the educational elite.

We can characterize these processes of exclusion as *strategies of social reproduction* used by educational elites (Bourdieu and Passeron 1974). Changes in property relations have over time eroded the ability of privileged classes to directly transfer their advantages to their children. As a result, they have turned to the educational system to transmit their status intergenerationally. This, unlike the direct inheritance of property, is broadly seen as socially legitimate, even meritocratic. Thus, in a strong credentialist position, the linkage between education and socioeconomic success lies not in merit in Young's sense of IQ plus effort, but in processes of "social closure" by which educational credentials are "misrecognized" as merit (see also Parkin 1971; Murphy 1988; Weeden 1998).

How do systems of credentialism develop?

I have taken a bit of a detour around credentialism, and it is time to return to it. I do this by returning to the earlier discussion of Berg and Collins. Collins, it will be recalled, understood credentialism in the United States as rooted in cultural and ethnic conflicts that took place one hundred years ago. Berg, in contrast, saw credentialism as arising from managerial indifference to rationality. These are contrasting views of how credentialist systems come into being, but there are other possibilities as well. How else might we understand how systems of credentialism develop over time?

This is a more difficult question than asking how systems of meritocracy develop. Indeed, the idea that societies evolve toward meritocracy is derivable from most classic sociological theories of social change – Weberian ration-alization and bureaucratization, Durkheimian changes in the division of labor, functionalist theories of convergence or industrialism, and (as we will see in the next chapter), postindustrialism. Human capital theorists would be unlikely to take the "origins of meritocracy" question seriously, simply assuming employer and worker rationality and utilitarian decision-making that lead to the right people being matched to the right jobs.

Because they follow less neatly from these standard sociological theories (although Collins did of course base his credentialist theory on Weber), the social origins of credentialism are more difficult to unravel. To show how some scholars have thought about this, I now describe a few particularly insightful efforts to shed some light on this question. None of these is in any sense the last word on credentialism, but each brings a distinctive point of view – different methods, different premises, different settings – that help move our understanding along.

Ronald Dore's influential volume *The Diploma Disease* (1976a) actually predates Collins' *The Credential Society*. This volume grew out of different concerns than those that motivated Collins or Berg. Dore's concern was with the possibilities of developing countries reaching prosperity in an in-creasingly competitive world economy. Based largely on a careful analysis of Britain, Japan, Sri Lanka, and Kenya, Dore observed that schooling has come to be less about learning and more about acquiring the credentials and qualifications that one needs to get a job. His analysis is firmly in the "credential inflation" camp. He sees this "qualification escalation" as socially destructive, particularly in the developing world, where the combination of rapidly expanding enrollments and a lack of middle class and professional jobs associated with higher levels of education is a recipe for social unrest. Reflecting on his "diploma disease thesis" 20 years after its publication, Dore (1997) concluded that credentialism was more rampant than ever (see also Little 1997).

A badly overlooked analysis by French sociologist Bertrand L'ain (1981) explored why some sorts of educational credentials have "certifying effects" while others do not. Using French business schools as an example, L'ain demonstrated that the specific sorts of interactions and relationships between the institutions granting a given degree, the employers who pay for it, and the professional associations who regulate the positions to which it provides access collectively determine how great the "certifying effect" of the creden-tial is. For example, by limiting entrance to a program of study, educational institutions can virtually assure that entrants will eventually secure positions associated with the credential that they grant. This in turn enhances the economic value of the credential to those fortunate enough to be admitted.

Moving to the United States, in 1988 David Labaree published *The Making of an American High School: The Credentials Market and the Central High School of Philadelphia, 1838–1939*. Labaree's strategy was to demonstrate how credentialism developed in a specific institution. This was Philadelphia's first high school, Central High School. He shows how the fundamental purpose of American schooling came to be at stake at Central. That is, the conflict was over a vision of schools as a means to build citizens in a republic versus schools as a means to confer status and social mobility on their graduates. To oversimplify a complex analysis, in the end credentials won and political equality lost.

David Brown's *Degrees of Control: A Sociology of Educational Expansion and Occupational Credentialism* (1995) is a notable analysis for recasting the credentialist thesis as one pertaining not to individual mobility or status attainment, but rather *collective mobility*. Brown sets himself the task of explaining why participation in higher education in the United States has historically been so much greater than in comparable nations. He notes that this expansion predates the implementation of the GI Bill or the widespread growth of community colleges. The trend toward mass postsecondary education was apparent one hundred years ago.

Brown is uncomfortable with the explanations offered by both sociologists (Trow 1961) and economists (Goldin 1998b) that this expansion was primarily a means to build the human capital demanded by an increasingly complex economic system. He is, however, equally uneasy with credentialist accounts that focus only on the strategies of elites to use the schooling system to monopolize opportunities for themselves and their children. In a wide-ranging sociohistorical analysis, Brown demonstrates how other factors – local efforts to build colleges to promote community economic development, land speculation, considerable regional wealth – worked together to tighten the linkage between educational credentials and jobs. Like other credentialists, Brown sees no necessary connections between the content of schooling and the demands of the workplace, but his analysis goes further in conceptualizing credentialism as growing out of broad political, cultural, and economic processes, rather than merely the behaviors of employers and job seekers (see also Dougherty 1994 and Brown 2001).

Li and Walder (2001) broaden the literature on credentialism even more. Their concern is with how party membership in China might operate as a credential. They believe that the literature on this has been uncertain and inconsistent because researchers have failed to carefully conceptualize the role of party membership in occupational mobility. They focus (pp. 1373–4) on what they see as some:

key questions about the attainment of party membership and the role this plays in individuals' careers. How exactly does party membership operate as a credential? Is it obtained by individuals based on open competition, or is it systematically granted by the party and party officials based on family background or other political considerations? Is it primarily an alternative career strategy for those with little education or a qualification that enhances the careers of all highly motivated individuals?

Li and Walder's treatment of these questions is conceptually and empirically compelling. Their resolution draws in part on the timing of party membership in a person's life course. As they conclude (p. 1376), "We propose that party membership should be conceived not as a credential but as something roughly analogous to membership in a club that can confer advantages upon members throughout their lives."

A final example is historian Nancy Beadie's (1999) analysis of how the Regents of the State of New York in the ante-bellum era developed a system of standardized examinations intended to "provide evidence of actual merit." Beadie observed that the Regents wanted to rationalize the relationships among secondary and postsecondary educational institutions (much as present day community colleges and universities attempt to accomplish with articulation agreements). She demonstrates how credentials came to acquire their value as currency in a broad "field" of higher education, the state, public education, and other social actors.

Rethinking credentialism

Where does all of this leave us? Obviously, there are different ways to think about credentialism. One way to impose some order on all of this might be to move from the specific to the general. That is, I earlier discussed what educational credentials consist of in a very concrete sense (i.e., degrees, licenses, and the like). In a more general sense, though, educational credentials represent a wider range of social practices and institutions. Specifically, credentials, educational or otherwise, provide a means by which social actors can send and receive information under conditions of social uncertainty and anonymity.

One important effort to bring some conceptual order to the role played by credentials is sociologist Steven Nock's 1993 volume *The Costs of Privacy: Surveillance and Reputation in America*. The interesting question for Nock is how people come to trust strangers in a large, complex, and impersonal society. How, for instance, can employers or clients trust that a person claiming a level of occupational expertise actually has that expertise, until actually watching that person perform the work (by which time considerable damage may have been done).

Nock maintains that societies solve the problem of how to trust strangers through surveillance. Avoiding the sinister meaning often attached to the concept, Nock defines surveillance as "overt and conspicuous forms of credentials (e.g., credit cards, educational degrees, drivers' licenses) and/or ordeals (e.g., lie detector tests, drug tests, integrity tests)" (p. viii). Unless these credentials and ordeals receive broad social legitimacy and acceptance, people have little reason to enter into exchanges with strangers, and as Nock observes, large modern societies are primarily societies of strangers. The use of educational credentials to allocate their holders to jobs, then, grows directly out of their ability to "produce reputations that are widely accessible, impersonal, and portable from one location to another" (p. 1). In short, educational credentials provide a reason to have confidence in the ability and reliability of strangers.

Nock's analysis is useful in placing educational credentials in a broader understanding of how societies solve problems associated with increased complexity and uncertainty (see also Brown 2001). Educational credentials, like credit cards and drivers' licenses, give some assurance that strangers can be trusted to have the skills and abilities that they claim to have. Whether in fact educational credentials do indicate this, as meritocrats would claim, or if there is widespread deception and exclusion taking place, as many credentialists would have it, is generally an open question. One would hope that these are questions that can be at least provisionally settled through appeal to the empirical evidence on the relationship between education and work. I turn to this evidence in the next chapter.

4

Is the United States a Meritocratic or a Credentialist Society?

The question that grows from the previous chapter is whether the United States can best be characterized as a meritocracy or as a credentialist society. Stated this baldly, the question can yield no clear answer. Societies are rarely if ever either "this" or "that" in any unambiguous sense, but are rather hybrids of competing and often contradictory logics. Ascription will creep in to even the most meritocratic systems, and talent will often be rewarded in even the most rigid social hierarchies. The questions then become "How much ascription does it take to negate a meritocracy?" or "To what degree do schools have to instill relevant skills to preclude credentialism?" There is no simple answer to these questions.

Moreover, even if there were clear answers to these questions, how to devise the proper statistical tests of the theories is far from self-evident. I noted earlier that even what appear to be straightforward measures of ascription and achievement are often ambiguous. As Breen and Goldthorpe (2001) observed, there is no common or natural "metric" of meritocracy. That is, there is no means by which we can compare x units of merit against y units of non-merit. Similarly, there is no readily interpretable metric to determine the degree to which credentials do or do not correspond to the skills that are demanded at the workplace.

Breen and Goldthorpe (2001) suggest that we can best assess meritocracy (and there is no reason why their argument would not apply to credentialism as well) by examining stratification processes over time. That is, there may be no definitive standard to apply to when a society is or is not meritocratic, but perhaps we can determine with some assurance if it is more or less meritocratic than it once was. Thus, the declining importance of ascription over time would mean something quite different than its persistence.

But the problem with adjudicating the meritocracy and credentialist models is not limited to the fact that the real world will inevitably contain elements of each, or in determining that the statistical trends are moving one direction or another. A more fundamental problem is that the same empirical evidence is almost always consistent with either theory. That is, data used in support of the credentialist position can usually be used to support the meritocracy model, and vice versa. The main reason for this is that, with some exceptions, we have not yet produced enough research that has been explicitly designed to test and compare the most basic, and typically unstated, premises of the theories. We have plenty of data portraying in a broadly descriptive way how credentials, jobs, incomes, and so on are related to one another, and how these associations have changed over time. We know far less about the mechanisms that produced those relationships.

Goldthorpe (1996) has described this issue with exceptional clarity. For Goldthorpe, there is no way to choose between meritocracy and credentialism strictly on the basis of observed empirical relationships because sociologists have not advanced an "underlying theoretical narrative of action." As he states:

> Thus, simply to show a strengthening association over time between educa-
> tion and occupational status is itself of rather little help in evaluating the
> theory of an increasing meritocratic emphasis in social selection . . . such a
> finding is equally consistent with a rival theory that sees the dominant tend-
> ency as being not so much towards meritocracy as "credentialism": that is,
> an increasing use of formal qualifications in selection, promoted by interested
> occupational associations and educational bodies, and in which manage-
> ments connive more for reasons of convenience than demonstrated efficiency.
> (Goldthorpe 1996, p. 111)

Goldthorpe's reasoning is persuasive, but may be discouraging for readers who would like a conclusive answer to the "meritocracy or credentialism" question. Discouraging or not, however, any serious appraisal of the relationship between education and work needs to come to grips with this question. If definitive answers may not be forthcoming, we can still examine the degree to which the empirical evidence leans in one direction or the other, or which hypotheses receive greater or lesser support, or perhaps most importantly, what questions remain to be asked.

The relevant literature encompasses social stratification, status attainment, and social mobility, and can be modestly described as immense. By necessity, as I explained in the first chapter, I will focus on the United States, but this is a focus with considerable costs. Whenever possible, I will make unsystematic but hopefully illustrative forays into the cross-societal literature.

This is also a literature that is often technically complex and often inaccessible to those on the outside looking in. Nonetheless, grappling with it is not a purely academic exercise. Important policy implications follow from a better understanding of the empirical adequacy of the models of meritocracy and credentialism. Knowing what kind of a society we are – who gets ahead and why – has implications that go beyond sociological theory. As Stephen Herzenberg and his colleagues (1998, p. 80) have observed (the bracketed material is mine):

> The conventional interpretation of labor market inequality leads to policy prescriptions emphasizing education and training [i.e., human capital or meritocracy theory]; inequality can be reduced by giving more schooling or training to the less skilled. But if entry requirements for the better jobs simply ratchet upward as more people gain credentials [i.e., credentialism], economywide wage differentials will not change much.

The Status Attainment Model as an Organizing Framework

I will review several large bodies of work that might shed light on the relative value of meritocratic and credentialist accounts of the relationship between education and work. Each of these is enormous. I make but the briefest foray into each of them.

Making sense out of this massive body of theory and research requires some sort of organizing or orienting framework. I adopt the *status attainment lifecourse* perspective. This model, as I will explain, posits education as the pivot of socioeconomic inequality. It directs attention to both the range of factors associated with unequal access to schooling, and the range of outcomes to which unequal schooling provides access. One need neither accept the model in toto nor dismiss the many (if often misplaced) critiques of it as functionalist or astructural to see its value as a way to organize an enormous amount of information.

In 1967, Peter Blau and Otis Dudley Duncan published what became the landmark volume *The American Occupational Structure*. The title is somewhat misleading. The book was not really about theorizing and empirically investigating the American occupational structure as much as it was about how people (or more accurately, how White men) advance or fail to advance throughout that structure. Along with the concurrently developed "Wisconsin Model" of William Sewell and his colleagues (more on this below), Blau and Duncan's status attainment model established the template for generations of research.

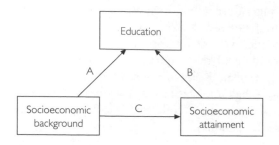

Figure 4.1   A model of the socioeconomic life cycle
Source: Adapted from Blau and Duncan (1967).

The status attainment model itself is remarkably simple. Figure 4.1 presents a diagram of the model in its most basic form. The model contains three variables: socioeconomic background, educational attainment, and socioeconomic attainment. We can think of each of these here as shorthand for much larger collections of variables. The diagram also contains what at first looks like three relationships, but which is really four relationships. The first three are: (A) the effect of socioeconomic background on educational attainment; (B) the effect of educational attainment on socioeconomic attainment; and (C) the effect of socioeconomic background on socioeconomic attainment. Scholars too often overlook (A × B), the effect of socioeconomic background on socioeconomic attainment as mediated by educational attainment. Each of these three variables and each of these four relationships merits some discussion.

"Socioeconomic background" refers to the ascribed and achieved characteristics that influence life chances. This potentially includes anything that exists or takes place prior to one's educational and socioeconomic attainment (or as the language of status attainment research has it, is "exogenous" to these). As I explained earlier, examples of ascribed statuses are parental education, occupation, and wealth, race, ethnicity, gender, and residence. Achieved statuses might include GPA, ability, aspirations, or non-cognitive behaviors. Other factors rest between ascription and achievement (e.g., parental, teacher, and peer encouragement and expectations). A given factor might well influence both educational and posteducational attainments.

Not all resources are on the level of the individual. Many are based in such social processes and structures as social networks, social capital, social contacts, community structure, and so on (Granovetter 1992; Lin 1999; Rosenbaum et al. 1999). That is, one's personal resources are embedded in relationships and networks in ways that can enhance one's life chances.

"Educational attainment" is likewise a complex construction. At its simplest, it denotes simply the number of years of schooling that one has completed. More fully, it extends to other characteristics of schooling – type of program, type of degree, quality of schooling, institutional reputation, and so on. Educational attainment also includes such school experiences as GPA, credits earned, degrees or certificates awarded, and track placement.

"Socioeconomic attainment" is usually taken to refer to occupation and income. It might also include such socioeconomic outcomes as the possession of authority in the workplace, how much autonomy one has over one's work, job satisfaction, and workplace benefits. While they take us too far afield to investigate here, one might also include such outcomes as health, happiness, or civic involvement.

What then of the series of relationships between these variables? By "the effect of socioeconomic background on educational attainment" (Path A), we mean all the processes by which schooling comes to be unequally distributed. Some of these are material – some parents simply have more money to send their children to school. Others may reflect such long-term processes as class-based differences in childhood socialization. Despite the importance of this relationship, both to sociological research and to those concerned with a fair society, we will not be terribly preoccupied here with this stage of the model, except as it pertains to the relationship between education and work.

By "the effect of educational attainment on socioeconomic attainment" (Path B), we ask about the mechanisms by which schooling leads to socioeconomic success. Muller and Shavit (1998) have noted that of all the "Blau–Duncan" relationships, the one between education and occupational destination varies the most across societies. It is probably the most complicated and least easily explained. This is of course the question that is most at stake in this book, raising important questions about meritocracy and credentialism.

Path C, "the effect of socioeconomic background on socioeconomic attainment" takes us to the area of intergenerational mobility. The guiding question here is somewhat different than that of how job assignment takes place. Researchers here are more interested in the general "openness" of a society – about the prospects for those of modest origins ascending into loftier destinations (Sorokin 1927 is only the beginning of a huge literature). Again, I only pursue this literature to the extent that it bears on the education–work connection.

Finally, A × B, "the effect of socioeconomic background on socioeconomic attainment as mediated by educational attainment," refers to processes of social reproduction in which educational institutions are in some way involved. Analysts here ask such questions as "Does schooling contribute to or detract from social inequality? Is the educational system a ladder up the occupational system or a way to maintain privilege across generations?"

Some General Findings on Status Attainment: What Are the Overall Trends and Patterns?

When fully explicated, the status attainment perspective can illuminate both schooling and labor market processes (Kerckhoff 1996). In fact, the narrative established by the Blau–Duncan model holds up pretty well. It goes something like this. Social background goes a long way in the United States in determining educational opportunity. Those from more privileged social backgrounds get more schooling than do those from less advantaged origins. This effect is significant, but is not deterministic, and in fact most of the variance in educational attainment cannot be explained by traditional measures of parental background. The schooling that one completes has a great deal to do with subsequent occupational attainment and earnings. Again, the association is far from perfect, but it is greater than the effect of socioeconomic background on schooling. Finally, social background has at most modest *net* effects on occupational attainment. That is, among adults with the same level of education, there are limited benefits to be derived from having more prosperous parents.

Others, notably Sewell and Hauser (1975), went on to elaborate this story. The well-known Wisconsin Model clarified the ways in which such social psychological and other factors such as aspirations, parental encouragement, cognitive ability, and the influences of "significant others" mediated the effects of social background on education and the effects of schooling on occupational attainment. It also showed how the status attainment process differed for men and women and for racially and ethnically different subpopulations. To oversimplify only a bit, the general conclusion was that Whites and men were more able to benefit from achievement than were minorities and women.

With this as a baseline, what changes have we seen in the process of status attainment over time? On a broad empirical level, there is considerable evidence for a trend toward meritocracy. Featherman and Hauser (1978) explicitly designed their study to assess the shifting role of ascription and achievement relative to the benchmarks established by Blau and Duncan. Comparing their 1973 Occupational Changes in a Generation (OCG) data with the 1962 data used by Blau and Duncan, Featherman and Hauser concluded that the effects of social origins were generally declining while the returns to (or effects of) schooling were increasing. This indicated to them an increasingly meritocratic society.

Featherman and Hauser had only the 1962 and 1973 surveys from which to discern trends. In response to this, Grusky and Diprete (1990) examined

14 annual cross-sections from the General Social Survey (GSS). They were interested in extending the earlier trend analysis of Featherman and Hauser (1978), noting that a variety of demographic trends since the 1973 OCG rendered the conclusion of declining ascription and rising achievement potentially premature. In particular, Grusky and Diprete pointed toward large-scale immigration to the United States and the continuing movement of women into the labor market. They argued that either of these might mitigate any steady trend toward universalism. Grusky and Diprete also directed attention to changes that took place in the nation's political climate (especially the dominance of more conservative political administrations), the ongoing complexity of bureaucratic personnel systems, and the wider economic transformation of the postindustrial society (more on this in the next chapter). They observed that any of these could affect stratification processes.

In general, Grusky and Diprete detected some important trends away from ascription. They noted apparently declining effects of race and class on social outcomes. Gender was more ambiguous. That is, even while women were moving into the labor market in greater numbers, the returns that they received from their work experience and education were stable (or, one might say, stagnant). In contrast, the returns to experience and education increased for men. They posit that this may be because more college-educated women "crowded" and thus deteriorated the market.

Perhaps Grusky and Diprete's most important finding was the declining position of white males. The narrowing gaps between White men on the one hand and women and minorities on the other, however, could not be attributed to any great improvement in the prospects of women and minorities, but rather to the fact that white men started doing worse after 1973. One might of course see this as trend toward meritocracy, but in an almost perverse sort of way.

Many analysts accept this interpretation. Economist Robert Lerman (1997) believes that declining race and gender wage differentials indicate a trend towards meritocracy in the United States. He concludes that rewards are increasingly based more on education and skill and less on race and gender. There remain, however, race and gender differences in educational opportunity, which in turn lead to disparities in socioeconomic opportunity, indicating that the United States has yet to reach a full meritocracy. Trends in the effects of social class may also turn out to be more ambiguous than it appeared when Featherman and Hauser conducted their study. Class barriers to educational opportunity decreased from the 1920s to the 1970s, but then slowed and finally reversed for individuals born after 1960. In brief, money matters more for more recent cohorts than for their older brothers and sisters (Hout 2001).

Moreover, the supposedly improved labor market position of women and minorities is a delicate one. While the economic condition of African Americans steadily improved between 1940 and 1990, we have since witnessed a "stagnated wage gap between races" (Smith 2001, p. 52; Blank 2001). Smith notes that "the average economic status of Hispanics appears to be deteriorating at an even more alarming rate than that of Blacks" (p. 52). Further, the relative economic standing of Hispanics declined steadily from 1970 to 1990, with Mexicans having done the worst.

The trend toward a "long, sustained improvement in the wage position of working women" (Smith 2001 p. 61) is clearer. The largest gains have been for Black women, with the least impressive being for Hispanic women. Perhaps more important is the vast diversity in wage trends, which vary in bewildering ways across various combinations of race, ethnicity, gender, educational level, and age. Thus, some groups have improved their relative socioeconomic position while others have lost ground, but in no clear pattern. Given the broad sweep of the twentieth century, all of this points to a lessened role for ascription, but any progress is fitful, inconsistent, and subject to periodic reversals.

These trends in economic well-being can be rooted in any number of demographic, labor market, or political factors. Of particular interest here is the role of education in attenuating or widening racial or gender levels of reward. That is, everything else being equal, we might well expect narrowing educational gaps to ultimately lead to narrowing income gaps. Smith concludes (2001, pp. 71, 73) that education's role is surprisingly indeterminate:

> What role can changing education disparities play in accounting for changing wage disparities . . . since the 1960s? Until the mid-1970s, schooling continued to assume its historical role as the primary determinant of the male racial wage gap. Male education differences by race, however, cannot account for the timing and magnitude of the racial stagnation since the mid-1970s; nor can schooling account for the impressive narrowing of the gender wage gap since the 1960s. The stagnation and decrease in Hispanic wages relative to U.S.-born Whites, however, is consistent with the apparent lack of relative educational progress of the average Hispanic worker. The adjective *apparent* is necessary because the absence of progress is mostly the result of a compositional effect of the addition of new Hispanic immigrants with low levels of schooling.

On balance, one can read the evidence as a glass half full (we've come a long way) or a glass half empty (we have a long way to go). There are unmistakable trends toward meritocracy, but having said that, labor-market disparities across race, ethnicity, and gender lines are remarkably stubborn.

What of social class? An important feature of the status attainment model has to do with the enduring effects of social background on socioeconomic attainment. As reported by Warren (2001), the evidence is now quite clear that "the effects of family background on occupation are entirely indirect, operating through their effects on education and cognitive ability" (p. 268). This is quite a different finding than that established by Blau and Duncan. It is of course consistent with an "increasing universalism" or "meritocracy" interpretation, but also with a "strategies of reproduction" one. That is, the numbers do not allow us to determine if people are increasingly being "freed" from their class of origin, or if they are increasingly advantaged by it.

The effects of schooling on occupation decline as people get older (Warren 2001). Individuals are less able to "cash in" on their educational credentials, in particular their postsecondary credentials, as they move through the life course. This finding leans in the direction of meritocracy. Presumably, as workers age they are evaluated and rewarded more on the basis of their job performance and less on the basis of their previous success in educational institutions. Declining education effects as workers age points towards the ascendance of achievement-based effects.

Hauser et al. (2000 p. 193) have offered the most sustained and incisive effort to understand changes in the status attainment process in the United States. They state that "we think the most important questions are whether there has been any change in the degree to which family background influences occupational success through schooling and how the effects of schooling have changed across time." Their conclusion (p. 201) is important:

> the main story here is that there has been relatively little change in the effects of schooling on occupational status. . . . Public perception of the growing importance of schooling in social and economic success has played an important part in discussions of "the meritocracy." What accounts for that perception if the effects of schooling on occupational standing have not changed very much? . . . First, since the early 1970s there have been major changes in the effects of school on earnings, and these have increased the relative value of high school graduation and college attendance . . . Second, . . . schooling has become more important because levels of educational attainment have increased. More of the population has completed levels of schooling where the expected returns to schooling are high.

Their full story is even more complex than this. For example, even though the effects of schooling on occupational status are not increasing, they are still large. Moreover, the effects of postsecondary schooling on occupational status are greater than are the effects of graded schooling. Even more to the point, the effects of graded schooling have generally become less important as the United States has achieved mass completion of high school, although a year of high school is not the same for everyone (Lucas 2001). Students in more high-status tracks gain more from completing the eleventh grade than those in general tracks. Postsecondary schooling, meanwhile, has assumed greater social significance. But this simple dichotomy hides a great deal. There are all kinds and levels of postsecondary schooling, just as there are all sorts of experiences at the high school level. There is little reason to believe that all postsecondary credentials will lead to job assignment in the same way (Kerckhoff and Bell 1998).

The GED

Even below the postsecondary level, however, there is a key benchmark at the high school level. This is the distinction between a regular high school diploma and the GED – the test of General Educational Development. The GED has a distinctive relationship with economic attainment that makes it worth a closer look.

People who lack a high school diploma can obtain the GED by passing a 7½ hour battery of examinations. These are in the areas of writing, social studies, science, reading (sometimes referred to as interpretation of literature), and mathematics. In a typical year, about two-thirds of those who sit for the examination pass it successfully. This amounts to about one in six high school diplomas (Boesel et al. 1998).

As with much of the history of standardized testing in the United States, the origins of the GED lie in American involvement in war. During World War II, the Roosevelt administration recognized that their efforts to reward veterans with the opportunity to attend college could be hampered by that fact that many service members lacked high school diplomas. Following the generally unsuccessful effort to award high school diplomas for wartime service to veterans of World War I, a combined effort of the American Council for Education (ACE) and testing experts working for the US Army led to the development of the GED. This development used the Iowa Tests of Educational Development as a basis. The GED designers intended the tests to reflect everyday life rather than more abstract knowledge (Boesel et al. 1998).

For several years, most GED examinees were veterans and service members, but by 1959 civilian testees were the majority. For whatever reasons, as the test-taking population shifted, so did the success rate, as the extremely high rates of the immediate postwar years settled in at lower levels. This contributes to the generally low repute in which the GED is held in many quarters (Boesel et al. 1998).

In spite of this, people still take the GED in very large numbers. Over 860,000 people took one of the five GED tests in 2000, the second-largest test-taking population since the inception of the exam. About 60 percent of these individuals passed the test.

It would be of great interest to know how the GED compares to the high school diploma as a ticket into the world of work. This turns out to be a very difficult question. One reason for this is the GED's self-selective nature. Only a small percentage of those eligible to take the exam do so – only about 1.5 percent of the nation's 44 million adults without a high school degree have taken the exam (Boesel et al. 1998). This 1.5 percent have greater resources (e.g., cognitive ability, motivation, economic wherewithal) than the overwhelming majority who do not. Still, these resources are in general less than those of traditional high school graduates.

What are the labor market consequences of holding a GED? The simple answer seems to be "better than high school dropouts, but worse than high school graduates" (Cameron and Heckman 1993). The GED tends to operate as a "mixed signal." That is, the GED indicates to employers that individuals had the ability to pass a reasonably complex exam that offered at least some evidence of their suitability for the workplace, but also indicated that they had been unable to achieve a high school diploma in a socially standard manner (Heckman and Rubenstein 2001). As two labor economists put it, the GED signals to employers that GED recipients are "smart but unreliable" (Heckman and Rubenstein 2001).

Some researchers are a bit more optimistic about the prospects of GED holders. For instance, male high school dropouts with low levels of skills tend to benefit from getting their GED. Unfortunately, though, more skilled high school dropouts do not (Murnane et al. 1999; 2000; Tyler et al. 2000). Further, the GED carries different weight for women than for men. Boudett et al. (2000) reported mixed results of the GED for women who lack high school degrees. These women gain by getting a GED, and the initially modest impact on earnings gets bigger over time. This boost is not enough to get them out of poverty-level jobs. Thus, while the benefits to women of the GED are real, they do not bring economic independence.

The sub-baccalaureate labor market

A crucial but overlooked segment of the educational system is that residing between high school and the four-year degree. Grubb (1996) characterizes this as the "sub-baccalaureate labor market," and observes that it is the level at which many of the broad economic and technological transformations of the workplace have their greatest impacts. The postindustrial battleground is largely one that will be fought by workers with educational preparations that go beyond high school but stop short of four-year degrees.

Much of the sub-baccalaureate labor market consists of what are normally thought of as vocational degrees. In fact, though, the once-clear dichotomy between vocational and academic degrees is an increasingly blurry one. Grubb believes that those who are "working in the middle" will need to draw on a range of skills well beyond the more narrow (if stereotypical) "how to" of traditional vocational education.

Despite the neglect of sub-baccalaureate vocational degrees by labor market analysts, these credentials have considerable economic value to those who hold them (Kerckhoff and Bell 1998). Unlike Europe, American high school degrees provide little differentiated information that permits employers to distinguish job candidates (Bishop 1990). Sub-baccalaureate postsecondary credentials, in contrast, are more information-rich and provide many employers with a suitable means to select employees (Kane and Rouse 1995; Grubb 1993; Lewis et al. 1993; Dougherty 1994). The pattern of effects is complex. Some sub-baccalaureate degrees pay well and some do not, and women and men seem to realize different benefits.

The baccalaureate and graduate labor markets

Finally, not all postsecondary degrees bear the same relationship to socioeconomic attainment. In his comprehensive report *What's It Worth?*, Bruno (1995) examined the relationships between postsecondary field of training and economic status. He found, probably not too surprisingly, that the highest earnings went to those with degrees in Law and Medicine or Dentistry. The lowest were to individuals with degrees in Home Economics. There was great variation in the rewards garnered by students with bachelor's degrees. Engineering majors earned about double what Education majors earned. Business majors were not far behind.

The situation is actually a bit worse than this for those with degrees in less remunerative majors. Those who start off at low levels of earnings also have low rates of wage growth later (Horn and Zahn 2001). Thus, the differences between the haves and have-nots widen over time. The differences are not trivial. For those with advanced degrees, those in Medicine or Dentistry ended up earning nearly three times what Liberal Arts majors earned.

Nor are degrees the only way in which one college education differs from another. There are many reasons to think that differences in the quality and reputation of colleges and universities influence the life chances of their graduates. Why else would people want to attend (and pay for) "good" schools? What of things that institutions advertise and brag about, like selectivity, student/faculty ratios, or expenditures on instruction?

In his report *College Quality and the Earnings of Recent College Graduates*, Fitzgerald (2000) examined the effects of college quality on earnings five years after graduation. While institutional quality was not as important a determinant of earnings as was choice of college major, it was far from irrelevant. Fitzgerald found small net effects of quality on earnings for men (2–3 percent) and larger net effects for women (4–6 percent).

In a thorough review of some 25 empirical studies, Pascarella and Terenzini (forthcoming) concluded that while the effects of college selectivity on earnings are significant (in the neighborhood of 2–4 percent), they are probably not linear. Only a relatively small number of especially selective elite schools provide an earnings premium to their graduates. This may reflect what P. Brown (1995) calls the "reputational capital" of elite universities. Pascarella and Terenzini add that even the estimate of 2–4 percent is probably too high, since little of the research controls for student ambition. That is, at least part of what looks like an advantage afforded by going to an elite school is really the higher ambition (or some other unmeasured factor) of the students who attend them.

On balance, institutional quality, an admittedly slippery and imprecise concept, matters. It definitely does not matter as much as choice of major, and it is unlikely that it matters as much as what students do (i.e., study hard and take the right courses). More here than in the broader trends I discussed earlier, the evidence for or against either the meritocracy or the credential society is ambivalent. Merit matters, and it may well matter more than it used to. At the same time, merit matters in part because ascription opens the door that permits it to matter.

Cognitive ability and personality

Michael Young's fictional meritocracy was less about schooling than it was about the combination of ability and effort. What about this? Would knowing more about how ability and effort contribute to socioeconomic outcomes, independently of the role of schooling, help us to better understand schooling and the world of work?

The research literature yields tentative conclusions, but a few seem trustworthy. First, both "skills" (broadly understood) and educational credentials working together are now required for successful socioeconomic outcomes. That is, schooling has little effect unless the individual has actually learned something. Pryor and Schaffer (1999) have offered the most thorough statement of this position. In an ambitious and creative analysis, they suggest that the educational credentials that workers bring with them to the world of work are becoming less important than what workers actually know. They observe that this helps to explain why many highly schooled but underskilled people have been performing poorly in the labor market.

Second, a wide variety of noncognitive factors are associated with success in the workplace. We might collectively file these under Young's "effort," or we might follow the lead of Jencks et al. (1979) and call them "personality." Whatever they are, they influence socioeconomic attainments, but in ways that vary so much across types of work, occupations, and work settings that few generalizations are possible. Thus, schools make people smarter in ways that employers value, but this is not all that schools do. Bowles and Gintis (2000), in fact, see the ability of schools to teach cognitive skills as having relatively modest effects on attainments. They hold that schooling also enhances many non-cognitive characteristics that come to be rewarded in the workplace. They add that the concept of "skill shortage" is too narrow a conception of what happens in labor markets, because what employers really want is workers with a broader range of capacities than simply "cognitive skills."

Perhaps the most useful analysis of the joint role of schooling and ability/skills is that of Kerckhoff and his colleagues (2001). They acknowledge that previous research has found only weak net effects of cognitive ability on labor force outcomes, but believe that this is at least in part because cognitive ability has been too narrowly measured. They analyze a data set rarely used by stratification researchers, the National Adult Literacy Survey (NALS), which measures a comprehensive set of cognitive skills, and find that education and skills are not redundant measures, but indicate quite different characteristics of participants in labor markets. Schooling and skills are affected in different ways by social origins, ethnicity, and native language, and have different effects on occupational attainment and earnings. In general, the effects of education are larger than those of cognitive skills, although this is more the case for occupation than for earnings. These patterns vary across race/ethnic and gender groups.

What can we conclude about ability and effort? Clearly, both add to our understanding of the relationship between education and work. Simple, unitary measures of IQ are of limited explanatory power, but more detailed measures of ability are informative. Personality (or effort) helps differentiate the life chances of similarly educated people, but in ways that differ across jobs and settings. Finally, all of this varies for different sociodemographic components of the population, in ways we have barely begun to sort out.

School and work across generations

Finally, I turn to path C of the Blau–Duncan model (see Figure 4.1). This relationship describes the degree to which socioeconomic attainment is influenced by social origins. Hauser et al. (2000, p. 183) reported that "There has been a steady decline in the aggregate intergenerational status mobility of cohorts born after the end of World War II. At least at young ages, there appears to have been no net upward mobility among white men born after 1950." Intergenerational mobility has meanwhile increased irregularly for black men. Hauser et al. note (p. 184) that the finding for young white men need not indicate an erosion of the merit principle, insisting that "One should not jump to . . . the conclusion that net immobility will last throughout the lives of recent cohorts of U.S. men, for the status of men's jobs typically grows from career entry to midlife." In short, the verdict is still out about long-term trends toward or away from greater or lesser intergenerational mobility.

What can we conclude from this large body of literature? It is difficult to avoid the conclusion that socioeconomic success in the United States is achieved more meritocratically than it once was. There is an irregular, fitful, but still pronounced trend toward achievement as the basis for socioeconomic success. The ascriptive bonds of gender have loosened, while those of race and ethnicity appear to have loosened and then tightened again. The effects of class have generally persisted, although the point at which they differentiate life chances shifts from one historical period to the next. The pivotal role of schooling, skills, and ability in assigning status seems to be increasing. Employers are willing to hire highly educated workers and pay them more, even as the supply of these workers increases.

These conclusions apply only to the United States. An assessment of trends toward or away from either ascription or achievement in the rest of the world will have to wait for a more extended review. A full assessment, however, is unlikely to be available for some time. Most of what we know of trends in status attainment processes is from the industrialized world. We know far less about less-industrialized or developing nations. Buchmann and Hannum (2001) observed that, in part, this is because of both the lack of large representative data and the infrastructure to gather and analyze it in much of the less-industrialized world, and in part because sociologists have yet to mobilize the kind of international collaborations that they have for the comparative analyses of developed nations (e.g., Shavit and Blossfeld 1993). Buchmann and Hannum do note, however, that the available evidence shows relatively weak support for any convergence in the stratification processes of less-developed nations. Sorting all of this out needs to be high on the research agenda of those interested in the relationships between education and work.

How Do Employers Think About and Act Upon Education and Other Credentials?

The missing link to this point in this story has to do with the mechanism by which individuals "cash in" their educational credentials for better jobs and higher incomes. This does not just happen. There is no central clearinghouse in which degrees and jobs are exchanged. Instead, the primary reason that those with more schooling get better jobs and those with less schooling get poorer jobs is that this is how employers hire. The social actor whose "narrative of action" (Goldthorpe 1996) most needs to be understood is the employer.

The key here is how employers use information. The problem faced by employers is that, because they have not had the chance to directly observe job candidates in a work situation, they cannot be sure that the workers they hire will be effective and productive (Rosenbaum and Jones 2000). Thus, employers need to find "signals" of productive potential. Educational credentials are a cheap, easily observed, and socially acceptable signal than employers can use when they have little other information (Bills 1992b).

In response to these sorts of processes, many social scientists have turned their attention to examining how employers use and act upon the information available to them when they make staffing decisions, that is, decisions to hire and promote (Braddock et al. 1986; Useem 1989; Neckerman and Kirschenman 1991; Miller and Rosenbaum 1997; Rosenbaum and Binder 1997; Miller 1998; Coverdill 1998; Moss and Tilly 2001; Petersen et al. 2001; see Bills 1992b for a review of much of this material). A few points stand out.

First, employers rarely see deterministic linkages between schooling and job assignment. I mentioned earlier that the noted credentialist Ivar Berg found employers to be unreflective and arbitrary in their use of educational credentials. Indeed, employers are often vague and uncertain about what they want, and rarely if ever check to see if their standard practices are either efficient or effective. As Block (1990, p. 88) observed, there is "little empirical evidence that most employers are, in fact, rational in their calculations concerning employee turnover."

Second, the matching of a level of schooling with a specific job is often not so much a decision made at the discretion of a hiring manager, but rather a formal organizational policy. Civil service criteria, for instance, often specify the level of schooling needed to get a job, and earlier I described the role of different kinds of state-sanctioned certification. Equally important, over time given levels of schooling and given sorts of occupations simply become culturally associated with each other. These expectations can prove to be remarkably binding.

Within these constraints, though, managers often have great latitude to use educational credentials as they wish. In my own analysis of hiring practices in several Chicago-area organizations (Bills 1988a) I concluded that "The major findings concern the flexibility of hiring standards, the discretion available to managers to adjust standards, the substitutability of specific experience for education, the role of job history data,[1] and the evaluation of personality as a hiring criterion and the way this differs for male and female candidates." Thus, managers clearly link education and jobs, but have little reluctance to "trade away" educational credentials when it meets their needs. Similarly, managers often avoid atypically highly educated job candidates as being inappropriate to the skill demands of the position (Bills 1992a). Candidates can be overeducated as easily as they can be undereducated.

Surveys of employers have also shed light on racial and gender disparities in labor market outcomes. Holzer (2001, p. 106), for instance, reported that "Employers continue to be reluctant to hire Blacks for jobs that require significant cognitive skills and credentials, such as specific experience or previous training, even those jobs for which formal educational requirements are not high" (see too Moss and Tilly 2001). Thus, at least some of the differential relationship between education and work across racial lines is due to the different meaning of education that employers attach to Black and White job applicants. Similarly, I found that employers often attach different meanings to what appear to be similar non-cognitive factors when evaluating male and female candidates (Bills 1988a). Behavior that is seen as ambitious in men may be interpreted as pushy in women.

In an innovative study, Jackson (2001) conducted a content analysis of 3,533 British newspaper job advertisements. Her analysis led her to the conclusion that:

> While formal educational qualifications are important to employers, other "non-meritocratic" criteria also have a significant role. Some of these non-meritocratic characteristics may relate more to ascribed characteristics than achieved, and in many cases may be more accessible to particular people or

---

1 "Job history data" refers to such things as a history of job-hopping, a spotty attendance record, or a reputation for clashing with previous employers.

groups in society. Overall, this research suggests that in some cases other types of characteristics may be as important as educational qualifications.

Bills (1990) reported similar results, finding that employers either rewarded or penalized the sorts of "job history data" (such as irregular work careers or extended absences from the labor market) that were more accessible to some labor market participants than to others.

Adams and McQuillan (2000) interviewed human resources managers in Ontario firms, and wanted to know if their hiring standards had changed in response to the extensive workplace restructuring that had been taking place over the previous several years. They concluded that they had. Many managers were insisting on higher levels of education and training (and experience). Adams and McQuillen attribute this in part (and perhaps without evidence) to credential inflation, but also to managers' belief that "jobs require a more educated and knowledgeable worker. . . . In particular, education was taken as an indicator of an individual's ability to learn and adapt" (2000, pp. 400–2).

Internal labor markets and self-employment as special cases of employer decision making

Employers turn to educational credentials in large part because they lack direct information about job candidates, and credentials serve as a reasonable shorthand way to acquire information. This reasoning works when people are being hired from outside of an organization, but what of cases in which the employer has had the opportunity to observe the individual at work? If employers use education as a signal under incomplete and uncertain information, what kind of a relationship should we expect between education and promotions?

Sociologists and economists have written a great deal about how job assignment within organizations differs from the processes involved in bringing in new members. Much of this work falls under the rubric of *internal labor markets*, or "ILM"s (Doeringer and Piore 1971; Althauser 1989). ILMs are less markets than they are ways to avoid direct market forces. Under ILMs, arrangements pertaining to staffing, training, and job assignment are handled internally. Individuals join organizations at specific *ports of entry*, and then acquire skills and move through a series of promotions based on these internally designed and sanctioned rules.

Internal labor markets assume all sorts of forms. Some are organizationally based, while others are based on occupations. ILMs continue to be transformed as technology advances and workplaces restructure (Grimshaw et al. 2001). Their relevance to the present discussion is that they direct attention to how the role of educational credentials might differ for different kinds of job transactions. This raises the question of whether employers draw on different stores of knowledge when promoting than they do when hiring.

The research indicates that they do. In general, schooling has smaller effects on promotions than it has on hiring. Credentials generally get people through the entry gates of organizations far more successfully than they get them up organizational job ladders (Bills 1988b). Once hired, managers evidently reward workers more on the basis of the performance they can see rather than the potential performance that they can only anticipate. This does not mean, though, that schooling is irrelevant to promotion. Spilerman and his colleagues have conducted a valuable series of studies on this (Spilerman and Lunde 1991; Ishida et al. 1997; Spilerman and Petersen 1999). They reported that "employers reward schooling to the extent it is relevant to job performance; as a result, the particular educational features that predict to advancement vary with salary grade and, presumably, with other job characteristics as well" (Spilerman and Lunde 1991, p. 715).

Internal labor markets represent a sociologically interesting variation on how employers evaluate educational credentials. Another important complication is self-employment. Unlike the more common case in which employers estimate job candidates' likely future value based on their level of schooling, the self-employed have no employer to whom they need to send signals about their skills (Wolpin 1977; Riley 1979). But to say that the self-employed "evaluate" their own schooling in ways that correspond to what takes place elsewhere in the labor market seems naive. Lazear (1977) suggests that the self-employed use their educational credentials to signal their ability to clients (rather than employers), but this sheds little light on how educational credentials allocate people into self-employment.

A major project by Walter Mueller and several colleagues is beginning to clarify the relationships between education and self-employment. Arum and Mueller (2001) observed the increasing heterogeneity of self-employment across different occupations and sectors of the economy. Participation in traditional skilled craft-based self-employment is declining, while self-employment in professional-managerial and unskilled occupations is growing. Self-employment is often unstable, as people regularly move in and out of spells of self-employment.

People travel two routes into self-employment (Arum and Mueller 2001). The first is universalistic. In this model, individuals use specialized education and training to achieve often well-rewarded positions of self-employment.

The principles that come into play here generally correspond to those at work elsewhere in a market economy. In contrast, others move into self-employment through more traditional processes of inheritance. Arum and Mueller demonstrate the resilience of such "petty bourgeoisie" social positions across a range of societies.

Shavit and Yuchtman-Yaar (2001) examined the determinants of self-employment among 27–34 year old Israeli men. They distinguished three categories of self-employment. These were professional-managerial, qualified occupations, and unqualified occupations. Interestingly, they found no ethnic differences in the odds of reaching any of these kinds of self-employment. Membership in one or another ethnic group did little to influence the kind of self-employment that people pursued. There was, however, an interesting pattern of education effects. This effect was curvilinear in the qualified and unqualified classes. That is, those with low education and those with much education were least likely to be self-employed in these sorts of positions. In contrast, the education effect was negative in the professional-managerial class. This general finding characterizes the United States, but is far from universal across societies (Arum et al. 2001). In fact, the effects of education on self-employment vary greatly from one society to the next.

At least in the United States, men and women typically take different paths to self-employment (Carr 1996). Carr found that the standard "human capital variables of education, age, and past work experience predicted self-employment for both men and women. Women's path to self-employment, however, was also dependent on their family situation. For example, having young children constrained women's ability to pursue self-employment, while being married enhanced it. It appears that for women much more than for men, self-employment represents a kind of contingent work, permitting greater flexibility in work hours and schedules.

All of this takes us full circle to some of the observations that motivated this book. We actually know quite little about the ways in which schooling does or does not provide the sorts of skills that contribute to successful self-employment. Still, American faith in the ability of schooling to lead to economic rewards is unabated by this lack of evidence. Whatever the research evidence shows about education and self-employment, American higher education has certainly determined that it has a role to play. "Entrepreneurial education" has become extremely popular. As the Center for Entrepreneurial Leadership Clearinghouse on Entrepreneurship Education (CELCEE) has conceptualized it:

> Entrepreneurship Education is the process of providing individuals with the concepts and skills to recognize opportunities that others have overlooked,

and to have the insight, self-esteem and knowledge to act where others have hesitated. It includes instruction in opportunity recognition, marshaling resources in the face of risk, and initiating a business venture. It also includes instruction in business management processes such as business planning, capital development, marketing, and cash flow analysis. (http://www.celcee.edu/general.html#EntEd)

Perhaps entrepreneurship education can accomplish this, or perhaps not. The point is that American society acts as though it can.

Summary

We have covered a vast terrain in this chapter. The sociological community has over the past few years learned a great deal about the contours of the process of social stratification. While scientific questions are never closed, our understanding of the empirical associations at issue are quite solid.

S.M. Miller (2001), a sociologist with a long and distinguished career, recently reflected on his career in an essay entitled "My Meritocratic Rise." Reacting to recent and vociferous attacks on affirmative action as destructive of true meritocracy through its adoption of "preferential hiring," Miller describes how one position after throughout his career relied in greater or lesser measure on luck or connections. Certainly Miller needed to perform adequately once these factors led him to a position, but his point is that he was only in a position to benefit from the meritocracy given the activation of a nonmeritocratic framework.

Miller's observations speak to the nature of social stratification in the United States. Socioeconomic opportunities are restricted for many Americans. Bonds of ascription prohibit some from full realization of their life chances. Still, there is an unmistakable trend toward meritocracy. At the same time, formal schooling is increasingly central to how people build their socioeconomic lives, and judging from the persistent payoff to schooling in the midst of the proliferation of educated persons, this cannot be due solely to credentialism.

To conclude that the United States is becoming an increasingly meritocratic society in which the practice of credentialism (whether as credential inflation or as sheepskin effects) is under severe social pressure is not an unambiguous cause for celebration. This is not only because often large pockets of ascription remain, or because many employers still operate according to credentialist principles. It is rather to acknowledge that a meritocratic society is a demanding society, in which the subordination of education to the workplace threatens to become complete. Both the fairness of meritocracy and the capricious behavior of credentialist employers cut both ways, as fairness is transformed into greater inequality and the decline of selection on credentials can signal a shift back to ascription.

All of this ultimately turns on what sort of a society either meritocracy or credentialism is embedded in. I turn to this issue in the next chapter.

5

Education and Work in the Postindustrial Society

The Structure of Contemporary Society

In Chapters 3 and 4 I described meritocratic and credentialist models of the association between education and work and presented evidence for and against these models as depictions of how rewards are allocated in American society. I suggested that both models have implications for how to think about the relationships between education and work.

I shift the lenses in this chapter, and present a model for understanding the nature of the society in which either meritocracy or credentialism is embedded. This is the *Postindustrial Society*. The postindustrial model emphasizes a handful of basic social transformations in the United States and other nations. These include information technology, microelectronics, the shift from labor-intensive manufacturing to knowledge-intensive service industries, and a transformed set of social relationships emanating from these shifts. Underlying all of these transformations is the emergence of *theoretical knowledge* as a foundation for social change.

Daniel Bell, whose *The Coming of Post-industrial Society: A Venture in Social Forecasting* (1973/1999) remains the point of reference for understanding postindustrialism, maintained that postindustrialism is meritocratic in its logic. For Bell, as societies move toward more rational means of organizing and conducting work, the old bonds of ascription and nepotism will fade. While this logic seems sound enough, empirically this may or may not be the case. Versions of both meritocracies and credentialist systems could and did predate postindustrialism. For now, we can leave open the question of the compatibility between postindustrialism and both meritocracy and credentialism, and turn instead to how the postindustrial model might advance our understanding of the relationships between education and work.

My goal here is not that of advancing postindustrial theory, but rather using it as a wedge into understanding some of the relationships between education and work. Others have offered capable criticisms of the theory, some sympathetic (Block 1990) and some less so (Webster 1994). I will often follow a somewhat circuitous path, but the focus is consistently on the relationship of education and work in postindustrial society. As in the previous chapters, sometimes the research base underlying the discussion is solid and sometimes it is inconclusive. I will spend some time presenting and criticizing basic concepts, searching for connections in the literature, and raising a few unresolved issues.

Daniel Bell's Formulation of the Postindustrial Society

The phrase "postindustrial society" has slipped into the vocabulary of American culture as a shorthand term for an assortment of social and economic trends. As with many terms that serve both lay and technical purposes, much is often lost in the transition. I rely here on the most systematic elaboration of the postindustrial model, that of sociologist Daniel Bell. Bell's now classic analysis first appeared in 1973, although the concept had appeared in his writing well before then. The book was republished in 1999 with substantial new material reflecting on the trends in American society since the original publication.

Bell distinguishes postindustrial society from preindustrial and industrial forms. A preindustrial society is primarily extractive. That is, preindustrial societies are based on extracting their livelihood from agriculture, mining, fishing, timber, natural gas, or oil. In contrast, an industrial society is primarily fabricating. It coordinates the application of labor, energy, and machine technology for the manufacture of goods. Finally, a postindustrial society is primarily processing. Telecommunications and computers are strategic for the exchange of information and knowledge. To oversimplify only a bit, the transformation from industrialism to postindustrialism entails a shift away from machine technology, capital, and labor and toward intellectual technology, information, and knowledge.

The broad contours of the postindustrial society: Industrial and occupational shifts

The most visible feature of postindustrialism is a series of shifts in the industries and occupations in which people work. The shift from goods to services and from blue-collar to white-collar occupations is a familiar soc.-ological story. The story rests, however, on several concepts that need to be presented first to better understand these trends and their evidentiary base. These concepts have long histories, and many are now being challenged by the research community (Abbott 1989; Barley 1996; Zuboff 1996; National Research Council 1999). As analysts rethink these concepts, what is at stake is a trade-off between accuracy, validity, and realism on the one hand and comparability over time on the other. That is, a cost of improving outdated concepts is that it makes it more difficult to chart trends.

Occupations, jobs, and others

In Chapter 1 I described "work" as what people do voluntarily for economic reward. They do this in different settings. *Organizations* are "work systems directed toward the production, distribution, and consumption of goods and services" (Kalleberg and Berg 1987, p. 32). Two basic kinds of work organizations are the *firm*, which is the basic corporate group, and the *establishment*, which is the "physical location of a certain economic activity" (Bureau of Labor Statistics, http://www.bls.gov/bls/glossary.htm). Both the McDonalds corporation and the McDonalds on the street corner are organizations, but the former is a firm while the latter is an establishment. An *industry*, in turn, is "a group of establishments that produce similar products or provide similar services" (Bureau of Labor Statistics, http://www.bls.gov/bls/glossary.htm). Both of these McDonalds work organizations would be in the restaurant industry.

Another important distinction is that between *jobs* and *occupations*. We are used to thinking of people as "having jobs," but this has not always been the case. The idea of a job as a distinct part of one's life is really quite new, arising during the shift from preindustrialism to industrialism (Barley and Kunda 2001). For most working people in a postindustrial era, however, the job is the key organizing principle of their work lives. Analysts typically emphasize the greater generality and abstraction of occupation, and the greater specificity of jobs. As Hauser and Warren (2001, p. 282) describe this, "A job is a specific and sometimes unique bundle of activities carried out by a person in the expectation of economic remuneration. An occupation is an abstract category used to group and classify similar jobs." One might think of jobs as the intersections of occupations and organizations, or as the specific set of tasks and duties associated with a given position (Kaufman and Spilerman 1982). Given the greater specificity of what constitutes a job, we are unable to chart trends in the "job structure," or to examine the distribution of jobs in any nationally representative sense. Performing these

Box 5.1 Odd jobs from *The Dictionary of Occupational Titles*, published by the US Department of Labor, Employment and Training Administration

Barrel Scraper	Mother Tester
Bed Rubber	Pantyhose-Crotch-Closing
Belly Roller	Machine Operator
Blind Hooker	Parlor Chaperone
Blow-off Worker	Pickle Pumper
Bologna Lacer	Powder Nipper
Bone Picker	Prize Jacket
Bosom Presser	Puddler
Brain Picker	Puffer
Butt Maker	Pusher
Cereal Popper	Radioactive-waste Sampler
Chicken Fancier	Religious-ritual Slaughterer
Comedy Diver	Retort Forker
Cookie Breaker	Santa's Helper
Cracker	Scratcher
Crown Pouncer	Sea-foam-kiss Maker
Devil Tender	Seal Killer
Dice Spotter	Searcher
Dope-House Operator	Seed-potato Arranger
Dukey Rider	Side Splitter
Dust Sampler	Slimer
Egg Smeller	Smearer
Finger Waver	Smeller
Frickertron Checker	Smoke Eater
Hand Shaker	Stereotyper
Head Beater	Streaker
King Maker	Sulky Driver
Knocker-off	Upsetter
Marshmallow Runner	Wad Impregnator

Source: *Harper's Magazine*, August 2000.

tasks with occupations, on the other hand, is a vital part of what social scientists do.

Any given "occupation" can be extremely heterogenous. Occupations, initial appearances perhaps to the contrary, can be ambiguous things. Boxes 5.1 and 5.2 are taken from the August 2000 edition of *Harper's Magazine* and the April 2, 2001 edition of *The New Yorker*, respectively. Both are entitled, appropriately enough, "Odd Jobs" (although both actually pertain to occupations). In addition to their entertainment value, these items demonstrate the range of activities that people perform to make a living for themselves. Indeed, the occupations envisioned in Paul DeFillippo's collection of futuristic short stories *Strange Trades* (2001) are not appreciably stranger than many of the real occupations in these articles.

Jobs come and go all the time as work projects are completed, as businesses fail, or as people resign. Occupations are less ephemeral, but are far from permanent. Occupations die over time (there is little call now for slide-rule makers, for instance), and new ones emerge. A few decades ago, no one was classified as a web master, environmental engineer, or convention manager (Bureau of Labor Statistics 1998).

Finally, we need a few words about the *service sector*. The service sector is more complicated than it is often portrayed to be. Despite the shopworn image of a world of fast food workers (for whatever unfathomable reason, typically referred to as "hamburger flippers") and domestic workers, "services" comprises an extremely diverse array of activities. Any category that includes both Tom Cruise and a Burger King employer, or both software programmers and those who clean the buildings in which software is programmed is being asked to conduct an enormous amount of conceptual work.

There are any number of ways to classify the range of industries that comprise the service sector. As a starting point, we can distinguish the *human* services of health, education, and a range of social services from the *professional and technical* services of such areas as research, evaluation, computers, and systems analysis. A more detailed classification consists of transportation and utilities; wholesale and retail trade; finance, insurance, and real estate (often identified by the acronym FIRE); personal, professional, and business services; and government (including federal, state, and local levels). Other, often more conceptually based, categorizations have been offered as well, although their full explication is beyond what I can offer here (see especially Herzenberg et al. 1998 and Sayer and Walker 1992).

At their best, these schemes can be imprecise. Further, even with these distinctions *within* the service sector, we can question even the more basic

Box 5.2　And more odd jobs: The Census Bureau's idea of upward mobility

Every writer I know has at one time dreamed of finding a different line of work – less solitary and solipsistic, more remunerative or athletic, something of greater immediate utility to the human race. I would have liked to be a brain surgeon.

Last week, I was inspired to rethink my alternative-career plans. My husband had downloaded the 2000 census data to our home computer, including lists of the thirty-one thousand professions open to census respondents. One table orders them alphabetically; another groups them into twenty-three uber-categories, which are ranked according to somewhat inscrutable Darwinian criteria: "skill-level," suggested one census official, or "roughly descending socioeconomic status," according to an introduction to an older job index, or perhaps just muscle-to-fat ratio. Extrapolating somewhat recklessly, I admit, from macro to micro, from ontology through to taxonomy via toxicology (it was happy hour), I reached the following conclusions about our new social order.

Presidents and board chairmen (but not chairpeople) are, predictably top dogs, but so are liquor commissioners. Oil-lease operators and zoo directors share second place. Fashion stylists, along with liquidators, rate highly, at 5. Bank cashiers and bank presidents fraternize bolshevistically at 12. Farmwives, sharecroppers, and stallion keepers hover around 20, with rat and muck farmers, ahead of space physicists (170), animal and people bounty hunters (611 and 382, respectively), impregnators (881), soubrettes (270), blood donors (465), wort extractors (896), boarding-house keepers (34), and Web developers (111), though they may be in for a downgrade next time around; and easily ahead of test pilots (903), blow-off workers (961), milkmen (913), goat drivers (920), and the undervalued zanjero (an assessor of water rights in the Southwest), who, at 975, is close to the bottom.

It was refreshing to think that, in someone's estimation, welfare mothers (460) rank above yacht masters (931), and that cancer researchers (165) have more prestige than tax lawyers (210) – though not, alas, more than undertakers (32). Stripteasers and bull fiddlers move and shake at 274 and 275, respectively, alongside professional athletes (272), clowns and cowboys (276), and journalists (281). Tonsorial artists are a cut above hairdressers (450 to 451), while medical doctors (in the age of HMOs) rank just 306 – well behind *mohels*, at 204, and faith healers, at 206, but marginally ahead of naprapaths, at 326. House wreckers (22) and casino managers (33) are

highly prized members of society, at least by census officials. No one con-
fessed to being a home wrecker; although, apparently, various respondents
did admit to practicing the metiers of axeman, bootlegger, gang leader;
knockdown man, roughneck, roustabout, rabbit fancier; roving hand slasher,
skull grinder, sponger, and spooner. An unspecified number also carry out
the work of baggage smasher (453). But we knew that.

It should come as no surprise that pollsters (181) rank higher than
politicians (202) and political reporters (281), or that literary agents, at 50
– a nose ahead of horse traders, at 51 – outrank authors. However
anyone who has ever tried to put together a barbecue grill by flashlight on
a buggy summer night will question the assignment of assembly-instructions
writers to the top of the scribe hierarchy (284), while biographers and
novelists (socioeconomically indistinguishable) must content themselves with
a 285. I tarried in the book section, impressed that there was so much to
do besides write: book canvasser, cleaner, coverer cutter finisher; jogger,
mender, packer and sewer. But I also felt an instinctive professional kinship
with those who serve the public in certain other guises, for example, borers,
bucket chuckers, carnies, impersonators, morale officers, printer's devils,
puppet masters, riddlers, smoothers, smutters, snipers, snubbers, solution-
makers, sourers, and perhaps also bone pullers, pickers, and crushers.

So many jobs, so little time! Briskly scrolling through the populous categories of assemblers, apprentices, assistants, officers, repairers, sale-speople,
and teachers, I stopped to wonder about the workday of an aging room
hand, joy loader; legman, pond monkey, rabbler; rink rat, riprap man, anti-
squeak worker; bad-work gatherer skoog operator; size changer, sister
superior, snake charmer; and zoogler.

I found no listing for brain surgeon as such, though there is one for
brainer (781). Still, it comforted me to think that, no matter how tough
times get, I can always apply – confident of my fitness – for work as a
wrong-address clerk.

Source: Judith Thurman (2001) The New Yorker. April 2. Originally published in The New
Yorker. Copyright © 2001 Condé Nast Publications Inc. Reprinted by permission. All Rights
Reserved.

distinction *between* goods and services. Chajewski and Newman (1998) state
that "The distinction between the production of services and manufacturing
of goods is no longer useful (Reich 1991). It probably never was." It is difficult, for example, to see why buying a fast-food hamburger represents the

Table 5.1 Occupational distribution of the labor force, 1900–1990 (percentages)

	1990	1980	1970	1960	1950	1940	1930	1920	1910	1900
White-collar workers	57.1	53.9	47.9	42.3	36.7	31.1	29.4	24.9	21.4	17.6
Professional, technical	16.7	16.5	14.7	11.4	8.6	7.5	6.8	5.4	4.7	4.3
Managers, officials, proprietors	12.6	12.0	8.2	8.5	8.8	7.3	7.4	6.6	6.6	5.8
Clerical	15.8	18.6	17.9	14.9	12.3	9.6	8.9	8.0	5.3	3.0
Sales	12.0	6.8	7.2	7.5	7.0	6.7	6.3	4.9	4.7	4.5
Manual and service workers	40.3	43.2	49.0	51.4	51.4	51.5	49.4	48.1	47.7	44.9
Manual	26.6	31.1	36.3	39.7	41.0	39.8	39.6	40.2	38.2	35.8
Craft, supervisors	11.6	13.3	13.8	14.3	14.1	12.0	12.8	13.0	11.6	10.5
Operatives	10.9	13.5	17.8	19.9	20.3	18.4	15.8	15.6	14.6	12.8
Laborers (except farm, mine)	4.1	4.3	4.7	5.5	6.6	9.4	11.0	11.6	12.0	12.5
Service	13.4	12.1	12.7	11.8	10.4	11.7	9.8	7.8	9.6	9.0
Private household	0.7	0.8	1.3	2.8	2.6	4.7	4.1	3.3	5.0	5.4
Other service	12.7	11.3	11.2	9.0	7.8	7.1	5.7	4.5	4.6	3.6
Farm workers	2.9	2.9	3.1	6.3	11.9	17.4	21.2	27.0	30.9	37.5
Farmers, farm managers	N/A	1.7	1.8	3.9	7.5	10.4	12.4	15.3	16.5	19.9
Farm laborers, supervisors	N/A	1.2	1.3	2.4	4.4	7.0	9.8	11.7	14.4	17.7

Source: Goldin (1998a).

purchase of a service rather than a good, or why warehouses full of software reside in the service sector rather than in manufacturing. (Esping-Andersen (1999, p. 104) provides more detail on a variety of measurement problems in the service sector.)

Essentially, what people mean when they talk about the shift from goods to services is that not as many people manufacture things as they once did. This distinction becomes difficult to sustain in the real world of informated production and "smart" machines, but can perhaps serve as a convenient shorthand for a general trend in postindustrial society.

Back to the story: The changing American industrial and occupational distributions

With this definitional diversion as background, we can turn to changes in American industrial and occupational structure. Tables 5.1 and 5.2 (adapted from Goldin 1998b) present some data on these shifts. While I do not present comparative results here, the trends in other postindustrial societies are broadly comparable (Esping-Andersen 1999).

The change from goods to services

The most widely acknowledged characteristic of postindustrialism is the transformation from a goods-producing to service-providing society. Even with the ambiguity of the industrial categories, the move away from manufacturing and into services is clear. This followed an earlier shift from agriculture to manufacturing. While the trend toward service-providing industries accelerated in the years immediately after World War II, it is also one that has been taking place for a very long time.

Zuboff (1996, pp. 1106–7) acknowledges the great heterogeneity in services, but suggests that we should neither overemphasize nor misinterpret the shift from goods to services. She observes that much of the postwar growth in services to about 1970 was in both K–12 and postsecondary education (along with a range of services that support education) and government (particularly at state and local levels). Moreover, much of the growth was not in the private economy often portrayed as the basis of postindustrialism, but rather in government agencies involved in administering health, justice, and national defense. Zuboff believes that the shift from blue-collar to white-collar occupations (discussed below) and the immense shift out of agriculture are more revealing.

Still, the shift toward service industries is clear. This is a familiar sociological story, but there are a few complications. First, the data in this table

Table 5.2 Changes in US industrial employment, 1890–2002

	1890	1950	1970	1982	2002
Service-producing industries	26	51	65	71	78
Finance, insurance, and real estate	1	4	5	6	7
Business, personal, professional services	8	10	19	20	38
Trade: wholesale and retail	9	18	20	22	21
Transportation, utilities, communications	6	8	6	6	7
Government: federal, state, and local	2	11	15	17	5
Goods-producing industries	74	49	35	29	23
Manufacturing	20	29	25	21	13
Construction	6	4	5	4	7
Agriculture, forestry, mining, fishing	48	16	5	4	3
Total employed labor force (in millions)	23.3	58.9	78.6	98.9	136.5

Many of the detailed entries are not strictly comparable across time, although the broad patterns are more stable.
Source: Tausky (1984) and US Bureau of Labor Statistics.

pertain to the numbers of people in each industry category, that is, to the *employment share* of each industrial sector. This is not the same as the importance of that category to the economy. While it is true that employment in manufacturing and (even more) agriculture has declined, productivity (which we can define here simply as how much output is produced for a given level of input) in those sectors has increased. Put simply, we produce more products and more food than ever, but it takes fewer workers to do so. The result is a net employment shift out of goods-producing industries.

Understanding trends in productivity has been a major preoccupation of social scientists, in particular economists, for decades. This is a complex issue, which for our purposes raises a few questions. What can we make of the fact that the expansion of secondary and postsecondary education, economic productivity, and postindustrialism have risen together (each to an astonishing degree) over the past several decades? Are these trends causally related to each other? What is the effect of educational growth on productivity growth, and how has this in turn led to the postindustrial transformation?

Scholars have given these questions much attention, and we can present their answers only briefly here. The pioneering analysis is that of economist Edward Denison (1962). Examining the period from 1929 to 1962, Denison was concerned with the role of educational expansion as a source of economic growth. He was careful to distinguish two aspects of this expansion – the increase in years of schooling completed and the quality of that education per American worker over that time. Denison calculated that only 5 percent of total economic growth during that period could be explained by such conventional "factor growth" measures as changes in labor hours or physical capital per worker. He concluded that 28 percent of the residual (i.e., the other 95 percent) of the growth could be explained by increases in years and quality of education per American worker. Put simply, economic growth in the United States had depended a great deal on the expansion of schooling.

Economist Claudia Goldin (1998a) thinks that Dension's 28 percent estimate is too low. Updating Denison's estimates in a provocative series of articles (Goldin 1998a, 2001; Goldin and Katz 2001), Goldin maintains (1998a, p. 346) that: "Human capital accumulation and technological change were to the twentieth century what physical capital accumulation was to the nineteenth century – the engine of growth." That is, by assuming world leadership in the provision of education (particularly, in the first three-quarters of the twentieth century, at the secondary level), Americans established a base of literacy, numeracy, and general and transferable skills that provided the needed foundation for economic growth. For Goldin, this was the "Human Capital Century," built on a unique combination of American institutions and traditions.

Goldin's position is a compelling one. It seems reasonable enough that an educated workforce would be a prerequisite to rapid economic expansion. As we saw in earlier chapters, however, there are dissenters. Credentialists such as Collins and Berg see little relationship between what is learned in school and what is needed on the job. Others too doubt that formal schooling (at least beyond the elementary years) has much to do with economic growth.

Sociologists Chabbott and Ramirez have helped resolve some of the evident contradictions between these two positions in their careful review of the "mutual effects of education and development" (2000). The authors acknowledge that education is undeniably related to economic success at the individual level, even if the causal mechanisms behind this (i.e., credentialism versus meritocracy) remain unsettled. Of more concern to them how education and work are related at the societal level. They find that "the effects of education on development at the collective level are ambiguous" (p. 163), and set themselves the task of sorting out this ambiguity.

As it turns out, education and work are related to each other at the societal level in many different ways. For instance, the expansion of elementary enrollments influences economic development in ways quite different from expansion at the secondary level. Postsecondary growth has still different effects. In particular, Chabbott and Ramirez conclude (p. 166) that "primary and secondary schooling have stronger effects on economic development than higher education." They add that the "economic effects of expanded schooling seemed stronger for poorer countries." (Walters and Rubinson (1983) reached similar conclusions for the United States by looking at differences across states.) Further, some types of schooling contribute more to economic growth than do others. Vocational schooling often has more "payoff" than does academic education. Likewise, "greater enrollments in science and engineering positively influence economic development" (Chabbott and Ramirez 2000, p. 167).

Barro (1991) has further clarified how schooling is related to growth. He reported that for a sample of 98 countries from 1960 to 1985, economic growth was more an outcome of the *initial level* of human capital in the society (which he measured as the 1960 school enrollment rates) than it was a result of the *expansion* of any level of the educational system. To simplify only a bit, having lots of educated people around enhances economic growth. Barro suggests that it is only by having abundant stocks of human capital (relative to GDP) that poor countries can ever catch up to rich countries (see also Romer 1990, and Block 1990, pp. 176ff).

What can we conclude from this? Clearly, societies with educated workforces have a stock of human capital on which to build that less educated societies do not. Which level of the educational system and what types of schooling are most consequential for economic growth varies across historical periods and across societies. For example, as Goldin (1998a) argued, the wide diffusion of general literacy and numeracy skills fueled the industrial era. It may be, however, that the postindustrial era will be driven by a wider diffusion of interpersonal and microelectronic-related skills offered in specialized postsecondary programs. Whether or not this takes place, there seems little doubt that economic growth relies on an educated workforce.

Occupational shifts

Broad shifts across industry lines are basic to postindustrial society. We also need to look at trends within industries. For instance, an increasing share of people in manufacturing *industries* work in something other than manufacturing *occupations*. That is, office work now characterizes goods-producing industries in much the same way that it does the service sector. To gain some insight into this, we now turn to occupational shifts.

The major trends are clear. First, as shown in Table 5.1, Americans long ago left the farm. In 1900, over one-third of the labor force consisted of either "farmers, farm managers" or "farm laborers, supervisors." By 1970 this had fallen to about three percent, where it has generally remained.

American workers have also moved out of laboring jobs. There has been a steadily diminishing role for the less skilled over time. This went from about one in eight workers in the rapidly industrializing economy of 1900 to about one in 25 in postindustrial 1990. Those classified as laborers in 1900 were by no means the only low-skilled members of the labor force (Goldin 1998a). Particularly in the manufacturing and transportation industrial sectors, skill requirements were generally low regardless of one's occupational designation.

The overall shift out of the "manual and service workers" category is less dramatic than some of the shifts within it. The decline in the proportion of the labor force employed in manual occupations only began in earnest after World War II, with an especially steep decline in the 1980s. This trend corresponded with a shift into a range of "white-collar" occupations. One might characterize this as a shift toward an "office economy" or as a shift into knowledge work, but either way the extent of this change is unmistakable. About one in six American workers were in white-collar occupations in 1900 (Table 5.1). By the 1980s more than half were. Of course, the white-collar category is heterogeneous. White-collar workers, no less than blue-collar workers, often work with their hands, use tools and machines, and get dirty (Barley 1992). The broader theme is the ever-increasing "technization" of the labor force.

A particularly striking part of the broader shift is toward what are often called "PTM" occupations – Professional, Technical, and Managerial. These are diverse categories that in many ways personify postindustrialism. The rate of change in the shifts toward PTM work varies over time (for instance, the share of the labor force in managerial occupations grew relatively little from 1900 to 1970 before taking off), but their broad sweep is evident.

Despite some recent slippage, the largest relative growth over time has been in clerical occupations. The greatest gains here have been for women. Within service occupations, there has been a shift away from private household occupations, but a shift toward "other service."

The movement of women towards certain kinds of work merits a closer look. Bell (1999) argues that the economic opportunities available to women will be enhanced under postindustrialism. Unlike industrial work (at least some of it), "knowledge work" presents little in the way of physical barriers that favor one sex over the other (claims that have been made about both manual dexterity and physical strength). It follows that, all else being equal, postindustrial society will bring expanded employment for women.

In the previous chapter, I presented evidence for the improving status of women in the American labor market. This begins simply with their growing rates of participation. "Among the most dramatic changes, the labor force participation of women has risen sharply from 41.6 percent in 1968 to 59.8 percent in 1998, and the share of all jobs held by women increased from 37.1 percent to 46.4 percent of the labor force" (US Department of Labor 1999, p. 46 and accompanying footnote). While the details can be found elsewhere, women have made comparable gains in occupational status and earnings (Fullerton 1999; Bowler 1999; US Department of Labor 2001).

There are important "education and work" angles to this generalization. First, over the past several years, women's wage growth has outpaced that of men at all levels of education. Both less-educated and better-educated women have improved their status relative to comparably educated men. This is only in part because women have done "better" in some objective sense. Rather, men's earnings have been with rare exceptions relatively stagnant over the past three decades. Thus, much of the apparent increase for women is really the deterioration of the position of men, a trend that cuts across educational levels.

While it is clear that employed women have made strides under postindustrialism, there is some doubt that postindustrial shifts have benefited men and women equally. Esping-Andersen (1999) believes, at least for many European nations, that postindustrial societies have often been forced into difficult compromises between women's work experiences and their domestic lives. He adds that this has taken place in ways that often disproportionately make women the bearers of the risks of an increasingly competitive set of economic arrangements.

Likewise, Fountain (2000) questions the enhanced economic opportunities that postindustrialism will offer to women. She directs attention to the absence of women in many of the most quintessentially postindustrial positions, which she characterizes as "information technology design roles." In 1995, fewer than 30 percent of US computer scientists, computer systems analysts, or computer programmers were women (although these jobs became less gender-segregated in the 1980s, see Wright and Jacobs 1994). Until women move into these positions of postindustrial influence, their participation in postindustrial society will be limited.

Labor force projections

The industrial and occupational trends presented thus far point to a more service-oriented and knowledge-based American society. Can we expect these trends to continue? To answer this we need to consider *projections*. For that, we turn to the work of the United States Bureau of Labor Statistics (BLS).

Every two years the BLS, an agency of the Department of Labor, releases a series of labor force projections. They target these at a date 10 years into the future. Without going into detail about the methodology underlying these projections, what the BLS does is to combine population projections made by the Bureau of the Census with its own projections of labor force participation rates. The projections are regularly evaluated against actual trends. BLS's most recent projections (to the year 2010) were presented in the November 2001 issue of the *Monthly Labor Review*. As with earlier presentations of their projections, this issue featured chapters on the economy, the labor force, employment by industry, and employment by occupation. These are done separately for 136 different age, sex, race, or Hispanic origin groups.

By all evidence, the trends toward postindustrialism will continue. As Berman (2001, p. 40) observed, "Continuing the 1990–2000 historical trend, virtually all non-farm wage and salary employment growth will be generated by [the] service-producing sector." While the goods-producing sector is expected to add jobs over the next decade, the rate of growth will be slow. At the same time, consistent with the historical record I presented earlier, the goods-producing sector will maintain its share of output relative to services. Within the service-producing sector, the service industry division (particularly business services and health) will grow most rapidly, followed by retail trade. The growth in the service industry division will take place in both percentage and absolute terms. This is an important distinction. Relatively small industries that are growing rapidly in percentage terms may actually produce relatively few jobs. The opposite situation, in which large industries grow slowly but produce lots of jobs, can also take place.

Turning to BLS's occupational projections, the fastest growth is expected to be in two occupational groups (Hecker 2001). These are professional and related occupations and service occupations. These projections pertain to both percentage change and the number of new jobs. The important thing about these projections is that these two occupations are at the opposite ends of the education and earnings distributions. That is, professional occupations require extensive educational preparation and are generally well-rewarded. Service jobs require lower educational credentials, with correspondingly lower job rewards.

The slowest growth will be in several different occupational categories. These include office and administrative support occupations, production occupations, and farming, fishing, and forestry occupations. Collectively, the projected changes to 2010 are basically incremental ones. While they will lead to modest changes in the relative *size* of different occupational groups, they will not lead to shifts in the relative *rankings* by employment share.

What do these projections mean for the relationships between education and work? As the header to Hecker's article states, "Occupations requiring a postsecondary vocational award or an academic degree, which accounted for 29 percent of all jobs in 2000, will account for 42 percent of total job growth from 2000 to 2010" (p. 57). While accurate enough, this claim needs to be interpreted carefully. Hecker (p. 57) elaborates:

> The economy will continue generating jobs for workers at all levels of education and training, although growth rates are projected to be faster, on average, for occupations generally requiring a postsecondary award (a vocational certificate or other award or an associate or higher degree), than for occupations requiring less education or training. Most new jobs, however, will arise in occupations that require only work-related training (on-the-job training or work experience in a related occupation), even though these occupations are expected to grow more slowly, on average. This reflects the fact that these occupations accounted for about 7 out of 10 jobs in 2000.

The implication of this is that the pressure on labor market participants to acquire and demonstrate ever higher levels of skills (or, as many would have it, ever higher levels of formal credentials, whatever these credentials may indicate) will continue. Put simply, the costs of not being able to offer marketable skills are likely to get worse.

Occupational projections are valuable. They permit analysts and planners to anticipate areas of shortage or surplus, and to design programs and provide information and incentives that can ease the shock of industrial and occupational shifts. They provide social scientists with grist for theoretical and empirical speculation. Nonetheless, projections of any sort have limitations. Bailey (1991) notes two particularly important features of occupational projections that limit their usefulness for understanding changes in the demand for workers with different levels of education. First, he sees many projections as insufficiently attentive to occupational change that take place *within* given industries. That is, the composition of a given industry – what kinds of people work in it and the kind of work they do – can change over time. Second, Bailey is concerned with ways in which the content of work within particular occupations can change over time (1991, p. 13). Even if the occupational composition of an industry does not change, there may be shifts in the kind of work performed by the incumbents of a particular occupation. Neither of these trends is adequately described in most projections.

Even with these criticisms, Bailey believes that BLS projections indicate a steady upgrading of skills, which may even be a bit underestimated. He indicates the care needed to interpret projections, noting that at least one influential report (*Workforce 2000*) greatly exaggerated the level of upgrading. More important for Bailey is that projections tell us relatively little about how education might be reformed in response to anticipated changes in the workplace. Rather than discussing only the length of time that prospective workers should spend in school, we should be paying more attention to the content of that schooling.

More Specific Features of Postindustrialism and How They Shape the Relationships Between Education and Work

In the 1976 "Foreword" to *The Coming of Post-Industrial Society*, Bell lists what he sees as the 11 fundamental dimensions of the postindustrial society. One might add a couple more based on his more recent writing. My approach in the rest of this chapter is to use a few of these dimensions as a point of departure to further examine the relationship between education and work. This may sometimes take us fairly far afield from postindustrialism per se, but hopefully in a way that retains the focus on schools and workplaces.

The centrality of theoretical knowledge

Postindustrial society is a knowledge-based society – a society resting on "a set of organized statements of facts or ideas, presenting a reasoned judgment or an experimental result, which is transmitted to others through some communication medium in some systematic form" (Bell 1999, p. 175). While any society depends on access to and management of knowledge, postindustrial society represents something new in the extent to which it organizes itself around *theoretical knowledge*. As never before, postindustrial society harnesses knowledge "for the purpose of social control and the directing of innovation and change" (1999, p. 20). The organization of postindustrial society around knowledge "in turn gives rise to new social relationships and new structures which have to be managed politically" (1999, p. 20).

The dominance of theoretical knowledge under postindustrialism signifies a shift away from the kind of knowledge that characterized industrial society. But what *is* theoretical knowledge? We can follow Bell that theoretical knowledge represents "the primacy of theory over empiricism and the codification of knowledge into abstract systems of symbols that . . . can be used to illustrate many different and varied areas of experience" (1998, p. 20). To use an example that may be overly simple (but which tends to work with my own students), we no longer learn about the strengths of bridges by observing which ones fall down and which ones don't, but rather by running endless and sophisticated computer simulations of virtual bridges under every possible combination of weather, load, and stress. In short, abstract and generalizable knowledge has replaced more pragmatic and contextual knowledge as the fundamental means by which societies anticipate and plan for the future (Frenkel et al. 1999). As evidence for the change in the character of the kind of knowledge that most matters in postindustrial society, Bell points to "the exponential growth and branching of science, the rise of a new intellectual technology, the creation of systematic research through R & D budgets, and, as the calyx of all this, the codification of theoretical knowledge" (p. 44). An example of this is the growth of such science-based industries as computers, micro-electronics, and fiber optics.

The primacy of theoretical knowledge, even more than the shift from goods to services, or the computerization of the workplace, or any trend toward meritocratic selection, defines the postindustrial society. More and more workers will need to master more and more complex skills to prosper under postindustrialism. There is, however, reason to doubt that equipping potential workers *solely* with theoretical knowledge will prepare them for the postindustrial workplace. Sociologists have learned a good deal about how different kinds of knowledge are used in the workplace under different situations. Similarly, the distinction between postindustrial-age theoretical knowledge and industrial-age contextual knowledge often breaks down in actual work settings. In fact, providing potential workers exclusively with theoretical knowledge may well be counterproductive. A couple of examples illustrate this.

In *The System of Professions: An Essay on the Division of Expert Labor* (1988, pp. 52–7), Andrew Abbott objects to the idea that there is a body of professional knowledge, however abstract or sophisticated, that can be separated from its use. That is, Abbott wants to advance a view of professional (or workplace) knowledge as "knowledge in use." All knowledge, in this account, is inevitably applied knowledge, and the idea of an abstracted "theoretical knowledge" is harder to imagine. Abbott recognizes that professions do of course have abstracted bodies of knowledge on which they can draw for solutions to specific problems, but he adds that "this perfected abstract knowledge system exists only in the world of professional textbooks" (p. 56).

If Abbott is correct, the rift in the kind of knowledge upon which society most relies may be less definitive than postindustrial theory suggests. Both industrialism and postindustrialism, for Abbott, are based on how working people apply any sort of knowledge – abstract or more concrete – in real work situations. A postindustrial educational system that ignores the fact that knowledge must be applied to be of value risks the benefits that theoretical knowledge can offer.

Barley (1996) has also offered some helpful observations on the role of knowledge in the postindustrial society. Barley observes that the real "work" of postindustrial society – the activities that separate the postindustrial era from the industrial one – is largely performed by the vast if diverse category of "technicians." He argues that technicians are in many ways the exemplar of postindustrial work (see also Orr 1996). This leads him to ask "What do technicians do and what do they know?"

Indeed, technicians do quite a lot. The US Census Bureau classifies technicians ranging from those whose occupations are in "accounting" and "aerospace" through those in "mental health" and "microfilm" and on through those in "respiratory therapy," "sand," and "x-ray." While not one of the numerically largest occupational categories, technicians continue to grow at a rapid rate. More important than their sheer numbers is their strategic importance to postindustrial work organizations.

Technicians also know quite a lot, and this knowledge turns out to go well beyond the theoretical knowledge discussed by Bell. Barley describes the link between the content of what technicians learn in school (which, interestingly enough, is usually called "training" rather than "education") and the current demands of their work. A surprisingly large number of technicians lack formal training (although in many cases, of course, some form of certification is required). Not only are many technicians "untrained," but "Almost every technician with whom we spoke devalued credentials" (p. 424).

If technicians as exemplars of postindustrial work see little necessary linkage between their education and their work, how do they explain their own ability to carry out what are often complex and demanding tasks? Barley notes that "Technicians valued experience over formal training, in part because technologies and techniques changed so quickly that by the time they filtered into the classroom they were already outdated. Moreover, knowledge became relevant in practice only in light of the problem at hand" (p. 425). In other words, technicians believe they learn most from specific instances when they have to solve problems, depart from routines, or apply hard-won lessons to novel situations. Like Bell, Barley distinguishes formal knowledge from contextual knowledge. Unlike Bell, he argues for the persistence of contextual knowledge in postindustrial society.

Why present the work of Abbott and Barley at such length here? They offer an insistence that we think harder about the relationship between education and work in postindustrial society. None of what they have to say denies that theoretical knowledge is key to the postindustrial society.

The evidence for the ascendancy of calculable and non-local ways of understanding the world is simply too great. Their analyses do, though, suggest some caution against pushing the linkage between schooling, theoretical knowledge, and the emerging workplace too far. The postindustrial workplace evokes a range of skills, capabilities, and dispositions. The relationship of these factors to the educational system thus emerges as a central question of the postindustrial society.

The creation of a new intellectual technology

Even with the concerns raised by Abbott and Barley, we can concede that postindustrialism brings with it an increased importance of theoretical knowledge. This raises the issue of what sorts of "tools" the postindustrial society needs to operate and manage theoretical knowledge. Just as an industrial society requires a machine technology of lathes, presses, and forklifts, so does the postindustrial society require a specific form of technology. For Bell, this is an *intellectual technology*.

"Technology" is yet another of sociology's contested concepts (Liker et al. 1999). Orlikowski (1992, p. 398) notes that "there is little agreement on the definition and measurement of technology, and no compelling evidence on the precise role of technology in organizational affairs." The term "technology" is often taken as interchangeable with "information technology" or "microelectronic technology." In fact, though, as engineer Henry Petroski (1992) reminds us, technology is broader than that. A pencil, no less than a desktop computer, is a technology, and quite a sophisticated one. To recast cognitive scientist Donald Norman's argument only a bit, technologies are those "things that make us smart" (Norman 1993).

Technology includes not only the hardware of machines and tools, but also social technologies (Orlikowski 1992). That is, the ways in which "things" and people are socially organized into "sociotechnical systems" matters every bit as much as the things themselves. These social technologies include organizational practices, management techniques, ways of organizing work, and so on. The transition from the rigid and routinized Taylorist and Fordist workplace technologies to their "post" versions is as important as the transition from steam to nuclear sources of energy.

Still, the sorts of technologies most central to postindustrialism are those that we ordinarily think of as based on computers and microelectronics. An example of intellectual technology is *econometrics*. Econometrics encompasses a wide range of intellectual activity, but Paul Samuelson and his colleagues (1954) have captured it quite succinctly as "the quantitative analysis of actual economic phenomena based on the concurrent development of theory and observation, related by appropriate methods of inference." Evolving along with the ever-greater capacity of high-speed computing, econometrics provides the ability to develop economic forecasts and simulations that are increasingly central to the operation of a modern economy.

Another example, one of particular relevance to the relationships between education and work, is *psychometrics*. Psychometrics takes us to the realm of the measurement of cognitive and non-cognitive aptitude and achievement. Standardized testing has a long history and an entrenched place in the American educational system. Students throughout the K–12 system regularly take a variety of assessments (such as the Iowa Test of Basic Skills or the Iowa Test of Educational Development). The Standardized Achievement Test (SAT) offered by the Educational Testing Service (ETS) and the American College Test given by ACT (formerly the American College Testing Program) are institutionalized as college admissions exams throughout the United States. Standardized testing has much to do with students' trajectories through the educational system, and hence, if less directly, through the occupational hierarchy.

There are indications that standardized testing (again, an example of the intellectual technology that supports postindustrialism) is increasingly directly implicated in the relationship between education and work as well. An illustration of this is the *Work Keys* assessment developed by ACT. ACT describes Work Keys as a program to support "workforce development" by providing a means to assess employability skills. The development of the Work Keys instrument involves a complex process beginning with job profiling, which is performed by ACT-authorized profilers or trained employees. ACT has profiled over 5,500 unique job titles. This elaborate process of profiling is then followed by assessments of several kinds of work skills. These include applied mathematics, applied technology, listening, locating information, observation, reading for information, teamwork, and writing. ACT is currently working to develop assessments of other skills that they have judged that employers value – basic computer skills, listening for understanding, and work habits.

Many employers are quite receptive to using inventories of skills assessment as one of a number of criteria that they might adopt when making hiring decisions (Holland 2001). Some of the employers in Holland's study used Work Keys to allocate training opportunities, and a few even considered its use for assigning promotions. Some saw standardized assessment as a means to convince external agencies (most pointedly, the Equal Employment Opportunity Commission, or EEOC) that their hiring practices were fair and unbiased.

In an earlier chapter, I described how employers select job candidates based on educational credentials. Again, this is because employers have not had the opportunity to observe the job performance of these applicants, and credentials allow employers to make some estimates about what that performance is likely to be. Credentials give employers a means to solve the problem of incomplete labor market information.

While educational credentials are a cheap signal for employers to read, they are an expensive one for job seekers to acquire. Further, it is expensive for society to build and maintain the educational infrastructures and institutions within which millions of people are credentialed every year. More than a few efficiency-minded observers (mostly, as it happens, economists) have wondered if there may be a better way. That is, some have asked why employers do not minimize their information costs by seeking less costly screens – both to them and to society – than educational credentials. In particular, the puzzle has been why American employers, unlike their counterparts in much of the world, avoid standardized tests as a cheap alternative to massive public investments in higher education. For the most part the testing option is offered as a foil – even the most rationality-driven labor economists do not seem to anticipate seriously the development of a workplace counterpart to the Educational Testing Service (Altonji and Pierret 1997, p. 26).

Still, as the intellectual technology of postindustrial society continues to evolve, we might expect the drive for efficiency and calculability to lead to the adoption of more direct selection devices than educational credentials. If not Work Keys in particular as an answer to the high cost of schooling and certification, it is one plausible challenge to the persistence of the dependence of employers on educational credentials. Why should employers trust schooling as a signal of the ability to "read for information," if this can be assessed directly via the intellectual technology of postindustrialism?

The spread of a knowledge class

If theoretical knowledge and its accompanying intellectual technology are growing more central to postindustrial society, it follows that those with access to and control of these resources will gain social advantage. This might signal a shift from ascription to achievement. It signals too, though, a shift from one basis of meritocratic social advantage to another. That is, the "old" economic elite based on command of industrial resources will give way to those with access to the skills valued in a knowledge-rich society. This transformation to a "knowledge class" or a "new class" (Gouldner

1979) amounts to a peaceful if wrenching succession of one privileged class with another. Without getting into the large and inconclusive debate over the "new class" – which Bell himself has called a "muddled concept" (Bell 1979) – at issue here is the claim that "if the dominant figures of the past hundred years have been the entrepreneur, the businessman, and the industrial executive, the 'new men' [sic] are the scientists, the mathematicians, the economists, and the engineers of the new intellectual technology" (Bell 1999, p. 344).

Probably the most important evidence for the spread of a knowledge class lies in the changes that have taken place in the American occupational structure. We examined the broad long-term shifts out of some occupations and into others earlier in this chapter. The evidence was clear that American workers are employed in different occupations than they were just a few decades ago. We noted, though, that occupational categories are blunt instruments, and that examining the movement of people from one occupational category to another in itself tells us little about changes in what people actually do during their time in these occupations. Over time, things change within occupational categories.

Responding to the changes in the distribution of occupations from 1950 to 1990, Szafran (1996) asked what these changes meant for "the frequency with which certain kinds of tasks are encountered by members of the labor force." By using a variety of indicators of "work tasks," Szafran was able to dig beneath the surface of broad occupational categories to say something about the changing nature of work. He found that the shift to PTM occupations brought with it an intriguing pattern of shifts in work tasks. In particular, both the "substantive complexity" of work and the level of "social interaction" involved in it increased in every decade from 1950 to 1990. At the same time, the frequency of "gross motor skills" decreased in every decade. The general trend in both "fine motor skills" and "harsh climatic conditions" was also downward, although the former was stable in the 1960s and the latter in the 1980s. Szafran's results quite clearly point to a postindustrial workplace in which social interaction and the manipulation of information matter more than physical strength or dexterity.

Szafran's analysis provides even further evidence of a broad shift to "knowledge work." Whether this also signifies the emergence of a powerful technocratically and professionally trained elite that plans and controls an increasing share of social decisions is another matter. In fact, the evidence for this is slim (Brint 1994). The more important point for our purposes is that the knowledge class is a credentialed class – "High education standards are the most *evident* feature of the 'class of intellectuals'" (Inozemtsev 2001, p. 127). Even Barley's educationally indifferent technicians usually had to be formally credentialed, and Brint would concede that while postindustrial professionals may not gain political power by virtue of their advanced degrees, these degrees are still a prerequisite to their entry into the professions. There is little doubt that the *linkage* between schooling and membership in the knowledge class has tightened.

For many observers, this ever-tighter articulation between higher education and entry into the professions works to the advantage of the well-educated. Lipartito and Miranti (1998) emphasize the intricate linkages between professions and universities, but also observe an ever greater link between professionals and corporations. Contrary to some (for example, Abbott 1988) who hold that the linkage to the private sector hurts the power of the professions, Lipartito and Miranti believe that it strengthens it. Professionals can exploit their strong associations with educational institutions to avoid the "proletarianization" that many elite crafts positions experienced in the transition from preindustrialism to industrialism.

Others doubt this. Kleinman and Vallas (2001), for instance, have pointed out important variations in the likelihood of even the most highly skilled and credentialed workers benefiting from postindustrialism. They see a "subtle paradox" in which among "scientists and engineers in private industry [there is] a trend toward increased levels of autonomy and control, as corporate bureaucracies adopt more flexible practices and thus defer to these workers' technical expertise." But on the other hand, university-based scientists are subject to "the commercialization of the academy [which is] a significant threat to the traditional autonomy of academic researchers" (p. 451). In other words, the traditionally privileged position of university-based scientists has been eroded before the "industrialization of the academy," while the more constrained work lives of scientists in the private sector are beginning to enjoy "the collegialization" of industrial research.

Kleinman and Vallas thus see a convergence in which academic norms and values (e.g., egalitarianism, discovery as communal property) are finding their way to industry (or at least to some segments), while at the same time industrial norms and values (e.g., hierarchy, profit) are entering universities. They note that it is far from clear what the final outcome will be, other than to remark that there will be winners and losers on both sides. They portray an increased dualism within both academe and industry. That is, universities will employ both elite tenured faculty and marginalized adjunct faculty, while the private sector will maintain both highly credentialed and marketable scientists and skilled but insecure temps. Kleinman and Vallas conclude, perhaps pessimistically but with some basis in the historical record, that the process is one in which industrial practices will ultimately have the upper hand.

A change in the character of work

Work in postindustrial society is something altogether different from work in industrial society. Preindustrial- and industrial-era work built on the relationship of people with nature and with machines. Postindustrial work, in contrast, has become primarily a relationship between persons. That is, nature and tools are now less central to the work lives of most people than are their interactions and encounters at work with other people.

I argued in Chapter 1 that "work" covers a lot of ground (Licht 1988). Some postindustrial workers have moved into a high-tech world of shared decision-making, high wages, and satisfying work. Many workplaces have achieved the "informated" quality attainable through sophisticated technologies and enlightened managerial practices. For others, postindustrialism has brought heightened uncertainty and insecurity. Many, in particular those lacking educational credentials, find themselves in marginalized and low-wage jobs with little hope of advancement. Some continue to work in little better than sweatshop conditions.

There is simply no way to do justice to the full range of "the nature of work" in postindustrial society, let alone the many ways in which education and work might be related across this full spectrum. Rather than try, my strategy over the next few pages will be to focus on what seems to be at least in part new and distinctive about postindustrial work. This directs attention to *knowledge workers* (Cortada 1998; Kleinman and Vallas 2001). These are those credentialed and cognitively skilled individuals employed in the most information-intense sectors of society (Hage and Powers 1992).

While I focus here on the "winners" in postindustrial society, equally "postindustrial" are those who have been economically left behind by their lack of educational credentials in an environment that increasingly demands them. While the postindustrial society might well produce a class located in generally privileged knowledge-intense occupations, coincident with this is a growth or at least persistence of low-skill jobs. The postindustrial society is turning out to be a bifurcated one.

There are as many ways to organize the way we think about the changing nature of postindustrial work as there are observers of those changes. Sociologist Stephen Barley (1992, 1996) characterizes the chief tendency as the "technization" of the workforce. He sees contemporary work as increasingly rationalized and information-driven. What we have witnessed is not simply a reshuffling of jobs, but a transformation in what work is.

Barley maintains that the current changes in work are fundamentally different from what has gone before, at least since the second industrial revolution of the late nineteenth and early twentieth century. Contemporary technological change – in particular computer-based information technology – is not merely *substitutional*, or "the replacement of an earlier technology by a more efficient or effective successor" (Barley 1992, p. 7; see also Meyer 1995). Historically, most technological changes are substitutional. In contrast, we are now experiencing the rarer and more profound sorts of technological changes that are *infrastructural*, those based on "the relatively small set of technologies that form the cornerstone of a society's system of production during a historical era." Thus, contemporary technological change is best seen as comparable to the advent of steam power rather than as incremental improvements in existing technologies. As Barley explains, computers are not merely efficient typewriters, nor is electronic communication simply a faster way of moving the mail. Instead, "The ramifications of a computational infrastructure are potentially staggering" (Barley 1992, p. 8; for related portrayals of work transformations see Zuboff 1984 on "infomating" the workplace and Cappelli et al. 1997 on the "digitalization" of work).

Not only is the direct experience of work transformed under postindustrialism, but the settings in which work takes place are changing as well. Analysts have characterized "the flexible firm in a new century" in so many ways as to nearly defy classification, including high performance, flexible specialization, Post-Fordist, progressive, transformed, and Post-Taylorist, to name but a few (Kalleberg 2001).[1] What is ultimately at stake here is that the "American system" of bureaucratically organized mass production has run its course. After lasting what perhaps seemed like forever but which was really only the latter few decades of the industrial era, the "mass production" model of standardized products and standardized, relatively low worker skills is now held to be giving way to a "high-performance model" of highly skilled and intellectually engaged workers employed in flexible and fluidly defined work settings (Appelbaum and Batt 1994; Bailey 1995).

The high-performance model is an eclectic one, but has a few common features. High-performance organizations are designed to draw workers in to processes of solving work-related problems. High-performance organizations exchange hierarchy and bureaucratic authority for autonomy and shared decision making. Workers, not just managers, are provided with deep understandings of organizational goals and priorities, and given the means

1   Some basic works on the topic of the transformed workplace, many of which explore cross-societal issues, include Piore and Sabel (1984); Sabel (1984); Osterman (1994a, 1994b, 1995); Gittleman et al. (1998); Vallas (1999); Rothschild (2000); Miozzo and Ramirez (2000); Appelbaum et al. (2000); Eriksson (2001); and Brown and Campbell (2002).

to help attain these. The organization's commitment is to the continual training and development of its workforce.

It is difficult to say how deeply the high-performance model has penetrated the American workplace. Osterman (1994b) reported that surprisingly high numbers of American firms have adopted at least some of the practices typically associated with the high performance model. Pollert (1988, p. 281) disagrees, characterizing the literature as "an ambiguous futurology which slips between research reportage and 'best practice' policy." For Pollert, analysts have exaggerated the extent of the "flexible firm," which is little more than "old wine in new bottles." If true, this would not be the first time that what looked like revolutionary change in the workplace turned out to be more of the same (Bernstein 1997).

At the least, the dominance of the high-performance firm in the American workplace is incomplete (Koeber 2001). Bernhardt (1999), for instance, observes that the high-performance model is not common in the retail trade sector, one of the biggest categories of employment. Although there are some "good" employers in the retail trade sector (for example, Home Depot), job quality generally remains poor. A firm such as Walmart can be extremely organizationally efficient, but at the cost of job quality. Similarly, Hughes (1999) argues that job quality has deteriorated in the supermarket industry because of the same sorts of organizational changes that are elsewhere characterized as progressive. Although there are countervailing trends (for example, increases in technology and training have benefited workers in the particular firm she studied), overall managerial changes have made the workers' lot worse. Much the same seems to hold among smaller employers in manufacturing (Theodore and Weber 2001).

Even a brief journey into the vast literature on workplace change recalls the 1960s lyric: "There's something happening here. What it is ain't exactly clear." Volumes (indeed bookcases full of volumes) have already been written on the ways in which the workplace is changing, and I open the issue here only for its relevance to the relationship between work and education. What does the emergence of the high-performance model have to do with this relationship?

One question to ask has to do with the relationship between the growth of the high-performance firm and the direction and distribution of skill. We saw earlier that more-educated societies tend to be more economically productive ones. The same thing appears to be true of individual workplaces. That is, firms that both have more-educated employees and then make more use of those employees through high-performance structures and processes tend to be more productive. The evidence points toward a causal linkage. That is, employers who hire highly educated workers and those who invest more in the human capital of their workers benefit by doing so. Firms are rewarded for both the "buy" strategy of selecting skilled workers and the "make" strategy of providing them with skills (Knoke and Janowiec-Kurle 1999).

This seems to hold not only for "information" workers, but for workers throughout job hierarchies. Black and Lynch (1997) investigated a range of industrial settings and found that "the higher the average educational level of production workers or the greater the proportion of non-managerial workers who use computers, the greater is plant productivity" (p. 1). Gale et al. (2002) reported similar but even more finely grained results. They asked quite simply, "What, in fact, are the skills needed to fulfill the requirements of the modern workplace?" (p. 49). They concluded that the high-performance workplace requires not only more skill, but a wider range of skills. These skills include problem solving, interpersonal/teamwork, math, basic reading, computer, and "other technical." Different high-performance practices were linked to these skills in a variety of ways, but the "greater use of flexible technologies and work-organization practices was positively linked to reported increases in each of six skill requirements" (p. 75).

Education and Work in the Postindustrial Society

So where are we? The broad story is this. Postindustrialism brings with it a drive for efficiency and rationalization that depends on the development and dissemination of theoretical knowledge. This is impelled by processes of technization and digitalization, that is, work that is increasingly saturated with information. None of this means that work must become either easier and less cognitively demanding on the one hand, or more complex and difficult on the other. On balance, though, successful job performance in the postindustrial era will demand more of the mental attention of workers than was the case in the industrial age. While some work will become deskilled and some even "degraded" (Braverman 1974), there is little evidence for any trend toward deskilling. Rather, the transferal of worker tasks to digital systems instead calls for ever-higher levels of many kinds of skills. The degree to which this is true depends on the "contingencies" at work in a given setting (Spenner 1983). More than anything, the postindustrial society is a demanding one.

For Hage and Powers (1992), the growth of theoretical knowledge that characterizes postindustrial society will lead not to more routinized and rationalized work, but rather to work that has gone through a process of "complexification." Successfully navigating the postindustrial world is going to require broader and deeper understandings of how the parts are connected and of how to develop and maintain interpersonal as well as technical relationships. This will produce just the opposite of deskilling, and carries large implications for education. If work is going to become complexified under postindustrialism (granting often substantial pockets of deskilling for workers who lack the credentials to participate in an information-rich society), Hage and Powers's question and answer become urgent: "What kind of people will society need in order to meet the PI challenge? . . . people with creative minds and complex selves" (Hage and Powers 1992, p. 63).

This brings us full circle to Bell. For Bell, "The major problem for the postindustrial society will be adequate numbers of trained persons of professional and technical caliber" (1999, p. 232). Such workers "must acquire more knowledge so that they can recognize and respond optimally to individualized circumstances" (Hage and Powers 1992, p. 52). This knowledge is not strictly or even primarily technical, but rather must foster "the ability to engage in fluid relationships, creatively recast social roles, and invent new forms of social institutions" (p. 68). As it stands, all of this leaves a lot of people behind. For every trend toward the high-performance workplace with its ever-expanding demand for sophisticated skills, one can point to a potentially countervailing trend of work restructuring that has resulted in a lesser need for skills. None of this obviates the claim that the modern workplace is demanding much more of workers than it once did. Both skills and credentials matter more than they used to. Given "the increasingly competitive pressure to maintain one's competitive position in the work force" (Mare 1995, p. 165), there is little question that the prosperity of those at both ends of the labor market depends on the constant infusion of new learning opportunities.

The competitive pressure to which Mare draws attention is created in large part by the postindustrial processes that we have been describing. These are not, however, the only forces reshaping the relationship between education and work. Rather, the press of demography on work, education, and how they link to each other, while perhaps not as conceptually dramatic as information explosions and theoretical knowledge, is no less dramatic in its impacts. We turn to these issues in the next chapter.

6

Demographic Booms and Busts, Aging, and the New Cultural Diversity

A Demographic Perspective on Education and Work

In the previous chapter I described how the emergence of the postindustrial society influences the relationships between education and work. While my focus was on the United States, postindustrialism characterizes much of the world. The experiences of the United States may not readily generalize elsewhere, but many nations are being transformed by the growth of a service sector, the centrality of theoretical knowledge, and a range of institutional changes.

In this chapter I shift attention to the *demography* of postindustrial United States and the implications of demographic trends for the relationships between education and work. Demography is the science of tracking a population through time. It is built on the three deceptively simple processes of fertility, mortality, and migration. In short, people are born, people die, and people move. From these simple concepts has grown a rich understanding of society. These processes are fundamental everywhere, but their peculiar combination in the United States makes that story a distinctive one.

In this chapter, I discuss three demographic elements that have been especially critical in reshaping American society over the past several decades. These are fertility, immigration, and the changing life course. As always, my focus will be on the implications of these processes for the relationships between education and work. These implications turn out to be substantial. They include an American population that is both growing older and becoming more culturally diverse, a shift in the social contract between the young and the old, and for many what has been aptly characterized as a more disorderly life.

I first examine historically changing patterns of fertility. The United States has experienced distinct phases in fertility behavior over time. After briefly establishing some historical context, I discuss the baby boom of 1946 to 1964 (which some scholars have broken into the early and late boom periods), the subsequent baby bust (1965–76), the "echo effects" of the boom (1977–94), and the echo effect of the bust (post-1995). Virtually every social institution in American society has been affected, even transformed, by this shifting pattern of fertility.

The second demographic trend is immigration. Particularly when combined with racial and ethnic differences in age structures and birth rates, immigration to the United States is making the nation more culturally diverse. Immigration also acts as a brake on the aging of the US population. In general, migrants are younger than natives, helping to produce the striking pattern of relatively younger minority populations and relatively older majority ones. To speak of increased cultural diversity in the United States is primarily to speak of a more diverse school-age and young adult population.

This leads to the third demographic trend, namely changes in the normative American life course. Americans live more disorderly and non-linear lives than they once did. The sequence of major life events less often follows any particular pattern. The implications of this for the relationship between education and work are far-reaching.

A full consideration of the changing demography of the United States is beyond the scope of what I can offer here, and in any case others have already very capably offered more sustained analyses (Farley 1996; Smelser et al. 2001a, b). My goal in this chapter is not to replicate these portraits of the changing American demography, but rather to interpret them through the admittedly often broad lens of the relationship between education and work.

Some Demographic Preliminaries

We first need to define some terms. By fertility rate, or more accurately, *general fertility rate*, demographers mean "the number of live births in an area during a year per 1,000 women of childbearing age for that year, defined as the midyear female population age 15–44 in the same area for the same year" (http://www.umanitoba.ca/centres/mchp/concept/thesaurus/thesaurus_G.html). The point here is that for a fertility rate to be informative, it must be geographically bounded (typically by state or national boundaries), temporally bounded (usually one year), and pertain to a specified "at risk" population (women of child-bearing age, which is inevitably somewhat arbitrary).

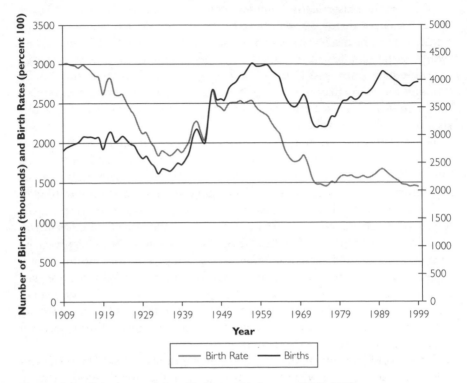

Figure 6.1   Baby boomer data: Births and birth rates 1909–1999
Source: Statistical Abstract of the United States and National Center for Health Statistics.

By *cohort*, demographers refer to "a group of people who have a common initial demographic characteristic, such as year of birth, and who are followed up in later years with respect to some other demographic characteristic, such as survival, marriage, or childbearing" (Siegel 2001, p. 9). Thus, the population of everyone born in 1940 comprises a birth cohort, or we could speak of those entering a particular graduate program in the same year as a different kind of cohort. In what follows, I will chiefly be concerned with birth cohorts.

Figure 6.1 illustrates the relationship between trends in birth rates and number of births in the United States over the past several decades. Consider first the (very) long-term trend in fertility. Clearly, this trend is toward ever lower birth rates. We could see this even more clearly by tracing this back well beyond Figure 6.1. White American women in 1800 averaged about seven births over the course of their lives. By 1890, this number had declined to a bit less than four, and by 1920 had fallen to 3.2. This is a remarkable decline in a relatively brief period of time.

What accounts for the long-term decline in American fertility? As always, there are many potential causes, but two large historical processes standout. The first is urbanization (itself, of course, closely associated with industrialization). Much of American demographic history is simply that of Americans moving off of farms and into cities. As they did so, the economic role of children changed from that of economic assets to that of economic liabilities. That is, whereas even very young children contribute productively to the farm economy, urban economies are not organized around the family in the same way. As the United States moved from preindustrialism to industrialism, children became, in this sense, more costly. One result was smaller families. Even today this is a major cause of the current decline in fertility throughout much of the world (Keller 2001).

A second factor leading to declining fertility was better health care. Improved nutrition and sanitation meant more children (and more mothers) stayed alive. This was true of both greater individual attention to hygiene and of advances in public health. With industrialization, families very simply did not need to bear as many children to raise a family of a desired size.

Figure 6.1 presents some very simple figures, but figures with immense implications. One way to "rearrange" these numbers is by applying the concept of *cohort succession*. This is the process by which one cohort replaces another in the population. Today's workforce, for instance, will in time be replaced by those who are now "pre-workforce" in some way. Cohort succession might be of relatively limited interest if the incoming and outgoing cohorts were demographically the same, that is, if their size and composition indicated little overall change. As we will see, this has hardly been the case throughout this century.

Table 6.1 gives a closer look at how this process of cohort succession operates. The entries in the table show the age that members of different birth cohorts were and will be at various times in the twentieth and twenty-first centuries. (I will describe these birth cohorts very soon.) It shows, for instance, that those whom we might consider the "very old" of today (those born before 1915) were already in their mid-thirties and older when the baby boom began. We can also see that the early old age of the baby boomer cohort is going to coincide with the prime working years of the boom echo cohort. Rather than going through this table at this point, we can use it as a point of reference throughout the following discussion.

As informative as Table 6.1 can be, it lacks an important dimension. One of the central aspects of cohort succession in the United States over the last several decades has been the strikingly different size of each succeeding cohort. Table 6.1 does not show the absolute or relative number of people in each of its cells. For this information, Figure 6.2 presents a series of *age pyramids*.

Table 6.1 The process of cohort succession

Year of birth	Current Year	1950	1960	1970	1980	1990	2000	2010	2020	2030	2040	2050
Pre-1915	Today's "very old"	35+	45+	55+	65+	75+	85+	95+	x	x	x	x
1916–45	Pre-boomers	5–24	15–44	25–54	35–64	45–74	55–84	65–94	75+	85+	95+	x
1946–64	Baby boom	Lt 4	Lt 14	6–24	16–34	26–44	36–54	46–64	56–74	66–84	76–94	86+
1965–76	Baby bust	x	x	5–	4–15	14–25	24–35	34–45	44–55	54–65	64–75	75+
1977–94	Boom echo	x	x	x	3–	13–	6–23	16–33	26–43	36–53	46–63	56+
1995+	Bust echo	x	x	x	x	x	5+	15+	25+	35+	45+	55+

The numbers in the cells represent the ages of members of each birth cohort at each point in time.

Source: Constructed from data taken from Statistical Abstract of the United States and National Center for Health Statistics.

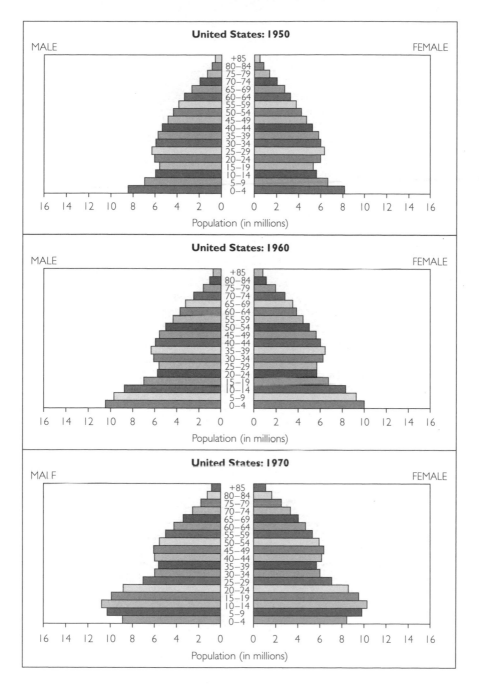

Figure 6.2 US population pyramids, 1950–2050

Source: US Census Bureau, *International Data Base*.

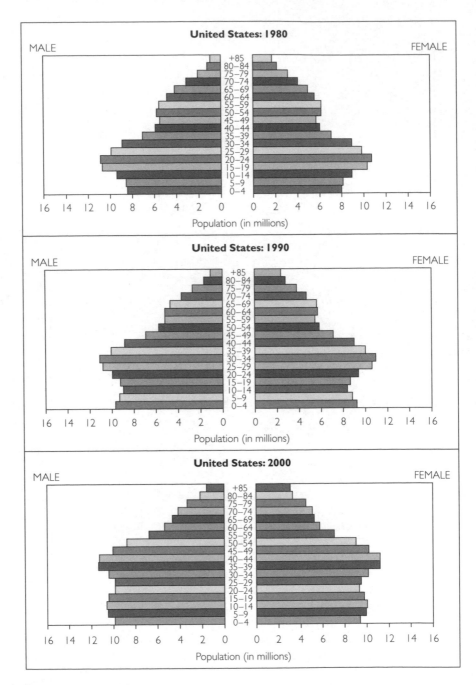

Figure 6.2 (*cont'd*)

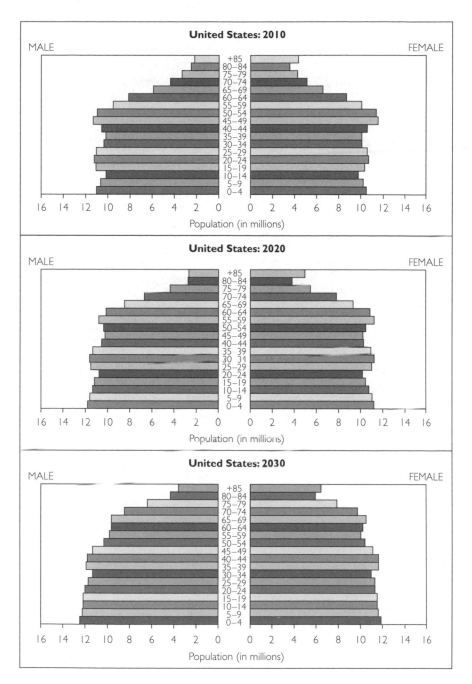

Figure 6.2 (cont'd)

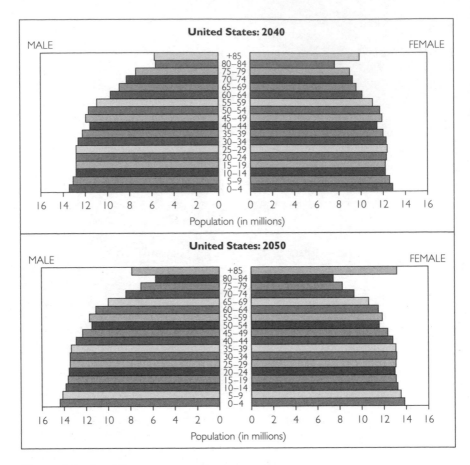

Figure 6.2 *(cont'd)*

These pyramids are constructed by stacking a series of horizontal bars on top of one another. Each bar represents the size of an age group, with the oldest groups placed nearest the top. Further information is added by putting males to the left and females to the right of the central vertical axis. Population pyramids thus provide a concise graphic portrayal of the age–sex structure of a population, and arraying several of them in sequence shows the trend in this structure over time (Siegel 2001).[1]

1 Population pyramids provide a more compelling graphical display when viewed as animations. I obviously cannot do that here, but readers should visit http://www.census.gov/ipc/www/idbpyr.html or http://www.ac.wwu.edu/~stephan/Animation/pyramid.html for excellent examples of this

The basic impression from this series of pyramids is that even referring to them as "pyramids" is growing increasingly misleading as the age structure of the US population changes. While other metaphors are possible, the "shape" of the American population has been steadily changing from a pyramid to something more like a beehive, if one can imagine a beehive that becomes ever-more asymmetrical over time.

Readers should regularly refer to all of the tables and figures that I have just presented through the following discussion. Demography is very likely the most "visual" sort of sociology, relying as it does on a range of such colorful visual metaphors as beehives, pyramids, and (as we will see) pythons. Keeping these broad patterns in mind should help amplify many of the points that are about to be made.

The Baby Boom, The Baby Bust, and So On

All of this is pretty striking, but how did we get to this point? Why do these pyramids look the way they do, and what does it mean that they look the way they do? We can pick up the story in the early 1920s. In 1921, shortly after the end of World War I, a little over 3 million American babies were born. This 3 million figure was not reached again until 1943. Births hit consistently low numbers throughout the Depression years of the 1930s. Because of the great financial strain it put on families, the Depression led many of these families to postpone births that they might otherwise have had. By the time the US had hit the depths of the Depression, there was every indication that the Unites States was facing a future of lower birth rates, smaller families, and at least relatively smaller cohorts.

All of this was soon to change. The 1940s were, of course, one of the most dramatic decades in US history. American involvement in World War II from 1941 to 1945 separated millions of young men from their families. Not surprisingly, the post-war reunion of veterans and their spouses led to an upturn in births. Demographers had anticipated this – wars are typically followed by higher rates of birth. They also anticipated, however, that the long-term downward trend in fertility would soon reassert itself and that the United States would once again be heading toward a future of slower population growth. It is probably safe to say that no one fully foresaw the length and depth of what became the baby boom.

While some increase in births was evident during World War II, the baby boom began in earnest in 1946. New records for births were set in 1946 and 1947, and then in every year from 1951 to 1957. Birth rates hit their postwar peak in 1957.

Scholars have debated for decades now why the boom was as deep and sustained as it was, and I would not pretend to reconcile the various sides of that debate here. More important for this chapter is that the United States became a different society after the advent of the baby boom. Part of the reason for this has to do with a distinction that demographers make between *cohort*, *age*, and *period* effects. The cohort effects on the life experiences of the baby boomers are only the most obvious, and I will describe soon how the sheer size of the cohort changed every institution the boomers passed through. The boomers were also, however, influenced by period effects, that is, differences that arise from the events of a given calendar year. Thus, the Korean War influenced the lives of eight-year old boomers very differently than did the Vietnam War when these same people were eighteen. Finally, ultimately boomers go through the same age-cycle changes as do members of any cohort – regardless of the historical period in which people are born or the experiences that they share with their age-mates, in the end no one escapes the mere process of getting older and the changes this brings with it.

The distinction between age, period, and cohort effects helps clarify why the boom was as consequential as it was. In particular, the fertility boom was accompanied by an extended and powerful postwar economic boom. Because of this extended period of economic growth, while the baby boom certainly produced social stresses and adjustments and while there were economic recessions, as a society the United States could afford the economic costs entailed by the baby boom.

In *Great Expectations* (1980), his highly readable account of the baby boom, Landon Jones characterized the effect of the baby boom cohort passing through life as resembling the way that a pig passes through a python (think again of the age pyramids presented earlier). That is, the sheer size of the cohort means that it has an exceptional impact on those institutions most closely associated with whatever age the boom cohort happens to be at a given moment (again, see Table 6.1). The baby boom has influenced all American social institutions – health care, housing, consumerism, retirement, even death and the projected "tomb boom" – but none more than education and work.

Beginning in the early 1950s, elementary schools that had been maintained for the smaller pre-boom cohorts were suddenly swamped with baby boomers. Not only were classrooms crowded, but American society had to construct an elaborate educational infrastructure around this. New schools had to be built, publishers had to publish and print more books (and writers had to write them), and colleges and universities had to train ever-greater numbers of teachers and administrators. Because of what quickly developed into an acute shortage of teachers, their salaries went up and the minimum standards for hiring probably went down (with effects perhaps on the quality of schooling the boomers received).

This process of cohort secession found its way into high schools a few years later. Again, different social trends reinforced the already substantial impact of the boom. Not only was the number of high school age people growing, but high school graduation rates were increasing. While we perhaps now take it for granted that most students finish high school, as recently as 1950 fewer than half did so. The result of this combination of many more young people getting many more years of schooling was an enormous expansion in the nation's stock of human capital in a very short period of time. The US economy quite suddenly had at its disposal a huge supply of young people educated and trained well beyond the educational level of their parents (or, for that matter, of their older brothers and sisters).

Just as the boom itself was finally starting to fizzle out in the early 1960s, the oldest boomers began to enter both postsecondary education and the world of full-time employment. The ranks of higher education had already expanded as a result of the postwar GI Bill, which provided veterans of World War II with a free postsecondary education at any institution to which they could be admitted. Enrollments grew even more as great numbers of new high school graduates not only entered, but also completed, college programs. Once again too, the persistently strong economy may have been stretched by the numbers of baby boomers setting off on careers, but never to the breaking point. As they had earlier had to compete for educational advantages with lots of other boomers, baby boomers entering the labor force had to compete with lots of other boomers for jobs. In one sense, this was "no time to be young" (Smith and Welch 1981), and the sheer size of the boom cohort does seem to have depressed their earnings in their early careers. The baby boomers' good fortune, however, was that there were lots of jobs to be had and the economy was generally buoyant, and these early disadvantages washed out over time (Smith and Welch 1981).

Without overdramatizing things, the baby boomers' luck ran out when they began to move into the mid-phase of their careers. As the American economy began to stall in the mid-1970s, the scenario of many people chasing many jobs switched to one of many people chasing fewer jobs and (equally seriously) fewer promotions. Everything else being equal, members of big cohorts face greater competition, and even the greater educational attainment of the boomers could not compensate for this as the economy soured.

What does all of this mean for the relationships between education and work? One thing to keep in mind is that the baby boom cohort entered the

1980s as the most highly educated generation in American history. Even if we grant the credentialist argument that levels of schooling have expanded more rapidly in the United States than have the "real" demands of the workplace, the fact remains that baby boomers brought an enormous amount of educated labor – a huge stock of human capital – to the economy.

The oldest boomers are now nearing age 60, and even the youngest of them are well beyond the typical age of full-time college attendance. What we are moving into is a situation in which the great size of the boomer cohort will create a special set of challenges as mid-career workers confront the growing demands for credentials and skills engendered by postindustrialism. Put simply, if postindustrialism brings with it greater needs for retraining or other forms of skill enhancement, the fact is that there are an enormous number of baby boomers to retrain. Not all boomers are highly educated, and even those that are often confront the reality of skill obsolescence engendered by postindustrialism. In a sense, Collins's often compelling argument that this skill obsolescence is more apparent than real misses the point. To the extent that employers insist on mid-career training (whatever its contribution to productivity), the consequences for the boomers will be real enough.

Stacey Poulos (1997) of the Urban Institute has examined the implications of the aging boomer population for the provision of training. While the boomers did attain what were at the time unprecedented levels of schooling, there are very high numbers of boomers with relatively low levels of education and skill, and often low incomes. From this, Poulos predicts a great increase in the demand for retraining services of the sort offered (at the time she wrote) by the federal Job Training Partnership Act (JTPA). Over the next couple of decades, the population eligible for federally funded employment and training programs will be aging, creating a large demand for public resources by a politically potent generation, yet a demand for which the United States has done little to anticipate or prepare.

Since Poulos' report, many of the programs that she saw as potentially meeting this need (for example, the Job Training Partnership Act's Adult Training program, Services of Older Workers, Dislocated Worker Training, and Senior Community Service Employment Program) have been replaced by typically less generous and far-reaching programs. For reasons that will become even clearer as we proceed through this chapter, the efforts to stretch these already thin training resources will be felt not only by the aging baby boomers, but perhaps even more so by younger members of society (both students and young workers) with their own needs for skill acquisition and development.

After the boom comes the bust

By about 1965, the baby boom had played itself out. Birth rates and the number of births began a fairly quick descent around 1964. The total fertility rate fell below 3.0 in 1965 (essentially returning to pre-boom levels), and by the mid-1970s had plummeted below 2.0. Never lacking in alliterative imagery, commentators began to speak of the baby bust.

The baby bust era is generally considered to have lasted until about 1976. While the beginning and end points of broad social trends are in the end a bit arbitrary, the bust was clearly not as sustained as the boom. Further, if we take the very long view, the bust was in one sense little more than a return to the fertility regime of long-term decline that preceded it, with the boom being the real aberration. Still, if less dramatic than the boom, the bust was in its own way transformative.

The baby bust set into motion a number of processes that were mirror images of those brought on by the boom. Over a period of years, the small cohorts of the bust followed the large ones of the boom through a sequence of social institutions. Thus, elementary schools that had been built or adapted to educate the boomers began to draw smaller numbers of busters. This cohort succession then played itself out in high schools, higher education, entry level work, and eventually the progression of careers. Without putting too fine a point on it, the United States shifted from being a society with too few teachers, too few schools buildings, and too few textbooks to a society with surpluses of all of these.

Further, the period effects – the social context – in which the baby busters found themselves were far different than what had been confronted by the boomers. For a variety of reasons that need not detain us here (e.g., high productivity growth in other national economies, the shocks brought to the US economy by the fuel crisis of the 1970s), the American economy settled into an extended period of slower growth.

The implications of all of this for the baby bust cohort are complex. Certainly the baby busters benefited from the continued expansion of American schooling, and in fact came to "outschool" their boomer predecessors. Because this happened in a less robust labor market, however, the prospects for translating these educational investments into economic returns became more difficult. More importantly, the weaker economy hit less-educated workers with more force than it hit their more-credentialed age-mates. Thus, as the buster cohort succeeded the boomer cohort, the costs of not having advanced educational credentials worsened.

Little boom

The baby bust came to a close about 1976. The birth rate then stayed fairly stable (at about 1.8) for another decade. There was a bit of a brief upswing from 1988 to 1991, with the total fertility rate creeping over 2.0 once again. Still, while birth *rates* remained generally low, the *number of births* began to edge back up around 1977 (again see Figure 6.2). The reason for this was that the baby boomers started to have children of their own. Even though the fertility rate of baby boom parents was low by historical standards, the fact that there were so many of them translated into high numbers of births. (It is important to remember that the total fertility rate and the number of children being born are indicators that can move in entirely different directions.) This has come to be called the baby boomlet or the echo (1977–94).

While the sheer number of boomers was the chief reason for this boomlet, there were other reasons too. Prominent among these was the increased volume of immigration that began around this time. Immigrants tend to be young, and the high birth rates among Hispanics and Asian immigrants added to the boomlet. By the early 1990s, annual births were of about the same magnitude that they had been during the peak of the baby boom.

Perhaps we can anticipate that in time the boomlet will set similar processes in motion as did the boom, if on a much smaller scale. It is simply too early to say. The oldest of the boomlet or echo cohort are just now entering full-time employment, and have yet to fully solidify their own school–work relationships. The youngest have yet to encounter what we will discuss in a later chapter as "Youthwork."

We can talk about with some assurance about the effects of the boomlet on educational enrollments (National Center for Education Statistics 1998). While the small size of the bust cohorts had led to contractions in the chain of social institutions from maternity wards, through all levels of schooling, and then beyond that to postsecondary education and the workforce, the echoers expanded anew US school enrollments. Beginning in about 1984, American elementary school enrollments began a steady increase. This growth reached into the secondary school level about 1991, and is expected to continue to 2007. With the inexorable process of cohort succession, the echoers will then move on to higher education in large numbers.

Once again, social trends reinforced the demographic ones. Elementary and secondary school enrollments increased in the 1980s and 1990s primarily because there were more kids. They also increased, though, because of choices that parents were making for their children and to some degree because of choices that they were making for themselves. Thus, enrollments increased not only for pure "demographic" reasons, but because of higher preschool and kindergarten enrollments and increasing rates of high school graduation. Much as with the original boom, all of this has created a greater demand for teachers and a greater pressure on other school expenditures (Frances 1998).

Little bust

When the baby boomers came of child-bearing age, the combination of low birth rates but many potential parents produced the large echo cohort. By the same set of processes, if in reverse once again, the combination of low birth rates and few potential parents that characterizes the baby bust cohort has produced the relatively small "little bust" cohort. In this fertility regime, which began about 1994, the total fertility rate and the number of births are moving in the same direction. Again, this is a generalization that applies to some parts of the United States more than others (more on that below), but we are now at the early stages of an era in which recently "re-peopled" schools will become "de-peopled" ones.

It is too early to say what sorts of education and work relationships members of the little bust will experience as they move through their socioeconomic life course. We do know that fertility at Year X will begin to have its "education/work" impacts in about Year X+20. It needs to be remembered too that these impacts will develop in what are unforeseeable combinations of age, period, and cohort processes. Still, we can anticipate yet another round of demographically induced changes about a decade and a half in to the new century.

Racial and Ethnic Differences in Fertility

To this point we have proceeded as if all groups in the United States have the same patterns of fertility. Of course they do not. Fertility rates differ greatly across sociodemographic lines. The fact that the fertility regimes of different race/ethnic groups are so different from one another says much about the kind of society the United States will be in the next decades. Groups with higher birth rates will be more highly represented in future generations than they are now. This is basic to the future of American education and work.

A useful concept here is that of *replacement rate* or the *net reproductive rate*. Without getting in to the fine points of how this number is calculated, it is roughly the number of children that a woman would have to bear to replace herself and her partner in the population, with some adjustment for the fact that some children do not survive to adulthood. We can think of this somewhat loosely as the rate that would lead to Zero Population Growth (zpg). Currently in the United States, a racial or ethnic (or any other) group needs about 2.1 children per female to maintain its share of the population over time.

As we saw earlier, the birth rate in the United States is currently about 2.0. This is a bit below the replacement rate. The US fertility rate, however, differs sharply across race and ethnic groups. Consider a few simple figures from 1994. Non-hispanic whites, who are for now and the next several decades the largest single group in the United States, have a fertility rate of 1.79. Non-Hispanic blacks stand at 2.34, and Hispanics at 3.00. Of course, to speak of a "Hispanic" population is to speak of a wide range of groups. Fertility rates among Hispanics range from 1.68 for Cubans to 3.82 for Mexicans. The rates for American Indians (2.08) and Asian-Americans (1.94) each stand a bit below replacement.

What all of this means, everything else being equal, is that in the future there will be proportionately fewer Whites, proportionately more Hispanics, and not a great deal of change (although certainly some) elsewhere. The "everything else being equal" clause is, however, an important one that rests upon any number of assumptions about fertility behavior. For example, there are reasons to expect the African-American fertility rate will continue to converge with the White rate. Unlike Hispanic and Asian populations, African-Americans get few new immigrants. Because immigrants tend to be younger and with higher fertility rates than non-immigrants, the effect of this is to keep the African-American rate relatively low. Moreover, as African-Americans continue to move into middle class positions, this may serve to make White and Black birth rates even more alike. This all seems reasonable enough, but the fact is that no one knows, and the gap between White and Black fertility rates may as easily begin to diverge.

Variable birth rates produce populations that have very different age structures. Mostly because of varying birthrates, the average ages of groups in the United States are quite different. Thus, in 1997 the median White American (that is, that hypothetical individual who is older than half the population and younger than the other half) was about 37.3 years of age. The median African American, at 29.8, was well below that, and the median Hispanic younger yet (26.5).

The implications of such numbers are both simple and striking. Put simply, the United States is growing more culturally diverse, but is doing so much more rapidly at younger ages. This results from both fertility differentials and, as we will see, patterns of immigration. To illustrate, while only 22 percent of the total US population is a racial/ethnic minority, African-American, Hispanic, and Asian children under age 18 now make up about 31 percent of the youth population. This will be 38 percent by the year 2010, and by 2050 many analysts expect that non-Hispanic whites will be a numerical minority in the United States (Pollard and O'Hare 1999). At the present, though, to speak of increased cultural diversity within the United States is largely to speak of the increased cultural diversity of young Americans. This is more the case in some parts of the nation than others.

The relevance of all of this for the relationship between education and work is largely that the increasingly diverse school-age population of today will become the increasingly diverse working population in the future. To fully grasp the import of this, we first need to think about the role of immigration.

The Movement of People: Immigration and Internal Migration

We have hinted several times about the role that immigration is playing in reshaping American demography. By its nature, immigration has its greatest impacts at the younger reaches of a population. Its most significant effects on the education and work relationship are thus on those who have yet to forge this relationship (children) and those just beginning to establish it (young adults).

Much is made of the currently heavy volume of immigration to the United States, but the Unites States has experienced major waves of immigration throughout its history. For reasons ranging from economic opportunity (largely driven by the need for unskilled labor in an industrializing society) to economic persecution to family reunification, the United States was in the nineteenth century demographically defined and redefined by immigrants.

The current wave of immigration follows a lapse of some half a century since the last great wave. Indeed, the United States "has become anew a nation of immigrants" (Portes and Rumbaut 1990, p. xvii). For various reasons, immigration slowed considerably after World War I, and only in the past generation (since about 1970) has the pace of immigration approached what it was many decades ago (Massey 1995).

Immigration is making the United States a more culturally diverse nation. This needs to be put in some context. Social commentators, including both those alarmed and those encouraged with the changing face of the US population, often describe what they see as unprecedented cultural diversity

in American society. In fact, the United States is in many ways less culturally diverse than it was a century ago. In many major cities at that time,
two-thirds to three-quarters of school-aged children had foreign-born parents. Then as now, schools had to find ways to accommodate a range of
languages and traditions (a task they approached with varying degrees
of good will and commitment). This was accompanied by widespread and
often ambitious efforts to provide adult education to "Americanize" their
parents – to make them not only informed citizens, but productive and self-
sufficient workers as well.

The educational backgrounds of today's immigrants are different from
those of a century ago. One hundred years ago, few people, immigrants or
otherwise, completed high school, and the consequences of not doing so
were virtually nil. The immigrants of 1880 to 1920 were drawn by the heavy
demand for less-skilled workers in an industrial society. The immigrants
of today, many disproportionately less educated than natives, are entering
a postindustrial society in which not only real job skills, but their formal
certification as well, are indispensable.

By far the greatest numbers of nineteenth century immigrants to the United
States came from Europe. This pattern held well into the twentieth century.
Today's immigrants come from strikingly different and more heterogenous
origins. Figure 6.3 presents some illustrative data, with the overall trends
being cogently summarized by Pollard and O'Hare (1999):

> Between 1980 and 1998, nearly three-quarters of all immigrants entering
> the United States came from Asia and Latin America; another 4 percent of
> immigrants came from Africa. About 20 percent of U.S. immigrants came
> from Europe between 1980 and 1998. This pattern is a marked change from
> the 1950s, when about one-half of immigrants came from Europe and 15
> percent came from Canada. Less than 40 percent of immigrants arriving in
> the 1950s came from Africa, Latin America, Asia, and Oceania, the source
> regions for the three largest U.S. minority groups.

Zhou (2001, p. 205) has made the simple yet crucial point that "The size
and composition of immigration has a lasting effect on the size and composition of the general U.S. population." And indeed, the current immigrant
population is distinctive in important ways from the native population.
One important difference has to do with educational attainment. Immigrants
represent all educational levels and many possess sophisticated and complex
occupational skills. Taken as a rather unwieldy and heterogeneous whole,
however, the immigrant population by no means mirrors the education and
skill levels of the native population. Immigrants include both highly trained
professional workers, and those lacking valued job skills.

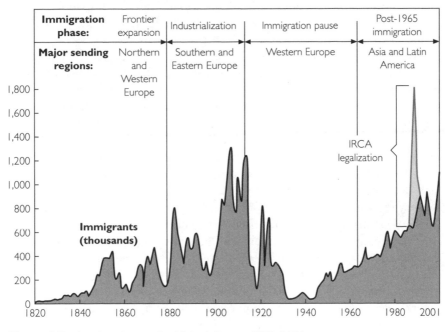

Immigration phase:	Frontier expansion	Industrialization	Immigration pause	Post-1965 immigration
Major sending regions:	Northern and Western Europe	Southern and Eastern Europe	Western Europe	Asia and Latin America

Figure 6.3 Immigration to the United States, 1820–2001

IRCA refers to the amnesty provisions of the Immigration Reform and Control Act of 1986, under which 2.7 million unauthorized foreign residents obtained legal immigrant status.
Source: US Immigration and Naturalization Service (2003).

For reasons having to do with the economies and political situations in their countries of origin, different immigrant groups bring very different mixes of credentials and skills with them. In a comprehensive analysis of demographic trends among several Latino populations, Perez and Salazar (1993) described an emerging Hispanic population that is "undereducated, youthful, and growing" (p. 188). They pointed out serious long-term implications of this, not only for the socioeconomic future of immigrants and their children, but for the longer-term productivity and prosperity of the larger workforce of which Latinos will be an ever-growing segment.

Enchautegui (1998) has further analyzed the experience of low-skilled immigrants. She reported that immigrants are found disproportionately in the less-schooled part of the population. Using 1990 data, Enchautegui found that 30 percent of all workers without high school degrees were immigrants. This translates into a quite large less-educated population. In 1994, for instance, there were 5.1 million foreign-born persons aged 15–55 in the

United States who were not in school and did not have high school degrees. About two-thirds of these had no high school education at all. Low levels of marketable skills were particularly common for men.

Not surprisingly, immigrants without high school credentials have high rates of poverty and exceptionally low wages. Enchautegui notes that both of these indicators of labor market marginalization were worsening more quickly for those without high school degrees than for those with high school diplomas, although both experienced difficult labor market positions. While non-credentialed immigrants were employed at fairly high levels, they usually held jobs characterized by low wages and low skills. Nor is there much evidence that these jobs serve as steppingstones to better jobs. In short, the lack of education is a serious barrier for low skilled immigrants, and there is every indication that their labor market prospects are likely to deteriorate further with the advance of postindustrialism.

While many immigrants lack the educational background typically demanded under postindustrialism, there are also large numbers of highly educated and highly skilled immigrants. As Farley (1996, p. 175) noted, "Immigrants have educational attainments unlike those of natives; they are greatly overrepresented in the upper and lower tails of the educational distribution." In fact, the number of highly educated immigrants seems to be increasing quite steadily. Pollard and O'Hare (1999) reported that "the number of minorities in the highest income brackets has more than doubled since 1980." While often portrayed in the popular media as reflecting solely the high educational levels of immigrants from Asia, there are in fact many less-educated Asian immigrants, and many highly educated immigrants from the Americas and Africa. The basic point is the striking heterogeneity of contemporary immigration.

One final point should be made about immigration. The most significant effects of immigration are not national, but local. Immigrants do not go to the United States so much as they go to specific places in the United States. We know quite a bit about these settlement patterns, and much has been written about Cuban immigrants to Miami or Hmong immigrants to Minneapolis (Zhou 2001; Portes and Rumbaut 1990). There are great differences across the United States in the extent to which the population has grown more culturally diverse (Frey and DeVol 2000; Pollard and O'Hare 1999). Not only is California more culturally diverse than New Hampshire, but West Liberty, Iowa is very much more culturally diverse than it was a generation ago, while West Branch, Iowa is not.

This is important for the themes of this book because any appreciable volume of immigration can change the nature of a small place very quickly. The transformation of the ethnic and racial composition of a community is only the most obvious. Such changes tend to bring with them changes in local age structures. Immigrant populations, as we noted, tend to be younger than native populations. Perhaps the most immediate local consequence of a changing age structure is a changing demand for educational services. Moreover, and following the cohort replacement concept introduced earlier, in relatively short order a community will find that it has a local labor supply quite different than it had a few years previously.

How all of this plays out in any given locale depends on the characteristics of the new immigrants. Thus, a local area can in a surprisingly brief period of time find itself needing to either expand its provision of GED, basic skills, and ESL classes, or to provide sophisticated and specialized training to already highly educated professionals.

Internal migration and the relationship between education and work

Before leaving the issue of immigration, one final point is worth mentioning. Immigration can change the "education and work" mix in a community or region by introducing a population with a different mix of educational preparation and job skills than that of the native population. Internal migration, the movement of people within national boundaries, can have the same effect. Americans frequently change their residence in response to educational or economic opportunities (Pastor 2001). The long-term shift in the United States of people and jobs from the Snowbelt to the Sunbelt has been going on for decades and is well known (US Bureau of the Census 2001). This redistribution is often quite complex, but regional realignments of jobs and people are an ongoing part of American history.

While being careful not to overstate the case, regions of the United States that were already demographically, educationally, and economically very different have become, in the last two or three decades, even more so (Morrill 1990). This matters because these flows of people can quite substantially transform the relationships between education and work at any given location. Internal migration, like immigration, is far from random. As Farley (1996, p. 288) noted, "the likelihood of making an interstate move increases with educational attainment." The result is that some parts of the country (for example, the Florida Coast from Miami to Jacksonville, or such cities as Las Vegas or Sacramento) are attracting large numbers of highly educated in-migrants, while other areas (especially older industrial centers) are losing the highly educated. While I cannot develop the point in any detail here (but see Rosenbloom 2002 and Kodrzycki 2000 on how this has played out in New England), *how* education and work are related has much to do with the constantly shifting mix of people in any given region, and internal migration is one of the chief determinants of this shifting mix.

The Changing Life Course

The appeal of demography is that knowing three things about a population – fertility, mortality, and immigration – reveals a great deal about that population. I have spent little time on mortality, but believe that an analysis of trends in fertility and immigration take us some distance in understanding the relationships between education and work. I now add one level of complexity by turning to one final set of factors. This is the changing American lifecourse.

Demographers conceptualize the lifecourse as the regularized patterns of roles that individuals hold and transitions they experience as they age. These roles are the standard "stuff" of introductory sociology – student, worker, parent, retiree, and so on. The transitions pertain to the processes by which people exit one role and assume another (for instance, how workers become retirees). The study of how the lifecourse has been changing has become a central preoccupation in contemporary sociology, both in the United States (Shanahan et al. 1997, 1998) and elsewhere (Mayer 1991).

At one time, the "location" of the "student to worker" transition in the lifecourse was reasonably clear. While there have always been exceptions, it made sense to think of the American lifecourse as including a discrete point at which individuals severed their participation in formal schooling and assumed the role of worker. Students either graduated from or dropped out of school, and went on to hold a series of predictably sequential roles in the workplace. (Many, of course, assumed such other adult roles as home-maker.) In this "Fordist" model of the lifecourse (Baizan et al. 2002), major life events and roles followed linear and generally irreversible paths – studying preceded earning, marriage preceded parenthood, work preceded retirement, and so on. This model was never entirely universal, but captured a sequence that was so broadly experienced as to be virtually normative.

More recently, the sequence of educational and work spells (as well as those pertaining to family life) has changed in ways that make this formulation less useful for understanding the linkages between education and work. As the United States has moved from a Fordist to a postindustrial model (Baizan et al. 2002), the notion of a single "school to work" (or even "school to family") transition in an individual's demographic career has been replaced by a persistent if irregular mobility between these diverse roles. There is evidence for this in other nations as well (Buchmann 1989), although perhaps not often to the same degree as in the United States (Mortimer and Kruger 2000). Put simply, the normative lifecourse of post-industrial Americans has shifted from a generally routine and predictable set of transitions to one in which lives are more "disorderly" (Rindfuss 1991), and in which people simultaneously hold a variety of roles. The consequences of these changing patterns of enrollment are far reaching (Nock 1993).

These changes in the lifecourse are not simply the result of people choosing to live more flexible and less constrained lives. On the contrary, as Shanahan et al. (1997) demonstrated, how people experience the life course is contingent on conditions that change over time. "Choosing" to leave school for work or to re-enter the world of work after having been a student is a very different choice in the midst of a depression or a war than it is during a peacetime economic boom. (Recall the discussion above of age, period, and cohort effects.) Shanahan and his colleagues believe that individual efforts to prepare for these sorts of historical contingencies – what they call "planfulness" – are rewarded when the "structure of opportunity" is an open one. Planfulness is perhaps of less consequence when those structures are restricted. As Shanahan et al. (1997, p. 55) state, "Adolescent planfulness is less predictive of adult attainment when social institutions, such as education and work, fail to offer viable alternatives." Sometimes schooling is a preparation for a viable employment future and sometimes it is little more than warehousing in the hopes that a more viable future will one day materialize.

In an earlier chapter, I presented the Blau–Duncan model of status attainment. I noted that the model depicts a world in which people at some discrete point figuratively cashed in their educational chips for a slot in the occupational hierarchy. Once this transition was made, that was essentially as complex as the lifecourse sequence got. Recent lifecourse research tells us that the Blau–Duncan model, whatever its great virtues as a way to organize our thinking about schooling and work, is becoming less complete as a template for understanding postindustrial lives. Rather than a single "education–work" relationship in any given biography, there may be many.

Both cause and consequence of the changing lifecourse are changes in the kinds of decisions made by American families. Families are vastly different than they were just a few decades ago (Levitan et al. 1988). As Preston (1996, p. 97) observed, "Perhaps the most significant social change of the past half century has been the reformation of the American family." These changes are both broad and deep, but I wish to focus here only on how they help form the context for the relationships between schooling and work.

The central changes in the American family involve work and children. Women have been increasing their involvement in the workplace for decades, and now comprise at the younger ages nearly half of the labor force. Increasingly, the expectation is that the typical household arrangement is to have two working adults. Other changes have been afoot as well. Describing shifts in family structure between 1980 and 1996, Farley (1996, p. ix) draws attention to "delayed marriage, more divorce, more childbearing by unmarried women, and more cohabitation, [so that] adults spend fewer years as spouses, and children less time living with both parents."

Quite properly, most of the attention given to the changing American family structure has focused on the consequences of these changes for the well-being of children (Furstenberg and Cherlin 1991). We now have a well-developed research literature on the effects of changes in family structure on children's cognitive development, anti- and pro-social behavior, and academic achievement. Certainly in the long term these effects will find their way to the education and work relationship as children mature to working age.

These same changes in family structure, however, might also lead to changes in the life events of the adults who are experiencing them. That is, the shifting family roles of adults both constrain and facilitate their participation in schooling and the workplace in ways unlike those that were prevalent under Fordist conditions. There is surprisingly little research on this, but there is little doubt that changing family dynamics collectively have the effect of altering the amount and distribution of time available to adults for pursuing adult educational activities. They also alter the mix of opportunity costs facing adult family members. We need more research on the extent to which adults living under this new regime of family structure use the time and resources that they are not with spouses or children to pursue educational and employment opportunities.

Putting the Demographic Changes Together: The Racialized, Disorderly, and Forevermore Aging of America

We have established a few simple generalizations about the shape and direction of the demography of the United States. The country is growing more culturally diverse, it is aging, and the normative life course is growing more variable. The ways in which the relationships between education and work are going to evolve over the next decades will take place in the context of a distinctive and probably unprecedented interaction between race/ethnicity and age, in which people are making different decisions throughout the "pyramid" than they once did.

I mentioned above that one of the most important consequences of these trends is the aging of the labor force. This aging will continue until at least 2015 as baby boomers continue to replace older members of the labor force, and will not abate until the boomers start to retire in large numbers (Poulos 1997). Some of the specifics of this can be further seen in a recent series of sociodemographic projections by the Bureau of Labor Statistics. Bowman (1997, p. 3) observed:

> While overall change in the labor force will be modest, significant shifts are expected in its demographic structure. Increases will be concentrated among older age groups, as baby boom cohorts swell the ranks of workers between ages 45 and 64. For the first time in 25 years, the number of young workers (16 to 24) will be growing faster than the overall labor force. Finally, a decline is expected in the number of those in the 25 to 44 year age range over the next ten years. The net result will be a continuation of the aging of the labor force seen in the previous decade. By 2006, the median age of the labor force will approach 41 years, a level not seen in the United States since the 1960s.

Other trends reinforce this. These include the longer life spans of Americans and trends toward earlier retirement (Moen 2001) Such forecasts are based on assumptions about trends in labor force participation rates that may or may not hold (the average age of retirement will probably increase, for example). Still, there are significant implications to "the impending decline in the share of prime-age workers" (Lerman and Schmidt 1999). Given the trends in fertility, immigration, and the life course described above, this decline means a labor force that has *both* more young workers *and* more older workers. This is a reversal from what the United States has seen in recent decades. Until recently, the pattern has been one in which youth's share of the labor force had been declining and (maybe more importantly) the biggest net gainers in the labor force were prime age workers (as baby boomers came of working age). What we now seem to be moving toward are fairly heavy declines among prime-age workers aged 25–44, and perhaps some increase in the share of those aged 45–54.

I will reserve consideration of some of the implications of this until chapter 8's discussion of life-long learning in the context of an aging population. For the present, the important point is that an aging labor force (along with changes in family structure and behavior) leads to changes in the *dependency ratio*. This ratio refers to "the number of those in the total population (including Armed Forces overseas and children) who are not in the labor force per 100 of those who are in the labor force" (Fullerton 1997, p. 37). In other words, to oversimplify a bit, the ratio estimates the extent to which the working population supports the non-working population.

We are currently witnessing shifts in the dependency ratio. Because of the aging of the population, women's increased labor force participation, and declining birth rates, the economic dependency ratio in the United States dropped 31 percentage points between 1975 and 1996. It is projected to continue to drop for the foreseeable future. This means that fewer and fewer workers are going to be supporting more and more non-workers, both young and old.

All of this portends increasing pressure between the needs of an elderly population and those of a young and increasingly ethnically diverse population. This pressure will become more pronounced as the baby boomers become the nation's elderly. This will be a powerful political force, one characterized by high rates of voting and sophisticated political mobilization. We can expect America's attention to focus increasingly on the elderly. This puts at risk the willingness of American society to make long-term investments in the human capital development of an increasingly outnumbered school-age population. The experience of the last two decades gives ample reason to worry about the extent to which future taxpayers (who will be less likely than taxpayers of today to have their own children in school, at least in much of the country) will pick up the tab for educating the next generation (Ladd and Murray 2001).

Nor is there any certainty that the commitments to human capital development across generations will be adequate as the young people of the next several decades enter the labor force. As Pollard and O'Hare (1999) stated with some bluntness, the future is one in which "In part because whites are concentrated in the older working ages and because of the history of discrimination against minorities in hiring and promotion, a largely white group of managers supervises a work force that is increasingly multiracial and multicultural." Postindustrialism brings with it the need for the continual upgrading of skills and capacities throughout the work life. The need to reconcile the demographic transformation that began in the early days of the baby boom with that emerging need for human capital development will be one of the great "education and work" policy challenges of this century.

At issue here is the level of *labor supply adequacy*. This is "the ratio of the quality-adjusted work force to the total consumption needs of the population" (Rogers et al. 1999, p. 5). This measure provides an indication of how able a working population is to provide for the needs of the whole population. Put simply, a society with a high labor supply adequacy index will live better than one with a lower score. Because of the demographic changes we have documented, labor supply adequacy will almost certainly decline substantially in the United states between 2010 and 2040 (Toder and Solanski 1999; Rogers et al. 1999, 2000).

The United States is not alone in facing an aging workforce and an increasingly inadequate labor supply, and is in fact better off than many nations. McDonald and Kippen (2001) examined the effects of fertility trends on the aging of populations (and hence the size of the labor supply) in 16 countries, and projected the likely outcomes from 2000 to 2050 (see also Kinsella and Velkoff 2001). They showed that in most advanced countries in the past 25 to 30 years, both fertility and mortality rates have been dropping, producing a rapidly aging population. This aging, as in the United States, will accelerate as baby boomers get old. The question raised by this pattern is whether future labor forces will be able to support such significantly older populations. Further, today's elderly will demand both more health care and more leisure, thus simultaneously creating jobs for younger workers and putting greater strains on the resources of those same workers.

They likelihood is that most advanced nations face either stagnation or decline in the absolute size of their labor forces. This is complicated still more by people going to school longer (increasingly required by the exigencies of a postindustrial economy) and retiring sooner (increasingly unlikely as dependency ratios shift). Again, the United States is in better shape than many other nations. Japan faces the least favorable prospects, while other nations face varying degrees of demographically induced pressure. Sommestad (2000) adds that one particularly pernicious consequence of all of this is that young cohorts in an aging society will have less incentive to invest in their own education. She sees this as a serious problem, among other reasons, for recruiting young people into science and engineering. Other analysts (e.g., Esping-Andersen 1999) have reached similar conclusions.

What Does All of This Add Up To?

I closed the previous chapter by remarking that "the press of demography on work, education, and how they link to each other, while perhaps not as conceptually dramatic as information explosions and theoretical knowledge, is no less dramatic in its impacts." In hindsight, this is probably wrong. Simple demographic processes – birth, death, immigration – offer enormous conceptual insight into how schooling and workplaces are related to each other. As with postindustrial processes, their effects are contingent rather than deterministic – people in some sense make "choices" about what to do with the demographic trends that confront them.

As I have shown here, the "social facts" of technology, trends toward meritocracy or credentialism, changes in the lifecourse, and so on affect members of different age groups in different ways. In the next chapter, I draw on the concepts and themes that have been developed to this point to analyze what has been called (perhaps not too gracefully) "youthwork."

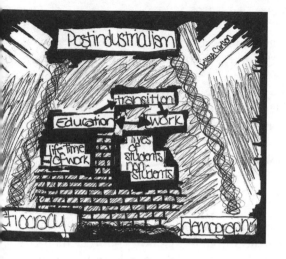

7

The Transformation of the High School, the Coming of Mass Higher Education, and the Youth Labor Market

Changing Linkages Between Education and Work

In the previous chapters I chronicled the often uneasy alliances between postindustrialism, meritocracy, and demography. A particular implication of the interplay of these trends is that the linkages between education and work are going to develop differently for young workers than they did for previous generations. Building on that idea, I turn in this chapter to the relationships between education and work for younger workers. There are three large sub-questions to this. The first involves schooling as preparation for (a lifetime of) work. The second directs attention to the work lives of students and non-students of traditional school age. The third involves how students make the transition from school to work.

Under the first question, I ask about what schools do or often do not do to help sort young people into adult work roles. This will include a consideration of the formal curriculum of courses, subjects, and skills that students encounter, but also of the "hidden curriculum" of less apparent processes and structures that help shape educational experiences.

The second question directs us to the "youth labor market." We can think of this as an arena of jobs and employers who draw their workers primarily from the ranks of young people. These "segmented" markets are often thought to consist of dead-end and poorly rewarded jobs. In fact, the term "youth labor market" can be misleading. Certainly some labor market segments are limited primarily to young workers. The prototypical jobs here are those in fast-food establishments, but even clearer examples are the lawn-mowing and baby-sitting jobs held by many high school students.

Even in this informal and unstructured segment of the labor market, though, older workers – often much older workers – compete for and hold these kinds of jobs.

Finally, analysis of the school-to-work (STW) transition has become something of a cottage industry over the past decade. American labor markets are structured (or, perhaps more accurately, unstructured) in ways that make moving from the status of student to that of worker much more difficult than it is in much of the world. I will spend some time examining proposals, often modeled on those that work effectively in other nations, to facilitate smoother transitions for young American workers.

The best way to understand the youth labor market is in the context of the trends I have introduced in earlier chapters. For example, a major consequence of shifting fertility rates is the absolute size of the cohort available to participate in schooling and in the workplace a few years later. Changing incidences of either credentialist or meritocratic selection procedures on the part of employers help determine the life chances of youth. Technological change has much to do with the ability of young people to negotiate the transition to employment. The postindustrial transformation from goods to services provides a very different context for the employment prospects of young workers than did the industrial-age industries that provided entry level jobs for the grandparents of today's entry-level workers.

Moreover, with what has become the near universality of high school education (that is, its emergence as a "mass" system), we have witnessed the declining value of the high school diploma as a route to middle-class employment or even stable working-class employment. As the United States continues to move toward the "massification" of higher education (Zemsky 1998), this threatens even the economic value of postsecondary degrees to younger workers.

Economic restructuring, postindustrialism, and the other broad trends I have been developing have hit young workers with particular force. The goal of this chapter is to examine these implications for the education–work linkages for younger workers.

The Shifting Role of High School as Preparation for Work: Schooling and Socialization

It may not be too much to claim that the educational institution most relevant to the world of work is the elementary school. Virtually all complex and sophisticated job skills ultimately build on the ability to acquire and display the "simple" skills of reading, writing, and calculating. Indeed, whatever its other roles in the building of community and passing on of moral and public values, elementary schools probably contribute more to the human capital stock of a society – postindustrial as well as earlier forms – that any other segment of the school system.

At the same time, the very universality of elementary school enrollment in the United States and most of the world makes them less relevant for our discussion. We can grant that elementary schools provide the bedrock of basic skills needed by any labor force, and that they provide the site at which the sorting and sifting of students throughout educational and eventually work hierarchies begins (Kerckhoff 1996). Social stratification starts young, and differences that take root in the early years have enduring effects. Elementary age students already know a great deal about adult occupations and the adult workplace. Even at a very young age, children have fairly elaborate mental maps of the world of work.

Still, the story has to start someplace, and examining the ultimate impact of the elementary years on the workforce preparation of children would open too big a box to adequately unpack here. I start instead with high schools (and to an extent, middle schools), both as institutions that prepare people for the world of work and as the setting that most competes with the workplace for the efforts and commitment of teenagers.

High schools play complex and contradictory roles in shaping the relationships between education and work. These roles have changed over time. The basic contradiction is that high schools are *terminal* for some students and *preparatory* for others. The implications of this were developed years ago in Martin Trow's classic analysis "The second transformation of American secondary education" (1961). Trow divided the history of educational enrollments in the United States into a few discrete periods on the basis of a small number of fundamental transformations.

Trow observed that "the mass public secondary school system as we know it has its roots in the transformation of the economy that took place after the Civil War (1961, p. 106).[1] This transformation is the one I described earlier as that from preindustrialism to industrialism. As the United States urbanized and industrialized, this brought with it a growth of a salaried white-collar class no longer tied to the land or to an economy of small shopkeepers. It also engendered a growth in the proportion of manual workers in the labor force (at least until about 1920, when this proportion began to level off). These changes in the occupational structure led to great changes in the organization of work, as an economy based on thousands of small farms and

1   Because the original Trow article can be difficult to locate, page numbers in the text refer to the reprint of the article in the more accessible Karabel and Halsey (1977).

shops was transformed into one based on large bureaucracies, characterized by centralized decision-making and administration carried out through co-ordinated managerial and clerical staffs.

This new economy needed a different worker than those who had carried out the work of a preindustrial, prebureaucratic society. Large centrally controlled and rationally maintained bureaucracies needed employees who could read, write, and calculate. For Trow (1961, p. 107), "the growth of the secondary school system after 1870 was in large part a response to the pull of the economy for a mass of white-collar employees with more than an elementary school education."

The challenge was that the American economy was evolving into indus-trialism while its educational system remained preindustrial. In 1870 there were only 80,000 high school students in the United States. Only about 2 percent of 17 year olds in 1870 were high school graduates. Most of these went on to college. Few high school students in 1870 were in public high schools, which were few in number and primarily in the Northeast. Instead, most high school students were in private tuition academies, which had tight linkages with postsecondary schools but virtually none with the emer-ging bureaucratic economy. The American secondary school system in 1870 offered a classical liberal education to a small number of middle and upper-middle class boys.

In the space of only 40 years, this situation turned upside down. By 1910, there were over 1.1 million high school students in the United States. Most were enrolled in a secondary system that had swelled to over 10,000 public high schools. Unlike high school graduates of 1870, however, few 1910 graduates went beyond high school. This massification of secondary educa-tion continued and by 1957, some 90 percent of the 14–17 year age group was in school. As this happened, the high school curriculum became steadily more practical and vocationalized, providing the skills presumably required by the new body of white-collar workers.

Trow concedes that these changes in the occupational structure do not provide the full explanation for such dramatic educational expansion. He points in addition to America's commitment to equality of opportunity, the importance it has historically attached to education, immigration, urbaniza-tion, the move to abolish child labor, and more. Still, educational changes were driven primarily by economic ones. The creation of a system of mass secondary education that accompanied the growth of mass economic organ-izations after 1870 could not be simply the extension of the old elite second-ary system. The new system had a different function (terminal rather than preparatory) and a different organizational form (public locally controlled rather than private tuition and endowed schools). Mass public schools needed to develop their own curricula and had to institutionalize relationships with teacher training programs. Moreover, the tremendous growth in enrollments led to changes in the characteristics of high school students. Many new students were in school unwillingly, came from poor homes, had modest vocational goals, or were the sons and daughters of immigrants. In short, the creation of a mass terminal system, with functions and orientations quite different from that of the traditional college preparatory system that preceded it, forced not only changes in the high school itself, but also a drastic shift in the basic assumptions underlying secondary education.

Trow continues his analysis with a look at the growth of mass higher education in the United States. During the decades when the institutions, curricula, and philosophies of mass terminal education were being created, the college population was rising very slowly. After World War II, however, college enrollments in the United States skyrocketed. This led to yet another transformation of American secondary education, from a mass terminal institution to a mass preparatory one. Trow maintains that the massification of higher education was driven by the same basic factors as those that led to the earlier massification of secondary schooling. The maturation of the postindustrial economy demanded yet higher skills of new workers.

This second transformation was even more socially painful than the first. Whereas the first had involved the invention and creation of necessary institutions, the second required the transformation of a huge existing institutional complex into something altogether different. After the second transformation, high schools had to be simultaneously terminal and preparatory institutions. In the process, the social meaning of *not* going to college (which had been the norm throughout US history) took on an entirely different character. That is, when most high school students make the transition to postsecondary education, those that do not are more likely to be seen and to see themselves as educational failures. The consequences are both psychological and financial. This transformation helps explain the declining labor market position of young workers who lack postsecondary credentials, a trend I examined in an earlier chapter.

Trow's explanation of educational expansion is a compelling one, even if in the end it is perhaps too parsimonious. As Chabbott and Ramirez (2000, p. 171) commented, "Historians and sociologists increasingly recognize that the rise of mass schooling cannot be adequately accounted for as an outcome of industrialization" (see also Meyer et al. 1979). Still, the thesis has generally held up, to the point that even such a conscientious reviewer as Baker (1999), responding to a vast post-Trow literature on the expansion of American mass schooling in the postbellum era, concluded that the weight of the evidence "revive[s] the possibility of more technical-functional based arguments about school expansion" (1999, p. 210). In other words, while there is healthy disagreement about many of the details, there is little doubt that much of the expansion of first secondary education and later higher education has been driven in great measure by the perceived exigencies of the workplace. Of course, other factors have been at work was well. Rubinson and Hurst (1997, p. 62), for instance, point to "the centrality of status competition, the lack of centralized political authority over schooling, and the loose connection between education and the economy." The "workplace exigencies" may be real (as they are for Trow, as well as functionalist sociologists and human capital economists) or more arbitrary outcomes of status competition and credentialism (Collins 1979), but the empirical linkage seems pretty clear.

Thus, we are now in an era in which high schools prepare the majority of their graduates to go on to higher education. This, of course, is an average across all American high schools. In some high schools virtually everyone goes on to college, while in others virtually no one does. Further, many of those who go on to postsecondary education are bound for two-year community colleges or trade schools, which are often vocational preparation for work. There are other high schools in which the blanket expectation is that graduates will go on to one of the nation's elite postsecondary institutions. These variations are important, and indeed are critical to understanding how social stratification operates in the United States. They do not, however, trump the main point, which is that what typical high schools do for typical students is to send them on their way to even more schooling.

Having said that, the fact remains that many high school graduates do not go on to postsecondary schooling, and even today many do not even compete high school. Some have taken to calling these students the "Forgotten Half" (Howe 1988). This phrase brings attention to the large minority of students whose schooling terminates with high school and who go straight to the workforce. As we will see, they are often – even typically – missed in policy initiatives to enhance the skill development of youth.

Non-college-bound students do not necessarily see themselves as non-college-bound, and there is evidence that they have over time become less likely to see themselves in this way. As a provocative analysis by Schneider and Stevenson (1999) demonstrated, "more than 90 percent of high school seniors expect to attend college, and more than 70 percent expect to work in professional jobs" (1999, p. 5). These aspirations and expectations, perhaps surprisingly, are nearly as characteristic of students who have done virtually none of the things they need to do to prepare for these attainments as they are of students whose aspirations and preparation are more "aligned." That is, many high school students who plan on college degrees have not taken even the minimum coursework required to effectively move through the postsecondary educational system. For Schneider and Stevenson, this "misalignment" of preparation and aspirations represents a serious threat to any hopes of successful transitions to the world of work for a large number of America's high school population.

How Schooling Prepares Students for the World of Work

For Martin Trow, the explosion in high school enrollments that began after the American Civil War was a response to the demands of an increasingly industrialized and bureaucratized society. Employers needed certain skills, and high schools appeared on the scene to provide them. While insightful, this story is incomplete. Most importantly, this account never shows *how* the increasing societal demand for higher levels of skills actually produced educational expansion (Walters 2000). That is, given a demand for education (or, maybe more precisely, a demand for educated labor), what mechanisms were put into place to ensure that the supply of schools, teachers, curricula, books, and the rest of the educational infrastructure actually came into existence? How, exactly, did the reputed demands of employers translate into the bricks and mortars of schools? And what does schooling actually do to people to make them acceptable to the needs of the world of work?

One would think that human capital theory would have much to say about this. Human capital economists see a clear link between a society's investment in education and its growth of productivity. Schooling, in this model, changes people in ways that employers value – it adds skills and dispositions that are close enough to those needed at work to make it rational for employers to prefer more- over less-educated job applicants. At least to the most devout human capital theorists, the question of how the demand for education and the supply of schools came into correspondence is barely worth asking.

As usual, though, things aren't that simple. Sociologists often accuse human capital theory of ignoring what exactly it is that schools do to people to make them acceptable to employers. The nature and extent of school learning is essential to human capital theory, yet this learning is far more often assumed than demonstrated (Baker and LeTendre 2000; Wolniak 2002). Indeed, economists spend little time examining the inner workings of schools (Bills 1998).

Functionalist sociologists have not done much better. For functionalism, the role of schooling in preparing people to work is straightforward. Parsons (1959), Dreeben (1968), and others saw schools as providing not only the cognitive skills, but also the affective orientations and demeanors needed to participate in modern economic institutions. Looking at schooling cross-societally, Inkeles (1969) said simply that schooling serves to "make men modern." Like human capital economists, functionalist sociologists posit a relatively clear linkage between what employers want and what schools provide.

To a point, this is unassailable. Even the most ardent credentialists are unlikely to doubt that schools teach people to read, write, and calculate. But *how* do schools socialize people for the world of work? Even when we restrict our attention to the socialization that takes place in schools, "socialization" is a vague term. Young people are socialized both in school and out of school, and there is no way to know what proportion of the socialization that children experience is derived from one setting or the other. Nor do we know, either in school or out of school, what the ratio of intentional to incidental learning might be. Schools certainly intend to teach certain things, but they at the same time they teach other less overt lessons simply because they are the kinds of settings that they are.

Given all of this, what does the literature show about high school socialization and the world of work? It might be useful to answer this question by constructing an ideal type (of the sort we introduced in Chapter 1) of the process of high school socialization. We can then compare this ideal type to any departures from it that might recur in the literature.

An ideal typical model of how schools socialize people to enter the world of work can be constructed from Robert Dreeben's classic *On What is Learned in School* (1968). Dreeben argues that the organization of schools – that is, the patterns of authority, division of labor, and formally sanctioned rules, roles, and relationships – prepare students to participate in adult institutions in ways every bit as powerful as those provided by formal instruction and curricula. For Dreeben, schools are fundamentally different from families. Some of these differences are obvious (schools are larger than families) and some perhaps less so (schools are more public places than are families). The effect of these differences is to teach children the norms of independence, achievement, and universalism and specificity. That is, schools teach children to understand when and how they need to act in self-sufficient ways, that they need to display some level of mastery, that they can expect to be treated as individuals rather than as representatives of categories, and that different aspects of their selves are open for inspection in different settings. Dreeben sees these norms as crucial in transforming naive children into functioning adults.

"Correspondence" models of schools and workplaces offer a useful extension to Dreeben's ideal type. The best known of these models appeared some time ago in Samuel Bowles and Herbert Gintis's *Schooling in Capitalist America: Educational Reform and the Contradictions of Economic Life* (1976). Bowles and Gintis drew attention to the class-stratified nature of the processes described by Dreeben. They held that schools play a subservient role in American society because they have always been shaped by the "needs" of the business community (see also Anyon 1980). Like Dreeben, Bowles and Gintis see the structure of schools as corresponding to that of the workplace. They add, however, that schools that serve different economic classes are structured differently, in ways that "reproduce" patterns of inequality over time. Thus, working class schools are organized in ways that produce docile and compliant students, while elite schools transmit norms of mastery and analytic ability.

While often presented as a rebuttal of such models as that offered by Dreeben, "correspondence" models do more to flesh out these models than to challenge them. In both cases, schools are organized in ways that socialize students to eventually move into adult roles. The major difference is that for Dreeben, "society" in general benefits from these arrangements, while for Bowles and Gintis some economic classes benefit at the expense of others. The thesis that schools change people in ways that employers value holds in either account.

Departures from the Ideal Type of Socialization for Work

With this as a template, what can we say about the ways in which high schools in the United States prepare people for the world of work? We can identify a number of major points that we can organize around a series of questions.

First, what do students know about the adult world of work? I stated earlier that students have reasonably complex mental maps of the adult world of jobs. On closer inspection, these maps turn out to provide as much misdirection as they do guidance. High school students know less than might be expected, much of what they "know" is wrong, and the accuracy of their perceptions has actually declined over time. DeFleur and Menke (1975) provided a useful baseline for these claims several years ago. Analyzing a sample of high school males, DeFleur and Menke determined that their understanding of the adult world of occupations was sketchy, and that what understanding they did have did not improve very much over the course of their high school years. Higher SES students had no clearer perceptions than did lower SES students, nor did academically successful students know much more about the workplace than lesser achievers.

Schneider and Stevenson (1999) have more recently provided evidence that what high school students "know" (or believe) about work is largely wrong. Surprising numbers of high school students view the opportunities that the world of work offers to them with far higher expectations than their level of preparation would seem to warrant. Others, although a much smaller number, seriously overstate the amount of education that they will need to achieve the job to which they aspire. Overall, high school students probably have a pretty clear sense of the youth labor market that they currently occupy, but a less clear vision of what the world of adult work entails (also see Wilson 2001).

A second broad question is "What are the constraints on the socialization process? How well does the ideal type model work?" As Bowles and Gintis recognized, not all students share the same socialization experiences. How do socialization processes vary in ways that differentially prepare people for work?

We can get some purchase on differential socialization by examining both the *formal curriculum* and the *hidden curriculum*. By formal curriculum we mean the array of differentiated subject matter that is offered to students. This expands the question beyond simply the growth in the amount of schooling that people have received toward changes in the content and context of that schooling. The formal curriculum involves such matters as course-taking and academic majors. More broadly, we need to ask what students do in school – what they study, what they learn, who makes these decisions, how these decisions are made, and so on.

These are important questions to ask, but any answers to them based on US data are unlikely to travel very readily to other societies. Generalizing from the education and work relationships in the United States to anywhere else in the world is a risky business. This is particularly true of the formal curriculum. Kerckhoff (2000, p. 457), noting the history of the common school and the comprehensive high school in the United States, observed that "A distinctive feature of the American educational system, in contrast with almost all of those of Europe, is its low degree of stratification into different curricular and status streams." US high schools award very general credentials that carry relatively little labor market information (a situation that also applies to many undergraduate degrees, particularly two-year degrees). In short, the formal curriculum of American high schools can be expected to have linkages with the world of work unlike those found in other postindustrial societies.

In contrast to the publicly visible formal curriculum, the hidden curriculum operates "underground." The concept of hidden curriculum is often distressingly expansive, and there is little consensus about what sociologists are talking about when they use the term. I will follow the usage proposed by Vallance (1973), who sees the hidden curriculum as "those nonacademic but educationally significant consequences of schooling that occur systematically but are not made explicit at any level of the public rationales for education" (p. 7). In other words, the hidden curriculum points toward the lessons that schools teach, at least to some degree unintentionally, strictly from the way they are organized (see also Jackson 1968).

With notable exceptions (Gamoran 1989; Benavot 1992), sociologists' understanding of the formal curriculum is surprisingly thin. According to McEneaney and Meyer (2000, p. 190), "Current work in the sociology of education gives surprisingly little attention to the substantive content of the curriculum." They add that when sociologists study the curriculum, they usually refer to either tracking or the hidden curriculum, but rarely to the content of the curriculum. I attack this question here largely via an appraisal of vocational education, but McEneaney and Meyer's observation raises broader questions about the relationships between course content and allocation processes (admittedly not the focus of their critique).

It is not always obvious where the formal curriculum leaves off and the hidden curriculum begins. Still, these concepts provide us with a vehicle to identify several factors whose operation call into question the validity of the ideal type that we established.

The Formal Curriculum

I begin with a little, if drastically abbreviated, history. With industrialization, American high schools became increasingly vocational institutions. This was "head" rather than "hand" vocationalism in that it focused on the basic skills of reading, writing, and calculating rather than on the technical and mechanical skills that came to be seen as "vocational education." Labaree (1997, p. 47) has commented on the emergence of this vocationalized academic curriculum: "The true significance of vocationalism is visible in the philosophical shift that took place in the general aims of American schooling in the period following 1890." This involved a shift away from education for citizenship to education for the development of human capital. Those who were in this era destined for white-collar jobs went to high school.

In a similar way, the locus of skill acquisition for those on a trajectory for blue-collar labor moved away from the workplace and toward institutionalization in formal school settings. To oversimplify a complex history that was not nearly this linear, the trend has led young people preparing for work from apprenticeships to vocational high schools to community colleges.

Apprenticeships provided the port of entry for most young people entering skilled craft and industrial trades in the early years of industrialization. Built on an older guild model structured along a hierarchy of apprentice through journeyman through master, apprenticeships provided an avenue for individuals to develop increasingly complex skills and the opportunity to independently practice them (Krause 1996).

We typically think of apprenticeships as characteristic of blue-collar trade occupations, but they predate that in the United States. Engineering may be the earliest example of training through apprenticeship giving way to preparation through formal academic programs (Collins 1979; Lipartito and Miranti 1998). This later happened in law, medicine, and business. The knowledge bases of most of what we now think of as the professions were passed along through apprenticeships before they moved into university settings. Universities had great competitive advantages over apprenticeships because of their large scale (Lipartito and Miranti 1998).

In time, the training functions of industrial and craft apprenticeships migrated to vocational high schools (DeYoung 1989; Kliebard 1999). This was not a case of high schools usurping the training function previously carried out by apprenticeships. In fact, apprenticeship as a form of industrial training was in substantial decline well before the growth of mass public secondary schooling in the United States (Elbaum 1989). Schools assumed the training role largely because employers were no longer willing to do so. Still, with industrialization, more and more job training for youth was carried out in educational institutions.

Dawson (1999) provides a fascinating historical account of how the shift from the work setting to the school as the site of skill acquisition took place. In his study of the Spring Garden Institute in Philadelphia, Dawson observed that "In 1878 the Baldwin Locomotive Works in association with the Spring Garden Institute, pioneered a new system of *industrial training* – a radical departure from nineteenth century apprenticeship" (1999, p. 143). Noting that historians have overlooked the preprogressive era manual-training movement, Dawson (1999, p. 144) maintains that: "Braverman suggested that the division of labor under industrial capitalism split the work of skilled mechanics by separating conception and execution of tasks. In the sphere of education, a parallel force led to the demise of apprenticeship and the triumph of industrial training. The classroom conquered the workshop."

Dawson's description of how all of this worked is richer than we can recount here. Its importance is that it once again highlights the tightening bonds between schooling and work. As he states, a small group of rich and powerful Gilded-Age business leaders, far from rejecting social intervention, were in the forefront of educational reform. Reform was not the product of an impulse to meddle in the lives of those they considered subordinates, but emerged concretely out of the conditions faced by a handful of workshop owners in the daily conduct of their businesses (Dawson 1999, p. 144). In time, Spring Garden led directly to the founding of Philadelphia's vocational high schools.

Apprenticeships greatly changed as the training function moved to high schools. Later in this chapter I will discuss various proposals to revive "youth apprenticeships," but traditional apprenticeships have become generally unimportant to the skill needs of young workers. In 1989 there were about 300,000 apprentices in the United States; with an average age of 29 (Bailey 1993). This amounts to only about 0.3 percent of civilian employment, and is located overwhelmingly in the building trades (Elbaum 1989). Apprenticeships in the United States have really become a means to upgrade training for already employed adults, rather than as an entry into a field (as they still are in much of the world) (Bailey 1993; Smith and Rowjewski 1993).

Still later, the functions assumed by vocational high schools passed on to community colleges. This moves us into the realm of postsecondary education and I will reserve a fuller discussion of community colleges for the next chapter. For now, though, the point is once again the historically strengthening link between the mission of the school and that of the workplace.

Vocational Education

While vocational high schools are less prevalent than they once were (but with recent signs of a comeback), there are few more contentious areas in the high school curriculum than that of vocational education. Supporters see vocational education as the best hope for young people for whom higher education is neither likely nor desired. Detractors counter with charges of blocked opportunities and class privilege. Even the term "vocational education" raises eyebrows, simultaneously connoting the lofty sense of a vocation as a calling with the despised sense of "vocational" as unworthy and degraded labor.

We can characterize much of the history of the US high school curriculum as a drift toward vocationalism. Finkelstein (1991), whose analysis of the early vocationalization of the American high school I presented earlier, demonstrated quite clearly that many educational reformers envisioned public schools as a service to industry. Curriculum analyst Herbert Kliebard (1999) believes that the American educational system was essentially vocationalized by the end of World War II (see also Perkinson 1991, ch. 4).

One effect of the trend toward vocationalization was the construction of distinct vocational education tracks. While the precise designations may have varied from place to place, four were prevalent: college preparatory, commercial, industrial, and domestic (Finkelstein 1991, p. 484). Not surprisingly, enrollments in these areas often lined up with socioeconomic hierarchies. Manual training as a curriculum basic was especially marked for African American and Native American schools. Moreover, women and children of the working class were commonly slotted for the tremendous growth of industrial jobs.

The vocationalization of the curriculum was fiercely contested, both pedagogically and politically. Finkelstein (1991, pp. 484–5) characterizes vocational education as having two "taskmasters." The first, associated most directly with educational philosopher John Dewey, consisted of "well-organized cultural minorities, seeking to transform the schools into instruments of democratic empowerment." On the other side was a contingent nominally led by "efficiency educator" David Snedden, representing "captains of capitalist enterprise and their allies, who in search of profit and efficiency, turned to schools to sort workers and legitimize inequalities among and between categories of workers."

Battles over vocational education were not joined only by educators. The Smith-Hughes Act of 1917, for instance, established federal support for vocational education. It was also instrumental in providing a steady stream of funding to support vocational education programs and initiatives. Much later, the Carl D. Perkins Vocational Education Act of 1984 (and subsequent reauthorizations), took aim at students unlikely to get four-year degrees. The Perkins legislation was particularly focused on those special populations that had traditionally been underserved by vocational programs (e.g., women, minorities, those with handicaps, and those with limited English proficiencies).

As important as the 1984 Perkins Act in many ways was its 1990 reauthorization. Known as the Carl D. Perkins Vocational and Applied Technology Education Act, this reauthorization was significant in that it emphasized academic as well as occupational skills. The 1990 Act called explicitly for greater "articulation" between secondary and postsecondary education. The mechanism here was "tech-prep," which was meant to institutionalize the role of high school vocational education as a preparation for future learning (Urquiola et al. 1997).

Funding for secondary vocational education took off in the 1960s and 1970s, growing from about 1 percent of public educational expenditures in 1960 to about 5 percent in 1980 (Arum 1998). Secondary vocational enrollments also rose during this period. In time, however, a consensus emerged that the Smith-Hughes and its successors defined vocational education too narrowly and in ways that contributed to the division in public schools between academic and vocational curricula (Urquiola et al. 1997). Thus, the 1998 reauthorization of the Perkins Act placed even greater emphasis on academic standards. The goal of the School-To-Work programs that were at the core of this reauthorization was to break down the old model of vocational education as isolated from the rest of the curriculum. At least on an official level, high school vocational education was no longer intended to be only for the non-college bound.

The uneasy nature of a vocationalized curriculum

The current US system of vocational education grows out of these tangled roots. For a curriculum that has been around in such a visible way for as long as it has, though, there is a surprising amount that we do not know about vocational education. Noting large and persistent gaps in the data on vocational education, Hurst and Hudson (2001) of the National Center for Education Statistics observed that:

> there is still much that we do not know. Most importantly, we do not yet have good information on what students learn from participating in vocational education, whether in technical courses alone or in combination with academics or other forms of learning such as youth apprenticeships or cooperative education. Additionally, while longitudinal studies have furnished better data on labor market participation by students taking vocational courses, one of the key labor market outcomes – earnings, immediately before and after participation in vocational education and over time – is not yet accurately or consistently measured. Finally, for a large and growing number of older adults using the postsecondary vocational education system for short-term skill upgrading, we know virtually nothing about learning gains or impacts on employment and earnings. In short, today we have much better information on who participates in vocational education but still know very little about what is accomplished as a result.

We do know with some assurance that academic course taking has increased in American high schools since the mid-1980s while vocational education has declined (Zemsky et al. 1998, p. 12; Levesque et al. 2000; Hurst and Hudson 2001). This is in part a response to more stringent high school graduation requirements set in motion by *A Nation At Risk* (1983) and such reports and in part because of a more demanding job market. Also, the high costs of vocational education came under increasing scrutiny on the 1980s as the economy slowed, leading eventually to diminished government support (Arum 1998).

The shifts in high school course-taking were quite dramatic, given that they took place so quickly. For instance, in 1982 vocational enrollments were about 33.7 percent of all enrollments By 1998 this had declined to 25.0 percent. During the same period, "general" enrollments fell from 58.2 percent to 42.6 percent, while "college" enrollments skyrocketed from 8.7 to 38.9 percent. These numbers need to be interpreted carefully. Hurst and Hudson show that the growth in academic enrollments did not come at the expense of vocational enrollments. Rather, many students simply increased the number of credit hours they took in high school. The major shift was from general education to college preparatory curriculum.

Not all vocational concentrations declined. The largest declines were in the two areas that began with the highest enrollments – trade and industry, and business. Enrollment in "personal and other services" declined, although these started off from low enrollment bases. Other areas that increased also started off from low enrollments. These included health care, technology and communications, food service and hospitality, and child care and education. Areas that changed little also began with low enrollments (agriculture and renewable resources, marketing and distribution). These trends broadly mirror labor market trends (Hurst and Hudson 2001).

Hurst and Hudson (2001) observe that it is fairly easy to see why college track enrollments grew, but less obvious why vocational enrollments went down. Certainly the trend in vocational enrollments was less dramatic than those in general or academic areas. Still, it is not clear why high school students would react to a harsher job market by shying away from at least some of the very courses most directly tied to the world of work.

The irony to this is that there is increasing evidence that for many high school students, vocational education is a good investment. This runs counter to what was at one time the received wisdom that vocational education provided a watered-down curriculum that consigned students to dead-end careers and foreclosed their options for postsecondary schooling and professional employment. This generalization may have held in the 1970s and into the 1980s, but is demonstrably untrue today.

Analysts have lately mined several nationally representative data sets to reexamine the benefits of high school vocational education. A particularly thorough analysis by Mane (1999) drew on three of these (The National Longitudinal Study of the High School Class of 1972, High School and Beyond, and the National Educational Longitudinal Study). His findings were quite clear that for students who were not college-bound, high school courses in vocational education produced significant short- and medium-term benefits. In fact, vocational courses did more to enhance the labor market prospects of students who did not go beyond high school than did academic courses. Further, the value of vocational education increased throughout the 1970s and 1980s. Mane's results replicate and extend earlier work by John Bishop (Bishop and Kang 1989), who found that vocational education students benefited greatly when they found employment in the area of their coursework (see also Rosenbaum and Jones 2000).

Such findings suggest that states would do well to invest in vocational education programs, and that the costs to the disinvestment in these programs over the past couple of decades as been disproportionately borne by the non-college bound. Students are especially able to benefit from vocational education programs when the state in which they live provides resources for those programs (Arum 1998). Because most vocational education action is really at the state rather than federal level, these differences in state-level investments are crucial. Arum's results challenge the belief (held by many sociologists as well as by many policy makers) that vocational education simply "cools out" people or offers them "false promises" or "diverted dreams." Indeed, vocational education can have beneficial effects on educational progression as well as on career success (see also Arum and Shavit 1995).

The Hidden Curriculum and School Socialization

A full exposition of the ways in which schools socialize some students differently than they do others, hence putting them on different trajectories into the world of work, could fill a book twice the length of this one. I briefly note a couple of the more obvious processes, and then discuss a couple of less obvious if perhaps more prevalent examples. In doing so, I shade from the clear province of the formal curriculum toward the murkier regions of the hidden curriculum.

Tracking may be the most visible means by which socialization is stratified in high schools. Tracking is much more complicated than it once was, or than we once thought it was (Lucas 1999, 2001; Rosenbaum 1976). There are any number of variations on the efforts of schools to compartmentalize instruction (Lucas and Good 2001), but at bottom probably most systems of tracking provide a means by which the courses of study that students take come to roughly correspond to their probable futures. The processes and decisions underlying tracking may be neither intentional nor even particularly visible, but at the end of the day some students have pursued coursework that moves them along to postsecondary schooling and from there to the middle and upper reaches of the occupational hierarchy, while others have pursued coursework that puts them on a more direct trajectory to the world of (often less rewarding) work. The scholarly consensus now seems to be that tracking does little to raise the level of achievement in a school, but does make achievement less equally distributed (Gamoran and Kelly 2001).

If we can accept some ambiguity and classify high school tracks as college preparatory, general, and vocational, it quickly becomes apparent that track placement in US schools is far from random. Zemsky et al. (1998, p. 12) showed that roughly equal numbers of high school seniors in 1992 reported their program of study as college prep (43 percent) and general (45 percent). (This, of course, is after about a decade of a decline in vocational enrollments and an accompanying growth in the general track.) About 12 percent of students report being in a vocational track. These figures were about the same for males and females, but there were large placement differences across race, ethnicity, and socioeconomic status. None of these differences was very surprising. Whites and Asian-Americans are more likely to be in college prep tracks and less likely to show up in vocational tracks. The reverse is true for African-Americans, Hispanics, and Native Americans. Students who do well on tests and students from socioeconomically advantaged families cluster toward college prep and away from vocational education.

High school *guidance counselors* provide another mechanism linking school and work The classic study here is Cicourel and Kitsuse's *The Educational Decision-Makers* (1963). These authors were concerned with how school gatekeepers provided organizational sponsorship for some students while withholding it from others. They found counselors to routinely, if not necessarily intentionally, favor the school's privileged members with better information about post high school opportunities, typically at the expense of more marginalized students.

Cicourel and Kitsuse conducted their research some 40 years ago, and in some ways the organizational role of the guidance counselor has diminished since then (Lucas 2001). Other features of *school organization* have emerged to provide new instances of the hidden curriculum. Powell et al. (1985) offered a powerful metaphor for understanding school organization several years ago in *The Shopping Mall High School*. For Powell and his colleagues, modern high schools resemble shopping malls in ways that limit the educational possibilities of many students. That is, the authors see schools as offering broad and shallow choices among course offerings to students. Much as in shopping malls, students can pick and choose between "boutique" courses and "fast food" courses, in a bewildering assortment of options and possibilities. Unfortunately, schools offer little guidance or structure for students to learn how to transform their course-taking into viable career paths. Schools come to favor those with the resources to capitalize on this excess of choice – those with the savviest parents and the most fully developed social capital. Other students are left to fend for themselves.

Economist John Bishop (1999) has provided another interpretation of how the hidden curriculum of schooling can socialize people in different and stratifying ways. In his innovative analysis of "nerd harassment and grade inflation," Bishop takes as his point of departure the claim that the major reason that high school students work hard is to get into college. Many students accurately see their academic performance as generally irrelevant to their prospects for employment upon graduation, so there is little linkage between hard work in school and the world of work outside of it. Bishop presents survey results that show that 79 percent of high school students worked hard to get the grades to get into college, but only 58 percent worked hard to get a better job. Hard work was even less strongly related to such factors as parental influence, intrinsic motivation, or the influence of teachers and peers.

Bishop believes that schools often respond to student motivations in what turn out to be dysfunctional ways. Because students are in the hunt for grades and credentials rather than learning itself, schools and students collaborate on developing norms against hard work, pushing students toward taking easy courses, and the dumbing down of courses. The fact that college selection decisions are based so heavily on such indicators as SAT, ACT, GPA, and class rank makes the situation even worse. For Bishop, SAT and ACT fail to assess most of what high school students are expected to learn. They leave out, for example, writing, art, literature, and foreign language. The result of this is to pit students against teachers. Teachers become judges rather than teachers or coaches. Bishop's solution is the use of curriculum-based external exams, which he believes would help solve the problem of low motivation and low achievement.

Interim Summary and an Unresolved Issue

Both the formal curriculum and the hidden curriculum of high school are related to the world of work in multiple and complex ways. While an oversimplification, we might conclude that a hierarchical formal curriculum helps send students on their way to a hierarchical occupational structure, and that a pervasive hidden curriculum systematically favors some students over others.

None of this adequately comes to grips with McEneaney and Meyer's (2000) observation that sociologists know far too little about the *substance* of the high school curriculum, that we are too little versed in the intricacies of social studies, science, language and literature, mathematics, arts and culture, and civics. Surely the content of what students learn is relevant to our focus on the allocation of young people to adult work roles. The fact is, however, that we lack a clear sense of how that works, and have "almost no evidence on the effects of high school curriculum on postsecondary education and on success in the labor market" (Altonji 1994, p. 409).

One can read the institutionalist theory of Meyer and his colleagues as suggesting that what students learn in school is less important than the fact that they were there and can be certified to have been there. This view has much to recommend it. It acknowledges that while socialization certainly takes place in schools, we can understand the linkages between schooling and work without having to rely entirely on an analysis of this socialization. Rather, if we see schools as "chartering" institutions – as institutions that are chartered by society to bestow official designations on those that pass through them (e.g., dropout, graduate, Advanced Placement student) – we can arrive at an alternative account of the relationship between education and work that avoids some of the difficulties of human capital and functionalist accounts.

Nonetheless, those making the transition from school to work now face a different world than those who preceded them. They evidently benefit more from knowing math when they enter the world of work, and there may be increased returns to other specific skills as well. At the same time, much of the traditional high school liberal arts curriculum is under increased criticism for its *lack* of vocational payoff. Sociologists have barely begun to examine the connections between the specific content of the high school curriculum – how this content is selected, delivered, evaluated, and certified – and the complex process by which young people shed the role of student and adopt the role of worker.

The Advent of the Youth Labor Market

Whatever high school does or fails to do to prepare people for the workplace, few students wait for the end of high school to make their first encounters with paid employment. This takes us to the youth labor market. As with most of the topics is this book, analysts come to the question of the youth labor market with very different perspectives and values. Some see "youth-work" (a term that may be inelegant but which has found reasonably wide acceptance) as providing the work ethic and orientations needed for a successful transition to adult employment (Barton 1989). Former US Secretary of Labor Alexis Herman, for instance, has described herself as "an avid supporter of jobs for young workers" (US Department of Labor 2000, p. v). Others see youthwork as exploitative and a drain on the time and commitments of young people (Greenberger and Steinberg 1986). Both sides often appeal to the same data to make their case.

Youthwork is nothing new. American teenagers have always worked, and in some times and places the odds of their participation in the labor force have been higher than their odds of staying in school. For much of American history the largest share of this work was performed on family farms. Indeed, American schools have quite often found themselves needing to respond to the pace and rhythm of farm life. Even as the share of American workers on the farm has plummeted to roughly 3 percent, most schools still operate on this calendar.

The industrial era brought with it a different youth labor market. Drawn by the seemingly insatiable demand for cheap and unskilled labor, the young sons and daughters of immigrants were often as attractive to employers as were their parents. Children, often at very young ages, in many industrial era factories worked alongside adults in often harsh, dirty, and dangerous jobs.

Gradually this changed. Late in Franklin Roosevelt's second administration, the Fair Labor Standards Act of 1938 placed serious restrictions on child labor. Even before this, states had begun to pass mandatory school attendance legislation. This was done less, in some cases, to educate a growing school-age population than to keep young people out of the labor force, where they competed with adults for scarce jobs, effectively lowering wages in the process.

Child labor remains an important issue throughout much of the world. It is of less pressing concern but not irrelevant in the United States. Indeed, there is extensive regulation at both state and federal levels covering child labor. Restrictions are much tighter for children aged 14–15 than for those aged 16–17 (US Department of Labor 2000). For example, 14–15 year olds are federally restricted to working outside of school hours, and face different restrictions for when school is and is not in session. There are also a variety of occupational restrictions, which differ across the agricultural and nonagricultural sectors. Still, there is considerable evidence of violations of many child labor laws. This is particularly the case when labor markets are tight (that is, when there are relatively more jobs than people to fill them). Many US employers (and many teen workers) seem willing to face the risks of prosecution when workers are hard to find.

If there is an underlying coherence to federal and state child labor legislation, it is that school comes first. Nonetheless, there is often tension between
schooling and employment for the commitment of young people. High
school prepares (or fails to prepare) people for work by providing skills and
dispositions relevant to the workplace, but it also does so by serving as the
foil of students' work lives. In many cases, it is work rather than school that
secures the primary commitment of high school students. US high school
students work in high numbers (much higher than comparable countries),
they start young, and they work a lot of hours.

Working while in high school

If one were to pay close attention to politicians, reformers, the popular
press, and even many social scientists, it would be easy to conclude that we
are experiencing great growth in paid employment among high-school-age
people. In fact, though, students today work at about the same rates and
with about the same level of intensity (that is, the number of hours worked)
as was the case in 1980 (Warren and Forrest 2001). This stability should
not obscure the fact that there have been demographic changes in who
works and how much they work, but the fact is that the United States is not
seeing a trend toward high school students entering the workplace.

To speak of *the* youth labor force is to speak too broadly. A report entitled
"The youth labor force" by the US Department of Labor (2000) drew a
crucial distinction between the young (12–15 years of age) and old (15–
17 years of age) segments of the youth labor market. The first group skirts the
edges of child labor, while the second approaches young adulthood. The
authors of the report also made much of the distinction between *freelance*
and *employee* jobs. Freelance jobs include such activities as lawn mowing
and baby sitting. Employee jobs, in contrast, entail an ongoing relationship
with an employer. In the United States, more than in comparable countries, both freelance jobs and employee jobs tend to be ends in themselves,
unconnected to future opportunities. They are rarely productive entrees
into the world of work, providing neither the first rungs on career ladders
nor the means to establish a career trajectory. As reported by the DoL:

> For the most part, the jobs held by U.S. teens are not conceived as stepping-
> stones on a life career path. Other developed countries, such as Germany,
> Denmark, and Switzerland, have long included adolescent employment as part
> of formal apprenticeship, School-to-Work, and Work Experience and Career
> Exploration Programs that are closely linked to the educational process and
> lead to specific adult jobs.

In addition to its loose linkages with the adult labor market, the youth labor market is a volatile one. Young people change jobs all the time, frequently interspersed between spells of being without work. Analysts are divided about the significance of this high rate of turnover, which is often referred to as "churning" (Osterman and Iannozzi 1993). Sociologist Krishnan Namboordiri (1987) calls this the "floundering phase" of the life course. Veum and Weiss (1993) found that between the ages of 18 and 27, the average high school graduate not continuing on to higher education held almost six different jobs and experienced more than four unemployment spells. While those with more schooling tend to have greater stability in the early career, for many youth the early career is an almost indescribably disorderly time (Cooksey and Rindfuss 2001).

In sharp contrast, some observers (Heckman 1994) consider high incidences of job changing as rational and productive job search. In this conception, youth move from job to job not out of any innate need for disorder or any inefficient functioning of the labor market, but rather as a means of seeking the best match between their interests and skills and the needs of some employer. If true, youth job shopping is probably as efficient as youth apprenticeship. In fact, if one can define employment stability as holding a job that will last between one and three years, most young people do enter stable employment by their early twenties (Klerman and Karoly 1995). Not only that, but job changes are often accompanied with wage increases, suggesting that something more than simple floundering is going on.

Youthwork starts young. Even 12- to 15 year old Americans have already established an active involvement in the labor market (US Department of Labor 2000). At age 14, 57 percent of youth had some kind of job. About 43 percent held freelance jobs, while 24 percent had employee jobs – 9 percent had both kinds. Rates of labor force participation are substantially higher for 15 year olds, but already the nature of these jobs begins to shift. While 64 percent of 15 year olds hold jobs, they are now about equally likely to hold freelance jobs (40 percent) and employee jobs (38 percent). About 14 percent hold both.

Youth aged 14 to 15 differ markedly in their likelihood of participating in the work force. White youth were more likely to have jobs than were African-American or Hispanic students. At age 15, males and females are about equally likely to work, although males tend toward employee jobs and females tend toward freelance jobs (largely, no doubt, baby sitting). Lower SES youth are less likely to be working than are those at higher income levels (US Department of Labor 2000).

The same general pattern holds for intensity of employment among 14–15 year olds. Males work more hours than females, Whites more than

African-Americans and Hispanics, and youth from affluent households more than those from less affluent ones. Even at age 14–15 signs of sex-stereotyping in occupations are beginning to emerge. This is particularly true in freelance jobs, where girls dominate babysitting and boys dominate yard jobs. Whites also have greater access to freelance jobs than do African-Americans and Hispanics.

The finding that more socioeconomically privileged students are more likely to work than are less-advantaged students deserves some comment. One might anticipate that students from families most in need of additional sources of income would be the most likely to send their children to the workplace. In fact, though, as Carr and her colleagues noted with only a little exaggeration, current working students are "junior and senior White males from intact, relatively well-educated middle-class families who are enrolled in college preparatory tracks and who are better-then-average students" (Carr 1996, p. 71; see too Lillydahl 1990, p. 307; Schill et al. 1985).

Probably the major reason for the positive correlation between social class and the likelihood of working is that less-advantaged youth (disproportionately minority) have less access to employment than do their more advantaged age-mates. This is in part because they live in neighborhoods with fewer economic opportunities, and in part because employers are less likely to hire them for the jobs that are available to youth (Neckerman and Kirschenman 1991). Seen in this light, the positive correlation merely reflects the stratified workplace that teenagers will eventually encounter as adults. Those left out of youthwork are generally those most at risk of being left behind by macroeconomic trends in the broader society.

If the ages of 15 to 17 are not exactly more of the same, they represent no great departures in the stratification of youthwork. There is an ever-growing participation of youth in the labor market as they age. For example, while only 9 percent of 15 year olds worked in a typical school month in 1996–8, this number grew to 26 percent for 16 year olds and 39 percent for 17 year olds. (Remember that this is the percentage of students who worked in a given month, and thus underestimates the percentage who worked at some point during the school year.) Males and females at this age participate at roughly equal rates, but the advantage of Whites relative to African Americans and Hispanics widens as young people enter their mid and late teens. As with younger students, 15 to 17 year olds from more affluent families held jobs at higher rates than those from poorer households.

As teenagers get older, not only are they more likely to work at all, but those who work also begin to work more hours. Once again, the persistent inequalities of race, ethnicity, social class, and gender are present. Warren and Forrest (2001) showed that the role of these factors grew throughout the 1970s, 1980s, and 1990s even as the level of youth participation in the labor force was stable. In a carefully conducted study of several data sets with information on the youth labor market, the authors conclude (2001, p. 23) that:

> Among seniors, the Black–White gap in employment rates has increased modestly over time, while the male–female gap has diminished and perhaps disappeared entirely. Considering only employed students, we find that senior girls have tended to work greater numbers of hours per week relative to male students. That is, race/ethnic and sex differences in employment behaviors among high school students – especially seniors – have changed over time.

The consequences of "youthwork"

Clearly, American youth have powerful commitments to working. But is it good for them? Does it give an advantage to participants as they prepare to face an increasingly harsh postindustrial labor market, or does it distract them from what would be in the long term better uses of their time? The balance between the costs and the benefits of high school students holding part-time and often full-time jobs has preoccupied many researchers in an often polarized and inconclusive debate. What does the evidence suggest?

There is no simple answer to the question of whether youthwork is good or bad for those who participate in it. One first has to distinguish between several kinds of effects. The most direct of these have to do with cognitive and academic performance. Does working help or hinder learning and achievement? Second, we can ask about the effects of youthwork on personal development and social relationships, although I will pay limited attention to that here. A third question pertains to a range of employment-related effects – wages, job stability, unemployment risk, and so on. Finally, we can ask about the effects of youthwork on these employment outcomes that are brought about via the earlier effects on academic performance and schooling. That is, to what degree does youthwork affect adult work not in any direct way, but rather through its influence on academic outcomes, which in turn affect adult work?

A host of methodological and conceptual problems have until recently limited our success in answering these questions (Marsh 1991; Bills 1997). Perhaps the major problem has been one we have encountered before – that of *selection*. That is, students who choose to work, or who choose to work more than a given number of hours, may be different in important and consistent ways from those who make other decisions. To put the issue simply and hypothetically, the question is whether students who work a lot of hours get bad grades because of the intensity of their work, or if students who are likely to get bad grades make decisions to work a lot of hours. Similarly, we can ask if students who work modest hours perform better academically because of this judicious employment decision, or if more high achieving students are the sort of students who make these employment decisions. At its extreme, even if all of those who worked during high school ended up as CEOs, we cannot say for certain if this is because their work experience changed them in ways that made that possible. It may be that if these individuals were different from their classmates even before embarking on youthwork in ways that made them more likely to become CEOs. Even with more contemporary state-of-the-art research on youthwork, analysts need to be cautious about this *unexplained heterogeneity*.

Other problems have plagued research on youthwork. For a long time the samples that many researchers used to assess the impacts of work on academic and employment outcomes were small and unrepresentative. The conceptualization and measurement of many critical variables was generally idiosyncratic. Analysts were often insensitive to the multidimensional nature of youthwork, which encompasses not only the simple fact of participation, but also its intensity, timing (e.g., weekends or nights, summer or school year), the nature of the work, the opportunities for meaningful learning and supervision on the job, and much more.

All of this made it difficult to sort out causation in ways that could inform both research and policy on youthwork. Fortunately, analysts have recently turned to more appropriate longitudinal data sets using a more sophisticated array of statistical techniques. By far the most valuable source of data has been the assortment of surveys conducted by the National Longitudinal Surveys Program of the Bureau of Labor Statistics. What have we learned?

On balance, there are academic benefits to be had when youth work modest numbers of hours, but academic prices to be paid when work commitment becomes excessive. What counts as "excessive" can be debated, although most researchers would put this at somewhere between 14 and 20 hours a week. This threshold is probably a bit lower for freshmen and sophomores and a bit higher for juniors and seniors. Neither the positive nor the negative effects are necessarily very large, but they are persistent and cumulative, lasting well into the students' postsecondary experiences (or in many cases, their lack of such experiences). The academic outcomes most strongly affected by excessive youthwork are entry into and completion of college.

Many opponents of youthwork claim that the consequences of youthwork for academic achievement have become greater than they once were. Data on this are sparse, but Warren and Forrest (2001) showed that the effect of intensive employment on dropping out of high school may have declined somewhat since 1980.

The results of the effects of youthwork on employment outcomes are somewhat different than they are for academic achievement. These differences generally run in a favorable direction. Working while young, at least to a point, often enhances post-high school employment outcomes. These benefits seem to persist, even as long as 12 years past high school. Youthwork increases the likelihood that one will be employed after high school, but has far smaller effects on the wages that one will earn.

Heavy doses of youthwork adversely affect academic achievement but can actually benefit employment outcomes. Of course, not all youth are or want to be college bound, and many of them are pursuing youthwork for precisely that reason. Such students may willingly accept the diminished odds of attending college (which was not in their plans anyway) in exchange for the short-term and long-term benefits that they accrue from early and extensive exposure to the workplace. If their aspirations are well-informed, perhaps the best advice and policy for such students is to encourage them to increase their work commitment during high school.

It remains to be seen at what point the benefits of youthwork outweigh the costs and how this differs for different kinds of students. We cannot know with certainty which high school students are not college bound, and prematurely facilitating the entry into the workplace of those whom we designate as terminal high school students could well close off future options for them. Still, we need to recognize that for many students, early and intense engagement with work provides an entree to the adult workplace every bit as secure as that provided by the advanced educational credentials of their former high school classmates.

All of this is complicated by race. As a general rule, minority youths gain less from working than do White youths (Leventhal et al. 2001). This is true of both education and employment outcomes. African-American youths in particular and Hispanics only a bit less have less access to the youth labor market and accrue fewer benefits from participating in it than do Whites. Steel (1991, p. 429), using 1979 data, reported no significant differences between White, Black, and Hispanic working youths in hours worked per week, job status, or the perceived opportunities in the job (see also Steinberg and Dornbusch 1991). Whites, however, worked at much higher rates than did Blacks or Hispanics, and were more likely to be employed in the private sector. This worked to the detriment of minorities, in that having a government job was associated with diminished employment in the early career. Steel posited that "employers do not view the early work experiences of Black youths as a signal of potential productivity or trainability in the same way that they view them for others" (1991, p. 443).

Gender relations do not seem to benefit anyone. Teenage girls move into sex stereotypical jobs at surprisingly high rates (Warren 2001). This can happen even in specific work sites. Bills (1999), for example, found fast food employers assign jobs that required contact with customers to girls and jobs requiring more physical strength (even if these demands were modest) to boys. Moreover, the negative effects of excessive youthwork are greater for boys.

On balance, we are left with a more favorable but hardly sanguine view of youthwork in the employment sphere than we are in the educational one (Ruhm 1997; Entwisle et al. 2000; Alon et al. 2001). At least over the past couple of decades, students who worked while in high school accrued measurable labor market advantages in their early work careers. New evidence suggests that this edge may stretch into later stages of the early career, staying with young workers as they approach age 30 (we need to await the availability of ongoing longitudinal data collection efforts to determine if the effects persist beyond that). All of this is true primarily for students who would have been unlikely to pursue postsecondary education.

The Transition from High School to Work in the United States

Whether they do so well or poorly, high schools prepare young people for the world of work through a long process of socialization. Further, high-school-age youth are often workers as much or more as they are students, again providing a form of preparation for adult work roles. At some point, however, the high school student role is cast off entirely, ushering in (in a phrase that has become something of an obsession among both academics and policy makers) "the transition from school to work" (Zemsky et al. 1998; Hughes et al. 2001).

Probably the most important thing to keep in mind about the "school to work" transition is that it is not a single identifiable and discrete event. Rather, it is a process that often can develop over an extended period of time. In the United States, more than in most comparable nations, the transition from high school to the workplace is remarkably informal and unstructured, to the point that at least one observer has observed that "The link between school and careers is largely absent for the vast majority of high school students" (Lerman 1996).

Not only is the transition from high school to work an ambiguous and diffuse one, but the early career of American workers is very fluid. Even thinking of this period as a "career," a phrase that suggests some direction and orderliness, stretches its meaning. Young people regularly change jobs. They move from jobs that are primarily "male" to those that are primarily "female" (and vice versa) with surprising frequency (Rindfuss et al. 1999). Even more to the point, they regularly move in and out of the labor force. This is especially the case for women.

There are important differences in the ease and success with which young people negotiate the school to work transition. Early career advantages consistently accrue to Whites more than to African Americans or Hispanics. Compared with racial and ethnic minorities, Whites have earlier work experience, earlier experience in full-time jobs, and a greater likelihood of making a transition from part-time to full-time jobs (Coleman 1984; Klerman and Karoly 1995). The youth market is also stratified by gender. Young women hold fewer jobs than do young men (that is, they do less "job hopping"), but make the transition to stable employment less readily.

One effect of the historic lack of formal institutional structures in the youth labor market in the United States (unlike that in such nations as Japan and Germany) is to increase the importance of personal contacts to individuals trying to establish themselves in the world of work. These contacts can turn out to be decisive. Rosenbaum et al. (1999), using an innovative mixture of both quantitative and qualitative data, found that when young adults obtain jobs through such personal contacts as relatives or school contacts, these jobs tend to have better long-term potential and more opportunity for development than do jobs found without personal contacts. Even when used successfully, though, these kinds of networks, which others have characterized as social capital (Arum 2000; Strathlee 2001), do not seem to function as equitably or effectively as have the institutional structures put in place elsewhere (Rosenbaum 2001).

International comparisons of school to work institutions

All of this is in sharp contrast to the school to work transition in many other nations. Virtually every postindustrial nation in the world has institutionalized the school to work transition more than has the United States (Muller and Shavit 1998; Heinz 1999). This does not mean that other industrialized nations are all of a piece. France has very active labor market policies aimed at youth employment and unemployment (Fougere et al. 2000). This includes such policies as youth employment schemes for unemployed and less-skilled young adults, on-the-job training arrangements, and payroll tax subsidies for minimum wage workers. Germany has established quite elaborate connections between school and work, while Great Britain often resembles the United States in its comparative "hands off" approach to how people move from school to work (Scherer 2001). Southern European countries such as Spain, Italy, and Greece do not fit easily on any "Germany–England" continuum of degree of institutionalization (Iannelli and Soro-Bonmati 2001; Lazaridis and Koumandraki 2001).

How we might go about comparing school to work transitions in different societies has become an especially vibrant area of research over the past several years, usefully bringing into collaboration researchers from many different nations and many different subfields of sociology. Much of the intellectual impetus came from an important paper by Allmendinger (1989). Allmendinger argued that national systems of education can be distinguished along two central dimensions. Systems are *stratified* to the extent that their various levels and curricula are hierarchically tracked. Swiss students, for instance, are tracked young and decisively, while Irish students are tracked later and with more potential for mobility. Educational systems are *standardized* to the degree that there are nationally accepted criteria about what counts as the components of education (for example, curricula, teacher preparation, and so on).

Many scholars have built on Allmendinger's relatively simple scheme. In an important extension, Kerckhoff added a third dimension that varies across educational systems – "the degree to which the educational credentials awarded are general academic ones or specialized vocationally relevant ones" (Kerckhoff 2000, p. 455). Using data from the United States, France, Germany, and Great Britain, Kerckhoff demonstrated the influence of these factors on three aspects of the school to work transition. These are the strength of the association between levels of educational attainment and occupational levels of first jobs, the extent to which workers return to school and change their levels of educational attainment during their early labor force careers, and the amount of job changing and occupational mobility during workers' early careers in the labor force (p. 463). In other words, the ways in which nations organize their educational systems make it more or less easy for their young people to establish themselves as productive workers.

Sociologist James Rosenbaum and his colleagues have approached national variations in the school to work transition a bit differently.[2] They set out

---

2   Rosenbaum has recently collected much of this research in his *Beyond College for All* (2001).

to examine three puzzles in the US educational system – "Why are most work-bound students unidentified in high school? Why don't employers use school information for hiring? and How do schools help students get jobs?" (Rosenbaum and Jones 2000, p. 412). In short, Rosenbaum et al. (1999) wonder how the United States, in contrast to Japan and Germany, gets by with such an unstructured approach. They conclude that the answer resides in the development of informal ties in US labor markets that serve the role of formal structures elsewhere. The authors are skeptical that such informality is in the long-run best interests of American youth.

Finally, a comparative project under the leadership of Walter Muller and Yossi Shavit has added a great deal to what we know about the transition from school to work (Muller and Shavit 1998). Muller and Shavit propose two ideal typical sets of institutional linkages between education and work. The first, which they associate most directly with Germany, is *qualificational space*. In this arrangement, employers use vocational qualifications to organize jobs and allocate persons among them. This is unlike *organizational space*, which occurs when "education is less closely related to the workplace and vocational skills are mainly obtained on the job" (Muller and Shavit 1998, p. 4). They see this as descriptive of the French system of education. Qualificational space leads to an emphasis on general and transferable skills, while organizational space leads to a focus on firm-specific skills.

These differences have important implications. For example, nations that tend toward the organizational space model experience greater pressure for credential inflation. Under an occupational space regime, in contrast, vocational credentials are more likely to reflect high levels of skill. There is little evidence that societies are becoming any more alike in how they manage these transitions.

The work of Kerckhoff, Rosenbaum, and Shavit and Muller is just the tip of the iceberg of a comparative literature on the relationship between schooling and work (Gaskell 1992; Genda and Kurosawa 2000; Mortimer and Kruger 2000). We can expect more, given the increasing availability of the sorts of data that allow better comparative research. Such data sets as the European Community Household Panel (e.g., Russell and O'Connell 2001) and the Third International Math and Science Survey (TIMSS, see Lippman 2001) provide exceptional opportunities to advance what we know about school to work transitions.

Nonetheless, there are a number of important conceptual issues that need continuing attention. Kerckhoff (2000) is particularly cogent in identifying three such issues. First, future work will need to define more effectively what is meant by the "first job" in the school to work transition. We also need a more adequate understanding of how the transition period itself should be conceptualized. Finally, Kerckhoff encourages researchers to be conscientious about defining the appropriate measures of educational attainment and occupational level of the first job.

The prospects for building American institutions to link school to work

The school to work transition in the United States is unstructured. Some see little problem in that, maintaining that young people eventually find their way into jobs that match their skills and interests (Heckman 1994). Most observers are less sanguine. The lack of explicit linkages between school and work almost certainly harms the life chances of less credentialed young people. Policy makers at all levels in the United States have turned to the models of other countries as guides to designing new institutions, while at the same time devising any number of "home grown" solutions to the employment problems that accompany the transition from school to work. The result has been a variety of initiatives across the United States. I cannot begin here to describe these in detail, but will try to provide a glimpse of what has been taking place.

The rationale for forging tighter institutional linkages between schooling and work has been set out in a forceful document entitled "Helping disconnected youth." As its author states:

> The main argument of the paper is as follows: 1) the evidence is strong that employers are increasingly demanding higher skills for many types of jobs potentially available to at-risk young adults; 2) the skills of many at-risk youth are often inadequate to meet employer demands associated with good careers; 3) while improving academic skills is critical, relying entirely on increasing academic standards within a school-based approach to remedy the skills problem is unlikely without improving student incentives to learn; and 4) only moving to a career-based approach that emphasizes well-structured work-based learning is likely to exert a major impact on the life chances of at-risk young people. (Lerman 1996)

School-To-Work (STW) supporters rally around the belief that "academic and occupational subject matter should be more closely integrated in high schools and two-year colleges; that work-based learning should be part of the curriculum for all or most students; and that clear pathways should be created from high school to postsecondary education, including four-year college or university" (Urquiola et al. 1997). For its advocates, STW brings the potential to move youth into meaningful work while avoiding the traps of socioeconomic inequality and restricted opportunity. Some counter that STW promises benefits out of proportion to what it can reasonably be expected to deliver. These critics point to the stigmatizing nature of participating in STW programs in a society that values "college" jobs above "vocational" ones, the role of general versus specific skills, the proper role of employers (who often turn out to be remarkably reluctant to participate) in STW programs, and the nature of involvement among postsecondary institutions.

Many proposals in the United States for programs that call for a tighter articulation between schooling and work are modeled (at least in theory) on the German model. The German "dual system" is noted for its ability to combine vocational training embedded in the workplace with vocational education located in the school. While perhaps never operating as smoothly as some advocates might suggest, the German system does offer a powerful principle of school–work integration that many Americans have found appealing.

Federal School to Work Opportunities Act (STWOA) of 1994

Any appraisal of the STW movement needs to begin with the Federal School to Work Opportunities Act (STWOA) of 1994. This was built in part on Goals 2000, a federal initiative that articulated the role of education (an increasingly vocationalized one) in postindustrial society. The supporters of the STWOA intended it to be both more inclusive and more expansive than the populations traditionally served by the Perkins legislation. More specifically, they wanted to extend STW to include the college-bound. This is basically to say that they wanted it extended to everyone, since the Perkins legislation already covered those not headed for college.

The STWOA was intended from its inception to be a temporary measure to provide seed money and give employers time to develop and institutionalize relationships (usually referred to as "partnerships") with schools. The National School-to-Work Office was closed in 2001. During its brief lifespan, the STWOA was administered jointly by the US Departments of Education and Labor (Levine 1994). The intention of its sponsors was to provide a guide for state plans for implementing sustainable school to work programs while giving states and communities discretion in how to do that (Recesso 1999). Participation in STW would assure students of a high school diploma and a "portable skill certificate" indicating their preparation to enter work, postsecondary training program, and either a two- or four-year school (Medrick et al. 2000). At its most ambitious, one might think of this an entailing "a national system of credentials that certify students' occupationally relevant skills" (Kerckhoff and Bell 1998, p. 152).[3]

The School to Work Opportunity Act, like the School to Work movement more generally, provided an extraordinarily broad umbrella. The full range of STW programs is practically unclassifiable, but we can indicate a few of the major forms it has taken. Readers who wish a broader introduction to these many programs might begin with Zemsky (1998) or Smith and Rowjewski (1993).

Career academies

One popular form of STW is the career academy. This is a high school program in which a group of perhaps 50 students stay together with the same teachers for two or more years. The curriculum is an academic one, but is organized around the world of work. Such industry or occupational themes might include health, finance, or computers. Career academies are intended to develop close linkages between teachers, parents, and employers.

Career academies are an outgrowth of a more perennial effort to integrate academic and vocational curricula (Urquiola et al. 1997). They have received a sustained look recently from economists Nan Maxwell and Victor Rubin (2000). These authors examined a large urban school district that included several career academies with different characteristics. While there were differences from site to site in how the model was implemented, the overall model called for "creating a 'school-within-a-school,' integrating academic and vocational learning around a specific focus (e.g., health, computer technology), building extensive employer involvement, and creating a cohort of students who take four core classes together throughout three years of high school, taught by a small groups of teachers."

Maxwell and Rubin reported that the career academies were generally successful. Participants gained more academic knowledge and skills than they probably would have without the program. This was especially significant because many of the students were marginal ones, so there is some warrant for believing that the academy did make the difference in getting them over the threshold. Some of this gain carried over into a greater likelihood of attending postsecondary education. There was, however, little

---

3   Not surprisingly, this legislation has had detractors as well as supporters. Levine (1994), for one, believes that all experience with these sorts of programs indicates that labor market trends and hiring policies will trump any proposed educational solutions. He worries too that the Act may perpetuate or deepen class and race-based tracking in schools, and that it uncritically accepts "vocationalism."

discernable effect on labor force outcomes in the early years of the career (see also Linnehan 1998; Kemple and Snipes 2000).

Youth apprenticeships

Apprenticeships occupy a middle ground between vocational education and job training, and this is particularly true of youth apprenticeships (Ryan 1988). While there is no single model of youth apprenticeships, all involve shifting some formal instruction from secondary or postsecondary schooling into the workplace. This can entail great effort to coordinate workplace and school learning. Variations on the traditional model of apprenticeship have long had great appeal for STW reformers (Hamilton 1990, 1993; Osterman and Iannozzi 1993; Bremer and Madzar 1995; Evanciew and Rojewski 1999). In many ways, the case for them is quite strong. Bailey (1993), for instance, sees them as providing an integrated and organized "system for moving the non-college bound into career-type employment" (1993, p. 5). He adds that youth apprenticeships, more than other STW initiatives, effectively build on emerging "developments in pedagogy and learning theory" advanced by such researchers as Resnick (1987). That is, apprenticeships are especially well suited to techniques that maximize how people actually learn (Mjelde and Daly 2000 make a similar case for Canadian apprenticeship programs).

Smith and Rowjewski (1993) note that the youth apprenticeship model that has caught the interest of the STW community is quite different than the school-to-apprenticeship version that was popular in the 1970s and which only recently fell out of favor. School-to-apprenticeship models were initiated in the late 1970s by the Department of Labor. As of 1993, there were about 3,500 students participating in over 400 programs. More than half of these were in machine trade occupations. These programs typically last two to four years past high school graduation, and often resembled co-op programs. This model has not flourished.

In contrast, the youth apprenticeship model is based on European models. It entails "a combination of academic instruction in secondary and post-secondary schools with employment-based training for students at a level of quality sufficient to certify the ability of individuals to perform entry-level tasks in skilled occupations capably and professionally" (Smith and Rowjewski 1993, p. 230).

Bailey, an astute observer of such efforts, is sympathetic but guarded in his assessment of them. He identified three problems that need to be addressed before we can be assured of the efficacy of youth apprenticeships. These are "securing employer involvement, assuring and improving the quality of on-the-job learning, and confronting the equity issues that arise from a public policy that incorporates the highly stratified world of work into the core educational system (1993, p. 4). Kantor (1994), on the other hand, is very skeptical of the concept of youth apprenticeships (at least as they were proposed by the Clinton Administration and developed by the Grant Foundation). Kantor sees these programs as not only ineffective in achieving their stated purposes of moving young people into meaningful and productive employment, but also as destructive. Basing his judgment on his reading of earlier vocational education movements, Kantor asserts that youth apprenticeships will actually hurt the employment prospects of the less advantaged, particularly racial minorities.

Tech-prep

As discussed earlier, the tech-prep concept was at the center of the 1990 reauthorization of the Carl Perkins legislation. The core idea of tech-prep is to allow high school students to avoid repeating their high school coursework when they reach postsecondary education. Not surprisingly, this pertains most directly to community college coursework. Such an arrangement would let high school students work simultaneously on an associate degree, two-year certificate, or technical preparation certificate. Tech-prep is normally in a field like health, technology, or a related vocational field. Again, the idea is that students get a high school degree and a two-year degree of some sort (Smith and Rowjewski 1993). Unlike the focus in youth apprenticeships on the integration of the school and the work sire, tech-prep supporters have pushed for much tighter articulation between high school and postsecondary education (Parnell 1985; Bragg et al. 1997; Pucel and Sundre 1999).

Co-op programs

Another effort to tighten the linkages between school and work is an assortment of co-op programs. While these do not involve the intense immersion that one finds in youth apprenticeships, the idea is that teachers and employers remain aware of what each other is doing. Each is expected to understand and visit the other's setting. The subject matter offered in school and the demands of the workplace are intended to be tightly integrated. Like all of the programs we are discussing here, co-op programs did not emerge full-blown in the 1990s, and date their origin in the United States to the early 1900s. As of about 1990, there were about 400,000 high school students participating in co-op programs.

Most high school students in the United States hold jobs while they are going to school, but few of these jobs are connected in any systematic way to their school work. If anything, these kinds of jobs widen the rift between education and work. The promise of co-op programs, according to Stern et al. (1997), is that they build on the concept of "community of practice" advanced by such scholars as Resnick (1987) and Lave and Wenger (1991). Thus, the underlying philosophy of co-op programs is that people learn best by doing. Co-op education at the secondary level usually means that students attend classes for part of the day and work for part of the day. At the postsecondary level the student usually goes to school for a quarter and then works for a quarter (Smith and Rowjewski 1993).

Work-based learning (WBL)

Work-based learning (WBL) is another example of STW (Urquiola et al. 1997, p. 5). WBL goes beyond co-op to emphasize "development of personal and social competence related to work, learning all aspects of an industry, and deepening students' understanding of concepts taught in academic classes." Lerman (1996) builds a strong case for WBL as a means to enhance the job prospects of "at-risk" youth. Largely because WBL calls for such a comprehensive integration of school and work, it is difficult to find many successful examples of its implementation.

Does STW work?

How well do these various STW programs work? This is a difficult question to answer for the same reason that it is difficult to examine the effects of high school employment on educational and employment outcomes (Ryan 1988). Students do not end up in these programs at random. Some students are more likely to pursue co-op, or tech-prep, or youth apprenticeships, or something else than are other students. This does not render evaluation impossible, but issues of selection and unexplained heterogeneity do make the world more complicated.

Given this, there is evidence that for some students, STW programs can be beneficial. Stern et al. (1997), for instance, compared co-op students with those in non-school-supervised-work-experience (NSWE). They observed first that co-op students were less academically inclined that were NSWE students. Over time, however, STW students developed closer connections with their employers than did NSWE students. Co-op students also were less likely to get further education than were NSWE students, which imposed some long-term costs. Ryan (1988) shows mixed results for apprenticeships,

an indeterminacy that seems to characterize much of the literature (e.g., Wieler and Bailey 1997; Wentling and Waight 2000).

Conclusion: Young People, Schooling, and Jobs

We have covered a lot of ground in this chapter. A simple but essential conclusion is that while there may once have been a time when American youths could be released into the labor market without a net and realistically been expected to successfully find their way to secure, steady, and rewarding work, those days are now over. The protestations of some to the contrary, the lack of institutions and structures to facilitate the transition from school to work has become too costly for American youth, particularly but not solely those without post-baccalaureate schooling, to have to bear. The relationships between credentials and skills on the one hand and the workplace on the other have simply become too tight to leave to the free hand of the market.

In the next chapter, we move to the relationships between education and work for adult workers. This brings different challenges and barriers than those facing youth, but ones that are equally affected by the broad features of postindustrialism, demography, and the contrast between meritocracy and credentialism.

8

The Possibilities of a Learning Society

In this chapter, I turn to the relationships between *continuing* or *post-compulsory* education and the workplace. Education, under the prevailing regime of postindustrialism and a disorderly life course, can no longer be seen as something that strictly precedes work. It becomes not only a preparation in the general and generic skills needed to make the transition to the workplace, but also a process that is interspersed with spells of working through the life course.

The idea of the "Learning Society" has become popular as a way to describe a set of institutions, policies, and orientations that many believe are needed to respond to the transformed relationships between education and work (Belanger and Valdivielso 1997). While not a precise term, the "learning society" directs attention to ways in which adults enhance their skills after they have "completed" their formal schooling. In a society characterized by rapid technological change, human capital depreciates quickly (Hage and Powers 1992, p. 39). Neither employers nor employees can rely on the stock of skills that workers have when they enter the workforce to carry them through their work lives. Simply, the need for lifelong learning is growing and gives every indication of continuing to grow. Advocates of the learning society typically favor solutions that move beyond traditional four-year colleges and universities, such as community colleges, technical institutes, job training, apprenticeships, and an increasingly complex assortment of alternative forms of instructional delivery, often generically called "distance learning."

Advocates of the "learning society" or "lifelong learning" are insistent about the benefits of their proposals. Often presented as a virtual cure for everything that ails postindustrial (and not coincidentally, aging) societies, discussion of the learning society has reached high levels in nations as different as England (Coffield 1998; Hillage et al. 2000) and Hong Kong

(Suen and Tam 2000), along with many others. The learning society movement transcends national borders, and is in fact a less fully articulated movement in the United States than in many other places.

The idea of a learning society is not an entirely new one, having origins in both utopian literature (Campanella 1982) and social science (Gorard et al. 1998). Indeed, one contemporary social scientist sees a certain utopianism in at least the more optimistic conceptualizations of the learning society. To Crouch (1997, p. 367), some advocates portray "a society almost without unskilled, low-productivity people, in which all mindless and physically demanding jobs have been robotized; everyone in the work-force has a source of occupational pride in their skills and knowledge; income differentials are compressed through the market-compatible device of reducing the relative scarcity of high skills." Such a utopian vision goes well beyond the generally reserved portrayal of the postindustrial society offered by Bell (1999). At the same time, though, Crouch acknowledges that postindustrial societies have made real progress toward this vision.

For many reasons, the idea of the learning society has enjoyed something of a resurgence over the past decade or so. Much of the intellectual foundation for the concept of the learning society has been developed by The Organization for Economic Co-operation and Development (OECD). OECD is an international agency whose membership consists of 30 of the world's leading economies. It collectively covers over half of all global economic activity. The mission of OECD is essentially the promotion of economic development. It is striking that the OECD has directed much of its traditional focus on broad macroeconomic policies and infrastructure development toward a "learning solution" entailing a greater emphasis on lifelong learning.

OECD's motivation is a practical one. In an ambitious series of reports (1994, 1996, see also Carnoy and Castells 1997), it has enthusiastically described how systematic programs of both individual betterment and organizational or community learning can alleviate the pressures that rapid technological change and globalization impose on the ability of workers to participate in modern labor markets. For OECD, the promotion of lifelong learning is critical to any global strategy of economic development.

There is, not surprisingly, skepticism from many quarters about the promised benefits of the learning society solution. Stephen Gorard and his colleagues (1998), for example, see a big gap between the ideal and the actual "learning society" in Great Britain. They doubt the real, as opposed to the professed, "skill shortage" (see also Livingstone 1998). Consistent with the credentialist thesis, Gorard et al. maintain that these shortages are more often asserted than demonstrated. They further question the ability of continuing education and training to improve economic outcomes, on the argument that the apparent positive effects of continuing education on workers' well-being may have more to do with the self-selection of workers or employers into training opportunities than to any authentic efficacy of the training itself.

Gorard and his colleagues also doubt that equalizing access to further education and training will make much difference in equalizing access to good jobs and decent wages. They state quite bluntly that "Claims of skill shortages by employers should always be treated with caution" (1998, p. 28). They add that "It may therefore be a delusion to think that creating more and more formal education can help with problems such as unemployment, social mobility and the conditions of working life" (p. 31).

Others see still more shortcomings of the learning society model. Frank Coffield (1998), a generally sympathetic observer of the learning society, has noted that while proponents of the learning society often focus on the admirable goals of skills growth, personal development, and social learning and communal activity, the model can also become a coercive one. Coffield worries that the model of lifelong learning can provide an intrusive form of social control. Particularly in a faltering economy, the unemployed may be coerced into "learning" opportunities as a condition of receiving employment assistance. For Coffield, learning that is constrained in this way compromises many of the better impulses that underlie the learning society.

Lifelong Learning and Adult Education in the United States

At this point, I will move off of the world stage and back to that of the United States. At first glance, the idea of the learning society has not caught on in the United States to the extent that it has in much of the world. Still, the idea is hardly dormant, and there are clear signs of a growing interest in lifelong learning throughout American higher education and policy circles (Carnevale and Desrochers 2001). Most of this discussion is firmly in the context of the economic purposes of education.

Americans have never been indifferent to postcompulsory opportunities to learn, often outside of formal educational institutions. Indeed, considered historically, it is not too much to see "adult education," if not necessarily lifelong learning or the learning society, as a cultural obsession. Historian Joseph Kett's engaging 1994 volume *The Pursuit of Knowledge Under Difficulties: From Self-Improvement to Adult Education in America, 1750–1990* describes in great detail the involvement of Americans in literary societies, university extension programs, Chautauquas (Johnson 2001), correspondence study (Pittman 1998), elder hostels, lyceums, libraries (Lewis et al. 2003), and virtually any other kind of informal learning that one might imagine. Clearly, the phrase "adult education" covers an enormous terrain. As Kett (1994, p. xi) has noted:

> Exploring the history of continuing and adult education entails making sense of astounding statistics, frustratingly loose terminology, lofty idealism, and base huckstering. . . . a lexicon that includes such terms as continuing, adult, further, recurrent, popular, and second-chance education, as well as educational extension and, more recently, lifelong learning. With variations, all of these terms describe education attained after the apparent conclusion of conventional schooling. In the twentieth century the clients of schools devoted to this type of education have usually been over the age of 21, hence legally adults, but adult education is best defined in terms of its function rather than by a targeted age group. The distinguishing feature of adult education has been its role in providing additional learning for those who believed that they had completed their education only to find that they desired or required more.

As this quote indicates, there are numerous problems of definition and measurement in the literature on adult education. Some post-compulsory schooling is easily observed and measured (such as participation in a post-secondary vocational or academic degree program), but other activities are more ambiguous. If instruction in ballroom dancing is to be counted as adult education, what of such self-directed activities as listening to foreign language tapes or watching the History Channel? Do activities only count if they are "offered" by educational institutions, or only if their successful completion is acknowledged with a certificate or credential of some sort? Such issues remain up for grabs among scholars of adult education.

Social scientists at the National Center for Education Statistics have offered perhaps the most serious effort to date to conceptualize adult education activities. The vehicle for this has been the Adult Education Interview of its National Household Education Survey (NHES). This survey, conducted several times since 1991, divides adult education into six categories, some very structured and institutionalized and some less so. These are adult basic education, English as a Second Language, apprenticeship, credential programs, work-related education, and personal development programs or courses.

Americans have greatly increased their participation in adult education over the past two decades, and probably even before that (Creighton and Hudson 2002). While only one-third of adults participated in some form of adult education in 1991, by 1999 nearly half (46 percent) were doing so. This increase held across most socioeconomic categories, although great differences persisted in the likelihood of participation. For the most part, those in their prime working ages who hold better jobs and who have more

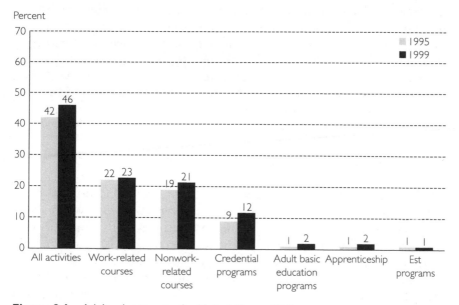

Figure 8.1   Adult education in the United States, 2001

Adults include civilian, non-institutionalized individuals age 16 or over who are not enrolled in elementary or secondary education.

Among adults ages 16–24, full-time participation in credential programs was not counted as an adult education activity.

Adults may have participated in more than one activity in each survey year.

Source: US Department of Education, National Center for Education Statistics, Adult Education Survey of the National Household Education Surveys Program, 1995 and 1999.

schooling take part more often in adult education than do those in less-advantaged labor market positions.

Most of the educational categories identified by NCES are directly related to the world of work. NCES asked respondents who participated in any of the types of adult education what their motivation was for participating. Figure 8.1, taken from Creighton and Hudson's summary of the NHES data, shows that the single largest category of adult education was "work-related courses." This figure, however, underestimates the extent to which adults pursue education to enhance their work lives, since many participants in credential programs, basic education, ESL, and (virtually by definition) apprenticeships did so primarily for work-related reasons. In short, more and more Americans are taking part in postcompulsory education, and the largest reason they do so has to do with their jobs. Certainly, this still leaves an enormous and often unacknowledged volume of adult education that is not driven by the demands of the workplace. People do take courses for self-improvement without regard to the economic consequences, and a great share of the enrollments in most community colleges is fee-based participation in economically disinterested learning opportunities. Nonetheless, the expansion of postcompulsory education and the demands of the workplace have proceeded hand in hand. Adults are willing, even eager, to learn, but largely for the economic benefits that this promises.

The Rise and Fall (and Rise and Fall) of Job Training

Clearly, we can characterize the lion's share of adult education as *workforce development* or *skill enhancement*. Skill enhancement covers a vast range of processes by which people learn to do their jobs. Some of what they know is from their schooling. Some is what they learn on the job. Much of the workplace knowledge that people acquire takes place informally and incidentally, or is structured more formally through internal labor markets. Increasingly, an understanding of skill enhancement has to turn to "how changes [primarily in workplace restructuring] may affect formal and informal opportunities for on the job learning, linkages with and use of education providers, and, more generally, approaches in workforce development" (Salzman et al. 1998, p. 6).

A crucial aspect of any strategy of workforce development is *job or worker training*. Researchers have written an immense amount about this. The training literature is, however, based in several different disciplines that do not always communicate with each other as fully as they might. Industrial psychologists are concerned with understanding how individuals learn and how to apply this knowledge to most effectively enhance the learning that takes place in training situations. Economists often have an applied bent of their own, and seek to understand such issues as the incentives for employers to offer training and the wage returns to the workers who participate in it. Training and development specialists of various kinds are interested in how training can be most usefully embedded in broader organizational structures.

With some exceptions (e.g., Knoke and Janowiec-Kurle 1999; Bills 2003), the sociological literature on job training is surprisingly modest (although this is far less true in much of the world than it is in the United States). Moreover, most of what sociologists have written about training builds quite directly on the human capital model of neo-classical labor economics. We are only beginning to develop a full sociological perspective on job training.

More than one analyst has characterized the American system of training as a non-system, or even more harshly, as "a complex and ill-defined system, often charged with overlap, duplication, waste, and sheer confusion" (Grubb 1996). Training programs are typically fragmented from one another, there is no coherent national or even state-level policy to guide training efforts, and employers, employees, communities, and states often seem to be working at cross-purposes. Governmental commitment to training waxes and wanes (hence the subheading of this section), ranging from seeing training as the cure-all for poverty and unemployment to a rejection of the training enterprise as futile. All of this is in considerable contrast to other postindustrial nations, which have developed often elaborate systems of training for adult workers.

In fact, though, characterizing the American system of skill development as a non-system misses an important point. Training in the United States is perhaps not so much a non-system as a markedly polarized one. Bartik and Hollenbeck (2000) describe the training system as two-tiered, both public and private, in which:

> The "first-chance" or conventional system allows individuals to proceed through an extensive public elementary, secondary, and postsecondary educational sector that is supplemented by private educational institutions and is followed by employer-provided job training and work experience. The "second-chance" system is designed for individuals who do not successfully traverse the first-chance system. The second-chance system includes public job training programs, public assistance, rehabilitation programs for offenders, and educational remediation.

The evidence on the comparative efficacy of these two systems is less than definitive, and both systems of training have their supporters. Nonetheless, there is little doubt that many American workers have access to better and more frequent episodes of training than do others.

European social scientists in particular have done much to conceptualize the differences between national training systems. Ashton et al. (2000), for instance, argue that the relationships between the state, the education and training systems, employers, and workers vary across societies in ways that lead to different models of "national systems of skill formation." They identify four of these. These are the market model, the corporatist model, the developmental state model, and the neo-market model. Regini (1997) examined training systems in four different regions in Europe, which do not correspond with national boundaries so much as they do with cultural and institutional variations within nations. These regions, collectively referred to as the "four engines" of Europe, are Baden-Wurttemberg (Germany),

Rhone-Alpes (Italy), Lombardy (France), and Catalonia (Spain). Regini's analysis of these training systems leads her to characterize them as a "redundancy-oriented" system (Germany and Italy) and a "appropriateness-oriented" one (France and Spain). The first system produces many highly skilled workers in greater numbers than economic demand actually merits. In contrast, the second is organized to make adjustments after the fact in response to shifts in demands for skill. Regini sees advantages and disadvantages to each arrangement.

The work of both Regini and Ashton and his colleagues is more sophisticated and comprehensive than I can recount here, and I will leave it to others to elaborate the fine distinctions between European systems of training (as well as of those elsewhere in the world). My point rather is to set some context for my discussion of training and work in the United States. Unlike the typically carefully designed and implemented training systems in many nations, by any account the United States has developed a system that virtually defies generalization.

How much and what kind of training is there?

American companies spend vast amounts of money and commit an enormous amount of time to job training. No one really knows how much. Part of the reason for this uncertainty is that employers lack the incentive or even the inclination to monitor either the extent of the resources that they commit to training, or the benefits they derive from doing so. Even more fundamentally, simply trying to measure training creates a host of problems. It is rarely clear how to distinguish between formal training and on-the-job training, how to account for the lost production time that occurs when workers train, how to measure the opportunity costs to both workers and employers (that is, the value of the time that they could have spent doing something else), and how to differentiate activity that is simultaneously learning and working.

Estimates of how much training takes place differ widely, often by an order of several magnitudes. It is almost self-defeating to try to offer precise estimates of the amount of training given the dispersal of these estimates. Marquardt et al. (2000) assembled data from various sources that give a good sense of the possible extent of training. In 1995 American employers spent $55.3 billion on formal training. This is an impressive amount of money, but seems somewhat less so when one considers that it represents only about 1.8 percent of payroll. On closer inspection, this figure may be nearer to 10 percent when indirect and opportunity costs are factored in (Bassi et al. 2000). Employers probably spent twice this amount on informal training. Much also depends on what sector of the economy is being considered. As a percentage of payroll, training expenditures are highest in the information and technology industry and lowest in the health care sector.

Not all training is provided by one's employer. Nor does all of it come from the business sector. Over half (52 percent) of participants in work-related courses receive this instruction from a provider other than business and industry (Darkenwald et al. 1998). A great deal of instruction comes from educational institutions or professional and trade associations.

There is little consensus about how to categorize the vast amount of worker training. Li et al. (2000) see the primary distinctions being those between occupational updating, advanced training, and retraining. At least in Switzerland, the first of these is not usually acknowledged with a credential and is typically paid for by the employer. The last two tend to be credential-oriented and are often financed by the worker. Other useful categorizations of training rely on still other criteria – for example, the content of training, its purpose, its formality or informality, or the characteristics of those served by it (Hollenbeck 1996; Frazis et al. 1997).

Who does and doesn't get training?

Clearly, there is an enormous amount of activity that we can sometimes generously characterize as training that is embedded in a vast if uncoordinated training infrastructure. As we might expect, not all employees have the same opportunities to participate. To oversimplify only a bit, the factors that sort people into better jobs, higher incomes, and more stable employment tend to be the same factors that determine who has the most access to training opportunities. There is abundant evidence that more highly placed workers, along a number of both ascribed and achieved dimensions, have more access to training than do less privileged workers. Much of this, however, is more complex than that. We examine a few of these inequalities next.

Perhaps the clearest finding in this literature is that those with the most advantaged labor market positions have the most access to further training. Professional-technical workers get far more training than do blue-collar workers (Osterman 1995). Employers also spend considerably more on more elite (or core) employees. Marquardt et al. (2000) found that 26 percent of training expenditures are for professional employees, 25 percent for managers, 12 percent for salespeople, and 37 percent for everyone else.

Often the strongest predictor of the likelihood of receiving training is how much education employees already have. Overall, employers are more likely to enhance the skills of workers who are already highly prepared than they are to invest in the provision of more basic skills to less advantaged workers. That is, employers apparently prefer to build on existing skills rather than to provide elementary skills.

Not only do workers in more advantaged positions get more training, but so do those in the "high performance" work organizations that I examined in an earlier chapter (Osterman 1995; Frazis et al. 1997; Lynch and Black 1998). This does not seem to be limited to the United States. Whitfield (2000) found this to be true (if somewhat tentatively) in Britain, although he notes that the main effect of moving to a high performance system is to increase the intensity of training to distinct groups of workers rather than to extend the coverage to wider groups of workers.

African-Americans and Hispanics generally get less training than do Whites. Younger workers and older workers get less than do workers in the prime years of their work lives. The evidence for sex differences is less clear-cut, but the best judgement is that women experience more disadvantages than advantages in their access to training (Knoke and Ishio 1998; Lynch 1998; Brown 1990). In both the United States and Britain, even though women often participate in training at comparable or even higher rates than men, this does not consistently translate into equally valuable credentials (Felstead 1994; Kerckhoff and Bell 1998).

Does job training pay?

Even though the amount of training in the United States is modest by the standards of other postindustrial societies, employers still put great effort into providing training, as do workers in participating in it. What are the payoffs? Are trained workers more productive and better paid? Do firms benefit from their investments in training?

Employers know surprisingly little about what the effect of all of this training is. In his discussion of how managers use educational credentials as a basis for hiring decisions, Berg (1971) noted that they make virtually no efforts to confirm whether or not this strategy really makes economic sense. Little seems to have changed since Berg wrote this. Managers operate as if credential-based hiring is a good idea, and have their own folk theories about it, but nothing is ever rigorously checked, audited, and accounted for. Employer provision of job training seems to follow a similar pattern.

We need to be careful when drawing conclusions about the effects of training (Li et al. 2000). There are many different kinds of training that are provided for many different reasons. There is little reason to think that all of these are equally effective (or perhaps ineffective), particularly when the goals of training are often radically different. Teaching a skilled craft worker how to operate a drill press, providing "diversity" training to university faculty, and offering "play therapy" workshops to child psychologists are such dissimilar activities that trying to measure their effectiveness along any common metric seems quite nearly futile.

Another problem in assessing the value of training is that it is an inherently longitudinal enterprise. Many analyses of training have relied on cross-sectional data, making any imputation of cause and effect suspect. Perhaps even more serious, examining the efficacy of training raises problems of self-selection into both occupations and training. Not all workers are equally likely to participate in training, and we need to distinguish between the characteristics of those who elect or are elected for learning opportunities and the actual effects of those opportunities.

These are large caveats. Even with them, however, the general conclusion seems clear – most training is of some value most of the time and under most conditions. Workers are better off when they know more, and their employers are better off with more skilled employees. As with all generalizations, this one has its limits. The conditions under which this is true, and how true it is, are complicated.

If we think of the effectiveness of training as the extent to which it leads to higher pay, more job security, and the like, then training is of the most value to those who are already in relatively skilled employment. Workers with a solid base of skill and experience on which to build are more able to translate training into increased chances of promotion and wage gain.

In contrast, training works less well for those without jobs at all. In general, training helps people do their jobs better and be rewarded for this, but it is less successful at putting people into jobs. Not surprisingly, it even less often leads people into what would generally be regarded as good jobs. The experience of training programs for the unemployed is mixed but not terribly positive. This is the case both for new labor market entrants trying to negotiate the school to work transition, and for those who already have some labor force experience. Economist Robert LaLonde (2001) reported that job retraining for workers who had been displaced from their jobs provides little benefit. This is of course an overly broad statement that does not generalize to every instance of training for those in less-advantaged labor market positions. LaLonde also reported that there are gains for displaced workers with greater skills to begin with and those who take highly focused and technically oriented coursework. From this he concludes that what displaced workers need are carefully chosen and pertinent job skills. The last thing displaced workers need, according to LaLonde, is a well-rounded education.

None of this is to indict training programs for the hard to employ. The demand for trained labor, once again, is a derived demand. Employers will not pay for workers at any skill level unless there is a demand for the goods and services those workers will produce. Put simply, training can be of little value if there are no jobs for the newly trained to move into.

Boyle (2001) sees even less payoff to training for less privileged workers. In a careful study of literacy training programs in 55 firms in Massachusetts, Boyle found that these programs did little to make workers at the bottom of the hierarchy any more skilled, productive, or well-paid than they were before their participation in the training. They did have the effect, however, of making workers more dependent on their companies, less occupationally mobile, and more likely to blame themselves for their lack of advancement. For those on the bottom, such narrowly conceived training limited rather than enhanced career potential.

A theme throughout this book is that many aspects of the relationship between education and work are going to change in the face of the ever-shifting mix of postindustrialism, demographic transformation, and changes in the welfare state. This is true too of the linkages between training and rewards, particularly perhaps for less-skilled workers. As Lundgren and Rankin (1998) observed, American welfare reform over the past decade has been based strictly on a model of "work first." That is, recent policy changes (specifically the Job Training Partnership Act and the Personal Responsibility and Work Opportunity Reconciliation Act) have had the effect of pushing people into any available job that the labor market has to offer, however dead-end or low-paying. At the same time, the incentives to invest in one's skills for the long-term have virtually disappeared. The unfortunate aspect of this, as Gangl (2002) has shown for Germany, is that unemployed workers with the opportunity to invest more time in job search and skill enhancement end up with better jobs as a result. The overriding philosophy of "work first" has done little to permit disadvantaged American workers to transform training into employment.

Do American employers invest enough in training?

There is considerable evidence about the value of job training to both workers and their bosses. Efforts to enhance the skills of workers more often than not pay off. Still, American employers (in combination with both the federal and state governments) provide less training than do other postindustrial societies. This raises the question of whether American employers invest enough (or perhaps too much) in training.

Any judgment about whether The United States as a society underinvests or overinvests in training needs to remember that training is only one way for employers to get the skills they need. Presumably, a highly functioning and responsive educational system, capable of churning out workers able to assume their positions in the division of labor, would obviate much of the need for employers to devise ways of imparting skills. We can characterize this as employers' "make or buy" decisions (Knoke and Janowiec-Kurle 1999). Put simply, firms can get the skills they need by hiring people with those skills, or they can train those skills "into" their current workers. Osterman (1995, p. 141) found that "firms that place heavy emphasis on hiring employees with previously acquired skills are less likely to provide training." This raises the possibility that even with effective programs of training, if employers can get the skills they need through a "buy" strategy, the possibility of overinvestment in training is there (Booth and Snower 1996, p. 3).

As it turns out, though, it is difficult to find an informed observer who believes that the United States is putting enough resources into training. Bassi et al. (2000) note that the mere fact that employers know so little about the effects and value of training in itself means that they will underinvest in it. That is, with investors putting increasingly unrelenting pressure on firms to justify every aspect of their operating expenses, employers have no means to rationalize the importance of training to investors. Lacking this rationale, American employers fail to make an adequate case for training dollars, a case that is not about to be made by cost-conscious investors. For this and other reasons, evidence for the underinvestment in training in American firms is persuasive. This has been the conclusion of the blue-ribbon report *No One Left Behind* (1997) that we presented in Chapter 2, as well as that of many labor economists. Lisa Lynch (1998) believes that increasing wage inequality in the United States relative to Europe indicates an American underinvestment in training. That is, even though training has clear returns for both individuals and firms, economic inequality is widening in part because the less-skilled are not being trained. In other words, the supply of skills fails to match the demand for them. Bassi et al. (2000) made a serious effort to actually measure the contribution of training to firm performance, and concluded that American firms need to spend a lot more on training.

Why should it be that American firms and workers invest so little in training? Much of the difficulty in the United States can be traced to the failure to build the sorts of institutions that produce some socially desired outcomes that markets are less capable of producing. This takes us back to the European model of training – or variations on this model – that we referred to earlier. As Streeck (1989) pointed out, any economy faces the problem of producing sufficient worker skill to ensure prosperity. Some do so by developing the communal bonds and institutions capable of engendering the reciprocal trust that will induce both employers and workers to invest in skill formation. Others trust the free market to provide employers and workers with the incentives to provide and acquire skills. On this analysis, because American employers need to worry about having their newly trained workers poached by other employers who are willing to offer a higher wage, they must spend more effort avoiding ways to offer skills that would be in the end most useful to someone else's workers than they do actually upgrading their workforces. The market, following this line of thinking, will naturally underinvest in skills (Streeck, 1989; Crouch 1997).

A strong collection of papers edited by Booth and Snower (1996) demonstrates that market failures in the provision of training – that is, the inability of the free market to provide enough skills in the absence of active state policies or employer collectivities – are far more serious in the United States and the United Kingdom than they are in Australia, France, Germany, Japan, or Sweden, to name just a few. The authors argue that each of these nations has built such institutions as apprenticeships, training levies, retraining, and career paths that make up for market failures. Despite occasional forays in those directions, the United States and the United Kingdom have not done so, and must tolerate more endemic skill shortages as a result.

Streeck has concisely noted that "skills are a peculiar thing" (1989, p. 97). Skills do not reside only with the individual workers who hold them, or even with the employer-controlled jobs in which skills are expressed. Instead, we need to think of skills as a collective good. That is, the skills that are produced by schools or other training institutions are more important in the generation of human capital to produce a skilled workforce than for individual social mobility. American policy makers (and many social scientists) have shown a reluctance to look at skills in this way. Too often, the recipient of training – the "vessel" into which training is poured – is taken to be the individual worker. As Streeck and others insist, however, training is more social than that. Skills reside in work groups as much as they do in individuals. In a similar way, the effects of training may be best expressed at the group level.

Apprenticeships, Community Colleges, and Other Adult Learning Settings

We have been speaking about training almost as if it were something that took place solely at the work site. In fact, the institutional makeup of training is complex. The US training "system" consists of a bewildering array of providers, brokers, partnerships, and other training actors. Two historically critical institutions for the provision of job skills are apprenticeships and community colleges. In some ways, the decline of the former is simultaneously the story of the ascendance of the latter.

I mentioned in the previous chapter that US apprenticeships have been transformed over a period of decades from an arrangement in which young people prepare for jobs to one in which experienced workers can retool. At the same time, the vocational preparation function that once resided in apprenticeships shifted to formal educational settings. As Resnick (1987, p. 17) observed, "the rise of vocational education in the skilled trades is simultaneously the story of the decline of apprenticeship." Not alone among those interested in building effective systems of skill acquisition, Resnick finds this divorce of learning and doing regrettable (Hamilton 1990).

The argument against apprenticeships essentially mirrors the argument for them. Their great strength is that they bring together different labor market actors – employers, workers, unions, the state – in ways that enhance a collective good. That is, by relieving employers of the worry of subsidizing the skills of their competitors and hence bearing undue costs, apprenticeships help align institutions in ways that facilitate the creation of a greater supply of skills. The cost of this, however, is that their institutional complexity sacrifices some of the flexibility that many feel is needed to compete in an increasingly globalized and technologically turbulent world. At least in some accounts, apprenticeship may be too cumbersome to provide the ever-changing skill mix demanded by modern times.

But the apprenticeship model is far from dead, and may not even be ailing as badly as some fear. There are signs, if less in the United States than elsewhere, of a return to models of apprenticeship that had been abandoned as outmoded only a few years ago. France, Italy, and Sweden, for example, have recently sought closer linkages between schooling and work by implementing apprenticeships (Crouch et al. 1998). This has caught the attention of many US observers.

An increasing share of training – in fact, an increasing share of all US postsecondary education – is taking place in the country's vast and diverse community college system. Both the stated mission and the actual activity of community colleges have shifted more than once since these institutions began nearly a century ago. Originally envisioned as academically oriented "junior colleges," community colleges have moved uneasily between the roles of preparing students to transfer to four-year colleges and universities, the provision of vocational training, personal development coursework, remedial instruction, and to an increasing extent, economic development (Dougherty 1994; Brint and Karabel 1989).

The important point here is that in the United States, when one is speaking of the "relationship between education and work," one is increasingly speaking of community colleges. Certainly former President Clinton's insistence that all Americans have the opportunity to go to college had more relevance to this expansive tier of two-year institutions than to the more elite, expensive, and exclusive four-year level. Moreover, much of the recent discussion of the "sub-baccalaureate labor market" (Grubb 1996, 1999a, b) is directed at this sector. Increasingly, community colleges are where the "learning society" action is.

While virtually everyone accepts that community colleges have grown, it is difficult to say how much. Their enrollments are tricky to calculate, but the long-term trend is clearly on the rise. Enrollments rose steadily from about 3.7 million in 1976 to roughly 5 million in 1990. They hit a peak of 5.3 million in 1995, and then leveled off until 1999. Since then, they have risen quite sharply. There are various reasons for this growth. Some of the increase is demographic. There are currently high numbers of college age people, although this varies greatly by region. Some of the increase is financial, as the growth in tuition costs at both private and public four-year schools continues to outpace inflation. Still more is largely economic. People who might otherwise hold full-time employment often go to community colleges when these opportunities are scarce.

Despite their growth and increasing embeddedness in American post-secondary education, Dougherty's (1994) depiction of the American community college as "The Contradictory College" cogently captures their position in the education–work hierarchy. The contradictions are legion. On the one hand, community colleges provide occupational preparation for tens of millions of mid-level workers (Grubb 1996). Much of this training is sophisticated, cognitively complex, and remunerative. At the same time, community colleges serve millions of academically underprepared and even marginally literate students. Much of the instructional activity at community colleges is remedial or developmental education. Grubb and Kalman (1994) have estimated that between one-quarter and three-quarters (depending largely on the state) of college students need remedial work. Community colleges get the lion's share of this. This is not necessarily a bad thing. Because community colleges have professional teaching staff (unlike adult education and job training), they are the best institutions to offer this kind of instruction.

Further, despite having what is generally regarded as a key and ever growing role in economic development and workforce preparation, this expressed commitment is not always matched with resources. Most community colleges have had to develop entrepreneurial strategies even beyond those of four-year institutions to secure operating expenses. Even in the area of their reputedly greatest comparative advantage, community colleges have to compete strenuously with high schools for federal and state vocational and technical dollars.

Largely because of the unreliability of public funding for what would seem to be the public good of a skilled workforce (Crouch et al. 1998; Labaree 1997), community colleges have been creative (one might say aggressive) about building linkages with the world of work. Dougherty and Bakia (2000) have described in detail the expansion of contract training in community colleges (see also Dougherty and Bakia 1998; Lerman et al. 2000). These programs, which deal in the most direct ways possible with employers (though often with public funding), include both inservice contract training and entry-level contract training. Dougherty and Bakia estimate that about 90 percent of community colleges participate in some form of contract training.

Community colleges face head-on the same issue that repeatedly surfaces about high school vocational education and apprenticeships – how, in a rapidly changing postindustrial society, can individuals be provided with skills that are general enough to be transferable yet specific enough to be valuable to specific employers? The question of what is to be taught and in what manner is thus particularly pressing in community colleges. While consensus is rare in higher education, there does seem to be emerging a shared belief that the most effective preparatory instruction will integrate academic and occupational instruction. There are examples of programs that apparently are successful at preparing workers with a solid background in both academic and vocational areas (Perin 2001), but such efforts are perhaps unusual.

Other Forms of Postsecondary Education

Apprenticeships have declined and community colleges grown, but a fuller story needs to acknowledge the great diversification and proliferation of providers of adult education. Employers and workers can now seek specialized skills and training through a range of institutions and settings that include, among others, corporate universities and other corporate centers, company certification, state-supported customized labor training, and largely unregulated and diffuse Web-based instruction. Even restricting our attention to institutions at the sub-baccalaureate level, we can add technical institutes, area vocational schools, proprietary schools, shorter-term job training programs, and firm-based training paid for in part by public funds

(Grubb 1996, p. xv; Hollenbeck 1993). Many of these are reputable institutions providing rigorous and carefully designed instruction. For others, Kett's (1994) "lofty idealism and base huckstering" comes to mind. Whatever monopoly four-year colleges and universities ever had on American higher education has proven to be historically short-lived.

Much of this expansion is coming and will almost certainly continue to come from outside of the traditional K–12 and postsecondary systems. A good example here is the growth in corporate universities, a near-textbook illustration of companies opting for the "make" rather than "buy" strategy of securing skilled workers. Meister (2001) notes that "a corporate university allows a company to coordinate and manage programs to train and educate its employees, customers, and suppliers." Increasingly, some corporate universities are going beyond this to offer instruction to the public. There is no single model of this institutional arrangement. Some use their own faculty and staff to provide instruction, while others do so in partnership with traditional universities. The number of corporate universities in the United States grew from 400 to over 2,000 between 1988 and 2001 (Meister 2001).

Much is being made of the decisions by many US firms to assume control and responsibility for providing education and training on their own, but such corporate strategies are hardly unprecedented. Nelson-Rowe (1991) demonstrated that 100 years ago many corporate leaders wrote off the ability of the public schools to supply competent workers. This disappointment extended beyond the comprehensive high school to manual training, trade schools, and apprenticeship programs. Nelson-Rowe maintains that much as now, corporate leaders saw industrial educators as insufficiently attentive to the practical needs of business. Faced with the "make or buy" decision that remains current in the US labor market, many firms chose to design and develop their own corporate schools or factory apprenticeships.

Another emerging model is the for-profit postsecondary institution (Bailey et al. 2001). These institutions were foreshadowed by the rapid growth of trade schools that took place in the 1970s, and even now are concentrated in a few business and technical fields. Largely because of the apparent ascendancy of such institutions as the more comprehensive University of Phoenix or Western Governors University, with which they share the profit motive if little else, these have received a great deal of attention over the past five years or so. For Bailey, these for-profit institutions (at least to this point) are more of a complement than competitor to community colleges. For-profits have become more regulated over the past few years because of several well-publicized incidents of mismanagement and scandal. This has led to their being designated as Accredited Career Colleges (ACCs). Much like community colleges, for-profits enroll high proportions of minorities and women (the latter because of the prevalence of cosmetology institutes). Despite the attention they have received, for-profits have a tiny share of two-year enrollments (about 4 percent), and even less (2 percent, but growing) of the four-year market.

Learning by Long Distance: The Possibilities of Information Technology for Bridging School and Work

Daniel Bell (1999) saw one of the great features of postindustrialism as its ability to use information technology to overcome many of the strictures of time and space. Nowhere is this more apparent than in the shadow postsecondary system that is emerging alongside the traditional, place-bound system of colleges and universities. Institutions can now deliver and certify instruction to adult learners without those learners ever setting foot on campus, or even being in the same country as the educational institution. Lenn (2002) notes that education and training in formats as diverse as "corporate courses, distance-education programs, branch campuses, and franchises, among others" is now one of the US's top five exports, generating close to $10 billion in 1999. The relationship between education and work is increasingly one of "distance" education and work.

Once again, the concept of social movements helps capture what is taking place. Foreseeing the inevitability of a modern technology that sweeps away tired bureaucracies and obsolete pedagogies, the "true believers" in the distance education movement have shown little hesitation about forecasting the imminent demise of traditional postsecondary education. They are understandably less clear about what will replace brick and mortar institutions.

In fact, any description of the partnerships, collaborations, and cartels that are emerging between postsecondary providers of skills, workers, and employers would be obsolete as soon as it was written. Ultimately, though, the point is less whether the University of Phoenix or Western Governors University survive and prosper than it is the fact that something like these institutions will in time become major players in adult education and training. For example, Roger Shank's online learning company Cognitive Arts has formed partnerships with Columbia University and Harvard Business School, and is evidently eying high schools and community colleges as particularly lucrative markets. Such enterprises are surely going to continue.

Certifying the New Modes of Training

There is a great potential for the proliferation of institutional forms in the postsecondary sector (particularly when coupled with distance learning) to transform or disrupt the entrenched credential system. As Lewis and her colleagues have noted, "what was once an eclectic assortment of individually accessed, non-credit educational courses is quickly being knit into comprehensive degree- and certificate-granting programs" (Lewis et al. 2000, p. 3). This brings us full circle yet again to the question of credentialism versus merit. If something called "instruction" is going to occur, some means to certify it cannot be far behind. The diversification (or perhaps fragmentation) of skill providers brings great uncertainty about the certification of the learning that presumably takes place. This poses challenges to the traditional postsecondary credentialing system. The legitimacy of a credential awarded by a corporation that has identified needed skills and designed the means to deliver them (a "competency-based" credential) seems straightforward enough, if probably often contested in practice. That of an Internet provider accountable to no particular accreditation agency or other form of oversight is something else.

The rapid increase in industry credentialing programs in the information technology sector now is built of a vast infrastructure of "testing centers, IT training companies, publishing companies, practice-test vendors, certification authorities, online mentoring, and resource providers" (Bartlett 2001, p. 11). This growing importance of this external certification of skills encompasses what have become quite standard categories – Cisco Certified Internet Expert, Microsoft Certified Systems Engineer, Certified Novell Engineer, and many more (over 1,000). A new hybrid version of the sturdy "make or buy" decision seems to be emerging.

The external certification of skills has as yet come nowhere near displacing the traditional college and university credentialing system. All available evidence suggests that both elite and technical degrees continue to matter. In the long run, though, external credentialing may be a viable alternative. Perhaps these new credentials, by being so closely and consciously tied to the world of work, will reflect merit more than the more ambiguous educational degrees that have traditionally been used to allocate jobs. Just as plausibly, they may become yet another instance of the empty but defensively necessary social badges cynically described by Berg (1971) and others. One can easily imagine the certificate training arena as being a revenue stream for economically stressed community colleges, having less to do with the certification of merit than the commodification of schooling.

Summary

A thread that runs through this chapter is that thinking about the relationship between education and work is to think longitudinally. If there was ever a time in which we could conceptualize this relationship as one in which a long spell of schooling preceded an even longer spell of work, those days are over. Postindustrial lives (Hage and Powers 1992) are lives in which people need to shift from the roles of learner to worker so readily and frequently as to make these shifts seamless.

9

The Future of Education and Work

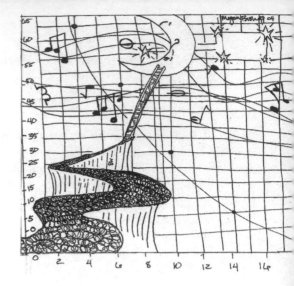

Perhaps the central theme that has run through this book is the historically tightening link between schooling and socioeconomic rewards. My focus has been on the United States, but the generalization applies widely if not uniformly around the world. Whatever else we expect from schools, there is little dissent about their role in preparing and credentialing people to work.

Evidence for this linkage can be seen in many ways. One is the ever-rising educational requirements for jobs. Stories of fleets of taxi-driving PhDs may be apocryphal, but the general principle that the educational standards for entry have risen for many, many jobs is a solid one. Young people entering today's workplace without academic credentials enter it disarmed.

Other evidence for the increasing interconnection between education and work is the vocationalization of the high school curriculum. I mean "vocationalization" in a broad sense, in that the experience of high school has become ever more oriented and attuned toward the world of work over the course of several decades even as vocational education per se has gone into decline. Indeed, it has become difficult to locate any public discussion of the American high school that does not emphasize the role of the school in the preparation of workers.

Still more evidence comes from the vocationalization of postsecondary education. Appeals by colleges and universities for a continued claim on public support increasingly rest on the legitimacy of these institutions as "engines" of economic growth. Governors and legislators are holding higher education institutions accountable for the job placement rates of their graduates, with programs that come up short in this sweepstakes facing a future of bleak and uncertain funding.

Evidence comes too from the increasing economic returns to schooling-acquired skill. It may be premature to jettison the advice that "It's not what you know, it's who you know," but this counsel lacks the force it once had.

Having connections on the job market certainly does not hurt, but postindustrial society is not proving kind to those who have not had their educational tickets punched.

Finally, we can point to the simple general cultural acceptance of the linkages between education and work. Schooling, as John Meyer (1977) so concisely reminds us, "works" as a theory of personnel allocation. One can call this legitimacy or one can call it hegemony, but Americans, together with most of the world, seldom imagine serious alternatives to schooling as preparation for work.

Of course, what this historically tightening linkage *means* is a different question entirely than the mere fact that the institutions of education and work are growing even more closely enmeshed. The tightening linkage could arise from the technical and cognitive demands brought on by the inexorable movement towards postindustrialism, or from the increasingly sophisticated strategies of reproduction adopted by elite and educated parents. It could reflect the relentless trend toward meritocratic selection, or the unceasing escalation of empty and irrelevant credentials. Of course, it is all of these things.

Is it inevitable that the linkage between education and work must get tighter and tighter? Is there a historical necessity here? Of course not. The strength of the relationship between schooling and work, like that of any social relationship, is a contingent one. As demonstrated in an extraordinary essay by Collins (2000), the extent to which occupational gatekeepers rely on educational institutions to provide them with new members follows no clear or unilinear path (see also Ringer 1991). Social arrangements change in ways that make particular markers of distinction more or less important.

But if there is no clear or unilinear path – no historical necessity – there has certainly been a path, and paths create dependence. Once the relationship between schooling and work has been established, the forces leading to the persistence and durability of this relationship are extremely hard to divert. The title *Work Is Here to Stay, Alas!* offered with some sense of resignation years ago by Levitan (1973) could be easily amended now to acknowledge that "Schooling and work is also here to stay, alas!"

Of course there are voices in the wilderness who would be more than happy to see education and work less intimately related to one another. Recall that Collins ended his agenda-setting *The Credential Society* (1979) with a plea for "credential abolitionism." Further, Labaree's social critique forces a reappraisal of the extent to which schooling has been hijacked by the workplace. Perhaps most to the point, historian Ben Hunnicut (1999) has argued that the cultural mantra of "JOBS JOBS JOBS" signals a work ideology that he believes has grown out of control. Hunnicut has extended this perspective to what he sees as the trivialization of leisure. It is a short step to extend it to the trivialization of schooling in the service of jobs.

These considerations lead to the second big theme that has worked its way through this book. This is that demand forces overwhelm supply forces. While stated a bit bluntly, this means that if the workplace expresses a demand for people with skills x, y, and z, schools will find a way to provide skills x, y, and z (or at least to convince employers and a broader public that they have done so). Despite reciprocities and interdependencies, schooling is still more often subordinate to the demands of the world of work than it is an innovative and proactive institution. This is not to deny Meyer's (1977) insight that schools do much to create the society in which they exist, but only to assert that schools more often than not find themselves in the position of dancing to the tune called by the economy. Of course, historically schools have done much to foster this relationship (Callahan 1962), and many school leaders would assert that the responsiveness of schools to business is as it should be. The point remains that what the economy "demands" typically takes precedence over what schools "supply."

The claim that demand forces overwhelm supply forces means too that "skills solutions" cannot succeed without a demand for those skills. That is, policies that proceed by "pumping" more and more skills into people – whether youth making their first school-to-work transition, middle aged participants in the "learning society," or a prototypical postindustrial PTM worker – can only succeed if a market exists (or can be created) for those skills. As Herzenberg et al. (1998, pp. 16–17) state:

> Finally, some might suggest that the best solutions to wage dispersion and dead-end jobs are found in education and training. Education is a good in itself. But education, standing alone, cannot make low-wage jobs disappear. . . . Indeed, more education and training absent other policies could simply make worker frustration more widespread. Rising numbers of Americans would face opportunities that fall short of their aspirations.

So where does all of this leave us? What can we conclude and where are we going? In this final chapter I will offer some speculation about ways in which the relationship between schooling and workplaces is likely to develop. I argue that the link between *education* and work may or may not continue to intensify, but the linkage between *credentials* and work will. If not inevitable, there are strong forces leading in that direcetion.

I see no difficulty in positing an increasing role for credentials in both meritocratic and credentialist senses. Postindustrialism has raised the stakes to the point that employers can no longer operate as they did when Berg described their behavior as capricious and unreflective. If not for every worksite and every occupation, credentials that repeatedly "mis-signal" productive capacity are likely to fall victim to other indicators that better secure employer trust. The irony, in what some have called the "Human Capital Century" (Goldin 2001), is that the ability of schooling to signal genuine skills is almost certainly greater now than it we when the "human capital turn" took place 40 years ago.

At the same time, one should not underestimate the resourcefulness of educational and class elites to make full use of the educational system. Credentialism, much like meritocracy, has proven to be an effective strategy of reproduction. Those able to "hoard" access to elite positions (Tilly 1998), to control the "entry gates and job ladders" of organizations (Bills 1998), and to make these social designations stick (Meyer 1970) will do much to ensure that some form of credentialism continues to operate.

Can the Linkage between Education and Work Tighten Forever?

For the relationship between education and work to endure, several things have to happen. First, employers need to continue to look to the schools as a source of human capital. Second, workers and job seekers (including students) will need to see the connection between the credentials they have or are accruing and those rewarded by employers. Third, schools will need to mediate what employers want and what job seekers have. Thus, we can ask: "Will the workplace continue to look to the schools?" "Will job seekers continue to stock up on credentials?" "Will schooling continue to 'feed' the workplace?"

These are complicated questions with lots of subquestions and subplots, but the answers to each are almost certainly going to be yes. The best projection is that employers, job seekers, and schools will continue to act in ways that tighten the linkages between education and work. We can spin out a simple three-act social play to illustrate this.

Act I: Will the workplace continue to look to the schools? What are employers likely to do?

In Act I, hiring is a decision made under uncertainty. Employers need indicators, however flawed, of productive potential. Educational credentials have been serving that purpose for some time, and will continue to do so. But employers have the upper hand. The business sector has always had considerable leverage over public schools, a relationship that has deepened lately (recall the earlier discussion of the United States Departments of Education and Labor). As shown in Chapter 1, the business community has rarely been shy about expressing what it expects schools to produce. Historically, too, business has rarely been very specific about what these needs are.

Labaree (1997) in particular has lamented the extent to which the nobler purposes of *education* have been sacrificed to economic exigency. At the same time, though, the relationship between school and work has worked in part to the benefit of *schooling* as an entrenched and potent institution in any society. Institutionalized schooling has received (at least until recently) a near monopoly on the production of the kinds of credentials that are of interest to employers. While it is not uncommon to read of employers' complaints about the quality of contemporary schools and the ability of those schools to deliver job-ready workers to the workplace, the overwhelming body of evidence suggests that employer trust in the schools remains high. Such employer complaints typically surface more as sniping at the inability of the school to provide workers with the *specific* skills that employers want than as any broadly felt critique of the ability of schools to produce endless supplies of human capital.

At the same time, the monopoly of schooling over the provision of credentials may be nearing its end. Private industry and a range of non-traditional providers of training are increasingly encroaching on the educational market. Thus, even if the magnitude of the relationship between "education" (very broadly construed) and work remains the same, or even grows, there may be ways in which the *specific* form of the relationship may change (Brown 1995; Bassi et al. 2000; Collins 2000). Other markers will almost certainly become of greater importance. These may assume the form of ACT's "WorkKeys" tests, or they may reflect new modes of corporate certification, but the signs are that employers will continue to look for opportunities to choose from a broader menu of credentials.

Act II: Job seekers

To continue to Act II, job seekers need to find ways to convince employers to hire them. To do this, they acquire "signals" that they can send to potential employers. Educational credentials have filled this role well for decades. Of course, educational credentials have never been the only signal of one's suitability for the workplace. At different times and different places, employers have been more swayed by work experience, or ethnicity, or race, or gender, or age, or any of a thousand other means of distinguishing among job candidates. In part, acquiring credentials has become a way to defend oneself in an increasingly credentialed environment, and in part it is a badge of admission that elites can display to other elites.

As long as employers reward educational credentials, job seekers will seek to acquire those credentials (just as a sudden employer preference for high WorkKeys scores would send job seekers scurrying for those). This is, however, more complicated than job seekers (again, including students) identifying the type of employer to whom they wish to send a signal, developing an educational plan to acquire that signal, and cashing in the credential in the labor market. There are two particularly important complications. The first is that many job seekers have dim perceptions of how all of this works, perceptions that are by some accounts getting dimmer all the time. Second, to an evidently increasing extent, job seekers are entering the labor market with the idea of deceiving employers with falsified but readily available credentials. Each of these merits some discussion.

Consider first how job seekers (and their parents) understand the relationship between the acquisition of educational credentials and the attainment of a job. In Chapter 1, I discussed Americans' commitment to the idea that schooling is the key to success. There are a couple of steps to this process. First, American parents see schooling as the means by which their children make their mark in the world. For less advantaged parents, schooling is a way for their children to move up, while for elite parents it is more a way to "reproduce" their advantages across generations. The second step is for children to develop the aspirations that their parents (and other significant others) have for them into aspirations and expectations of their own. In other words, to some degree the expansion of education is an outcome of expanded aspirations.

A massive loss of legitimacy of the idea that credentials lead to socioeconomic success could disrupt this linkage between schooling and work, and there are instances of historical precedent for this sort of thing happening. Still, the prospect of parents and children rejecting the American "folk norms" of upward mobility in a postindustrial, information-rich, technologically sophisticated but also increasingly unequal society are remote. The best evidence for this claim is that rather than declining, the career ambitions of contemporary American youth seem to be increasing faster than the ability of the occupational system to absorb these ambitions. Rather than a lack of faith in the ability of schooling to deliver the goods, the concern now is that students have aspirations out of proportion to their likely futures.

Over a half century ago, before the baby boom, postindustrialism, or rampant credentialism, Frances Carp (1949) concluded that "High school boys are realistic about occupations." While simple in design, Carp's study was persuasive that youth in the early postwar years entered the world of work with pretty clear visions of what that world had to offer. In sharp contrast, many of the difficulties facing American high school students do not arise from any lack of motivation or ambition, but rather from their failure or inability to "align" these ambitions with a realistic educational plan for reaching their occupational goals. An important statement here is Schneider and Stevenson's *The Ambitious Generation: America's Teenagers, Motivated But Directionless* (1999). Schneider and Stevenson argue that an evidently increasing number of students claim to want remunerative jobs, but have no clear idea of the educational paths that will get them there. Moreover, on even the most ambitious projection of occupational opportunity, more and more youth are aspiring to levels beyond what the occupational structure will be able to accommodate.

There is plenty of other research that supports Schneider and Stevenson's thesis of rising ambitions, along with an increasingly instrumental orientation to education as the means to realize those ambitions (Hanson 1994; Morgan 1996, 1998; Rindfuss et al. 1999; Reynolds and Pemberton 2000). This research shows important variations across such standard categories as race, gender, and social class, but the general point is the same. American youth want educational credentials for the economic benefits that they promise, and they are prepared to work persistently if not always in a clear direction to earn those credentials. Job seekers (and their parents) want signals that they can send to potential employers. The pursuit of educational credentials, even if unfocused and unrealistic, in filling that role is likely to continue.

The second complication in the likelihood of job seekers continuing to send signals in the form of educational credentials to employers is that an apparently increasing number of those credentials are fake. At least to the extent that the received wisdom of the business community is accurate, people lacking credentials are ever-more willing to invent them out of thin air. Their deception is abetted by a growing industry of diploma mills and other providers of falsified degrees (Potter 2003). Traditional higher education institutions have to compete not only with Governors University and Cisco Systems, but also Degrees-R-Us and Cooldegree.com.

For obvious reasons, securing reliable data on the extent of this fakery is difficult, but among those whose business it is to evaluate credentials, there is little doubt that the falsification of educational credentials is on the rise (Meredith 2001). By one estimate, the proportion of applicants who inflate their educational achievements grew from 14 percent in 1995/96 to 18.5 percent in 2000/01. Another estimate is that the fakery extends to over half a million people a year who lie to employers about their college experience (Foster 2003). Because of this evidently growing deception, such firms such as Credentials Inc and EdVerify are beginning to coalesce into an elaborate credentials verification industry.

Thus, the credentialist model of the future will grow more complex. As ever, credentials that legitimately signal merit will co-exist with those that reflect inflated expectations. To add to this, different forms of "shadow" credentialing systems will proliferate. One shadow system is emerging from the vast and unruly system of corporate certification, online learning, and the like. A second, even more deserving of the moniker "shadow," is a modest but expanding system of faked, forged, or otherwise false educational credentials.

Act III: Educational institutions

To complete the play, as long as employers and job seekers both accept the legitimacy and efficacy of the linkage between schooling and work, the only obvious thing for the schooling system to do is continue to expand. Only by doing so can it maintain its market share of employers' attention. Obviously, educational expansion has implications for what level of schooling and what specific degrees are associated with specific occupational attainments. If educational credentialism can be interpreted as credential inflation, meaning that it takes ever more schooling to gain access to a given job, it becomes of considerable interest to know what the prospects are for continued educational expansion. It becomes important to inquire both what might facilitate further educational growth, and what brakes there are on the system. The question then is how much can the educational system expand, and what does this mean for the relationships between education and work?

Educational researchers dedicate an enormous amount of time and effort to projecting postsecondary educational enrollments. These researchers are constantly aware of both the constraints on educational expansion, and the forces that might impel expansion to continue or even accelerate. The brakes are chiefly those of costs, both to the individuals aspiring to postsecondary schooling and to the society more broadly. The factors leading to expansion – the "gas pedals" – primarily have to do with occupational aspirations.

Others have written at length about the prospects for the durability of the trend toward universal higher education, and I will not elaborate on that debate here (Farley 1996; Dougherty 1997; Rubinson and Hurst 1997). To the extent that there is a consensus, it seems to be that postsecondary schooling in the United States is far from saturated, that there is still plenty of room for growth. More relevant for my focus on the relationship between education and work is that the increasing stratification of the educational system can take two very different forms. The first of these is *vertical expansion*, and the second is *horizontal differentiation*. We may well be up against some limits on the former, but limits on the latter are virtually nil.

By vertical expansion, I mean a greater share of the population going to school for more years in pursuit of more advanced degrees. This is what is typically at stake in discussions of educational expansion. Horizontal differentiation, in contrast, entails greater variability at any given level of the educational system. While perhaps less remarked upon than expansion, the long-term consequences of increased differentiation, both for trends toward meritocracy and toward credentialism, are greater yet (Breen and Jonsson 2000; Lucas 2001).

The prospects for horizontal differentiation are as far-ranging at the K–12 level as they are for higher education. At the K–12 level, horizontal expansion encompasses on the one hand such curricular and other programmatic differences within schools as early and competitive preschool, gifted and talented programs, Advanced Placement courses, and themed schools. Differentiation also matters across schools. If not the most important reason for the recent growth of charter schools, magnet schools, and the like, one thing this differentiation indicates is a more stratified signal of "employability" aimed at employers and the workplace. The K–12 system is endlessly capable of adding on differentiations within levels in ways that send different information signals to both postsecondary education and the labor market. In short, there would seem to be no brakes on the ability of the K–12 educational system to offer up diverse credentials to the world of work.

At the postsecondary level, this differentiation is vaster yet. It extends at the minimum to areas of study, institutional selectivity (sometimes referred to somewhat hopefully as "quality"), and institutional reputation. By all accounts, differences both across and within institutions matter more than they once did as a means to signal something distinctive to employers.

My judgement is that the ever-tightening link between credentials and the workplace will arise more from horizontal differentiation than from vertical expansion. The latter has historically been the predominant source of what is either credential inflation or the upgrading of occupations. It is likely to give way in the future to more varied (and presumably more information-rich) credentials. In general, whether the system of skill enhancement and certification expands or just differentiates, its ability to stratify is boundless. From the point of view of both job seekers and employers, the demand for credentials is virtually insatiable. Where these credentials are generated may shift in the future, but the credential society (whether meritocratic or not) is likely to persist.

Conclusion: Education and Work in the "New Modern Times"

Midway through *The Coming of Post-Industrial Society*, Daniel Bell stated a fundamental issue with characteristic clarity: "Today, not only does a child face a radical rupture with the past, but he must also be trained for an unknown future. And this task confronts the entire society as well" (p. 171). The observation is at once technocratic and normative. It raises the question of how we might go about designing and implementing an educational system capable of meeting the demands of postindustrialism. More urgently, it raises the question of what the education–work relationship that emerges from this *should* be.

It will take more than sociologists to answer these questions. Everyone in a postindustrial (or any other) society – parents, employers, labor, families, government, retirees – has a stake in how we shape the relationship between education and work. A discussion about what we expect schools and workplaces to mean to one another is a discussion about what kind of a society we want to be. Within broad limits, we can opt for some reconciliation of the three goals for schooling so carefully explored by Labaree (1997) – democratic citizenship, social efficiency, or social mobility. We can also opt for the increasingly tight relationship between schooling and work, and the continuing primacy of the social mobility goal.

But while this is a conversation that demands broad participation and many voices, sociologists do bring something unique to the table. Sociology does not settle the moral and normative questions at stake here, but it can bring a clearer empirical and conceptual understanding to them. Part of this understanding, as I have tried to demonstrate throughout this book, is that there remains much that we need to learn. My expectation is that the sociological imagination is going to be more important than ever as the relationship between education and work continues to unfold.

References

Abbott, A. (1988) *The System of Professions: An Essay on the Division of Expert Labor*. University of Chicago Press, Chicago.

Abbott, A. (1989) The new occupational structure: What are the questions? *Work and Occupations* 16: 273–91.

Adams, T., and McQuillan, K. (2000) New jobs, new workers? Organizational restructuring and management hiring decisions. *Relations Industrielles* 55: 391–412.

Adelman, C. (2000) *A Parallel Postsecondary Universe: The Certification System in Information Technology*. Office of Educational Research and Improvement: US Department of Education, Washington, DC.

Allmendinger, J. (1989) Educational systems and labor market outcomes. *European Sociological Review* 5: 231–50.

Alon, S., Donahoe, D., and Tienda, M. (2001) The effects of early work experience on young women's labor force attachment. *Social Forces* 79: 1005–34.

Altbach, P.G., Kelly, G.P., and Weis, L. (eds.) (1985) *Excellence in Education*. Prometheus Books, Buffalo, NY.

Althauser, R.P. (1989) Internal labor markets. *Annual Review of Sociology* 15: 143–61.

Altonji, J.G. (1994) The effects of high school curriculum on education and labor market outcomes. *Journal of Human Resources* 30: 409–38.

Altonji, J.G., and Pierret, C. (1997) Employer learning and the signaling value of education. US Department of Labor, Bureau of Labor Statistics, Discussion Paper, NLS 97–35.

Anyon, J. (1980) Social class and the hidden curriculum of work. *Journal of Education* 162: 66–92.

Appelbaum, E., and Batt, R. (1994) *The New American Workplace: Transforming Work Systems in the United States*. ILR Press, Ithaca, NY.

Appelbaum, E., Bailey, T., Berg, P., and Kalleberg, A.L. (2000) *Manufacturing Advantage: Why High-Performance Work Systems Pay Off*. Cornell University Press, Ithaca.

Arum, R. (1998) Invested dollars or diverted dreams? The effect of resources on vocational students' educational outcomes. *Sociology of Education* 71: 130–51.

Arum, R. (2000) Schools and communities: Ecological and institutional dimensions. *Annual Review of Sociology* 26: 395–418.

Arum, R., and Mueller, W. (2001) Self-employment dynamics in advanced economies. Prepared for the conference of the International Sociological Association Research Committee on Social Stratification and Mobility, Mannheim, Germany, April 26–28, 2001.

Arum, R., and Shavit, Y. (1995) Secondary vocational education and the transition from school to work. *Sociology of Education* 68: 187–204.

Arum, R., Budig, M., and Grant, D. (2001) Labor market regulation and the growth of self-employment. *International Journal of Sociology* 30: 1–26.

Ashton, D., Sung, J., and Turbin, J. (2000) Towards a framework for the comparative analysis of national systems of skill formation. *International Journal of Training and Development* 4: 8–25.

Astin, A.W. (1997) *What Matters in College: Four Critical Years Revisited*. Jossey–Bass, San Francisco.

Astin, A.W. (2000) *The American Freshman: National Norms for Fall 2000*. American Council on Education, University of California at Los Angeles.

Attewell, P. (1987) The deskilling controversy. *Work and Occupations* 14: 323–46.

Bailey, T. (1991) Jobs of the future and the education they will require: Evidence from occupational forecasts. *Educational Researcher* 20: 11–20.

Bailey, T. (1993) Can youth apprenticeship thrive in the United States? *Educational Researcher* 22 (3): 4–10.

Bailey, T. (1995) The integration of work and school: Education and the changing workplace. In Grubb, W.N. (ed.), *Education Through Occupations in American High Schools, Volume 1: Approaches to Integrating Academic and Vocational Education*. Teachers College Press, New York.

Bailey, T., Badway, N., and Gumport, P. (2001) *For-Profit Higher Education and Community Colleges*. National Center for Postsecondary Improvement, Stanford University.

Baizan, P., Michielin, F., and Billari, F.C. (2002) Political economy and lifecourse patterns: The heterogeneity of occupational, family, and household trajectories of young Spaniards. *Demographic Research* 6 (8): 189–240.

Baker, D.P. (1999) Schooling all the masses: Reconsidering the origins of American schooling in the postbellum era. *Sociology of Education* 72: 197–215.

Baker, D.P., and LeTendre, G.K. (2000) Comparative sociology of classroom processes, school organization, and achievement. In Hallinan, M.T. (ed.), *Handbook of the Sociology of Education*. Kluwer, New York, pp. 345–64.

Barley, S.R. (1992) *The New Crafts: The Rise of the Technical Labor Force and its Implication for the Organization of Work*. (EQW Working Paper WP05.) National Center on the Educational Quality of the Workforce, University of Pennsylvania.

Barley, S.R. (1996) Technicians in the workplace: Ethnographic evidence for bringing work into organization studies. *Administrative Science Quarterly* 41: 404–41.

Barley, S.R., and Kunda, G. (2001) Bringing work back in. *Organization Science* 12: 76–95.

Barro, R.J. (1991) Economic growth in a cross section of countries. *Quarterly Journal of Economics* 106: 407–43.

Bartik, T., and Hollenbeck, K. (2000) *The Role of Public Policy in Skills Development of Black Workers in the 21st Century*. W.E. Upjohn Institute for Employment Research, Kalamazoo, MI.

Bartlett, K.R. (2001) *The Perceived Influence of Industry-Sponsored Credentials in the Information Technology Industry*. National Research Center for Career and Technical Information, University of Minnesota.

Barton, P. (1989) *Earning and Learning: The Academic Achievement of High School Juniors with Jobs*. National Assessment of Educational Progress, Washington, DC.

Bassi, L.J., Ludwig, J., McMurrer, D.P., and Van Buren, M. (2000) *Profiting from Learning: Do Firms' Investments in Education and Training Pay Off?* (Research White Paper.) American Society for Training and Development, Alexandria, VA.

Batenberg, R., and Witte, M. de (2001) Underemployment in the Netherlands: How the Dutch "Poldermodel" failed to close the education–jobs gap. *Work, Employment and Society* 15: 73–94.

Beadie, N. (1999) From student markets to credential markets: The creation of the Regents Examination System in New York State, 1864–1890. *History of Education Quarterly* 39: 1–30.

Becker, G.S. (1964) *Human Capital: A Theoretical and Empirical Analysis, With Special Reference to Education*. National Bureau of Economic Research, New York.

Belanger, P., and Valdivielso, S. (1997) *The Emergence of Learning Societies: Who Participates in Adult Learning?* Elsevier, Tarrytown, NY.

Bell, D. (1999) *The Coming of Post-Industrial Society: A Venture in Social Forecasting*. Basic Books, New York.

Belman, D., and Heywood, J. (1991) Sheepskin effects in the return to education. *Review of Economics and Statistics* 73: 720–4.

Benavot, A. (1992) Curricular content, educational expansion, and economic growth. *Comparative Education Review* 36: 150–74.

Berg, I. (1971) *Education and Jobs: The Great Training Robbery*. Beacon, Boston.

Berman, J.M. (2001) Industry output and employment projections to 2010. *Monthly Labor Review* 124 (11): 39–56.

Bernhardt, A. (1999) *The Future of Low-wage Jobs: Case Studies in the Retail Industry*. Institute on Education and the Economy Working Paper 10. Columbia University.

Bernstein, P. (1997) *American Work Values: Their Origin and Development*. State University of New York Press, Albany.

Bianco, D.P., Moran, A., and Bianco, D.J. (1996) *Professional and Occupational Licensing Directory: A Descriptive Guide to State and Federal Licensing, Registration, and Certification Requirements.* Gale Group, Farmington Hills, MI.

Bills, D.B. (1988a) Educational credentials and hiring decisions: What employers look for in entry level employees. *Research in Social Stratification and Mobility* 7: 71–97.

Bills, D.B. (1988b) Educational credentials and promotions: Does schooling do more than get you in the door? *Sociology of Education* 61: 52–60.

Bills, D.B. (1988c) Credentials and capacities: Employers' perceptions of the acquisition of skills. *Sociological Quarterly* 29: 439–49.

Bills, D.B. (1990) Employers' use of job history data for hiring decisions: A fuller specification of job assignment and status attainment. *Sociological Quarterly* 31: 23–35.

Bills, D.B. (1992a) The mutability of educational credentials as hiring criteria: How employers evaluate atypically highly credentialed candidates. *Work and Occupations* 19: 79–95.

Bills, D.B. (1992b) A survey of employer surveys: What we know about labor markets from talking with bosses. *Research in Social Stratification and Mobility* 11: 3–31.

Bills, D.B. (1997) The effects of working on high school students: Youthwork is here to stay, Alas. In Hlebowitsh, P.S., and Wraga, W.G. (eds.), *Annual Review of Research for School Leaders.* Scholastic Leadership Policy Institute, New York.

Bills, D.B. (1998) Review of Gary Burtless (ed.). Does money matter? The effect of school resources on student achievement and adult success. *Educational Studies* 29: 166–70.

Bills, D.B. (1999) Labor market information and selection in a local restaurant industry: The tenuous balance between rewards, commitments, and costs. *Sociological Forum* 14: 583–607.

Bills, D.B. (ed.). (2003) *Research in the Sociology of Work: The Sociology of Worker Training.* Elsevier, London.

Bills, D.B. (2004) Credentials, signals, screens, and jobs: Explaining the relationship between schooling and job assignment. *Review of Educational Research* (Winter).

Bishop, J. (1990) Incentives for learning: Why American high school students compare so poorly to their counterparts overseas. *Research in Labor Economics* 11: 17–52.

Bishop, J. (1998) Occupation-specific versus general education and training. *Annals, American Academy of Political and Social Sciences* 559 (September): 24–38.

Bishop, J.H. (1999) *Nerd Harassment and Grade Inflation: Are College Admissions Policies Partly Responsible?* Working Paper 98–14. Center for Advanced Human Resource Studies, New York State School of Industrial and Labor Relations.

Bishop, J.H., and Kang, S. (1989) Vocational and academic education in high school: Complements or substitutes. *Economics of Education Review* 8: 133–48.

Black, S.E., and Lynch, L.M. (1997) *How to Compete: The Impact of Workplace Practices and Information Technology on Productivity*. Working Paper 6120. National Bureau of Economic Research, Cambridge, MA.

Blank, R.M. (2001) An overview of trends in social and economic well-being, by race. In Smelser, N.J., Wilson, W.J., and Mitchell, F. (eds.), *America Becoming: Racial Trends and Their Consequences, Volume 1*. National Academy Press, Washington, DC.

Blau, P., and Duncan, O.D. (1967) *The American Occupational Structure*. New York: Wiley.

Blaug, M. (1976) The empirical status of human capital theory: A slightly jaundiced survey. *Journal of Economic Literature* 14: 827–55.

Block, F. (1990) *Post-industrial Possibilities: A Critique of Economic Discourse*. University of California Press, Berkeley.

Boesel, D., Alsalam, N., and Smith, T.M. (1998) *Educational and Labor Market Performance of GED Recipients*. National Library of Education, Office of Educational Research and Improvement, United States Department of Education, Washington, DC.

Booth, A.L., and Snower, D.J. (eds.) (1996) *Acquiring Skills: Market Failures, Their Symptoms and Policy Responses*. Cambridge University Press, Cambridge.

Boudett, K.P., Murnane, R.J., and Willett, J.B. (2000) "Second-chance" strategies for women who drop out of school. *Monthly Labor Review* 123 (December): 19–31.

Bourdieu, P., and Passeron, J. (1974) *Reproduction in Education, Society and Culture*. Sage, Thousand Oaks.

Bowler, M. (1999) Women's earnings: An overview. *Monthly Labor Review* 122 (December): 13–21.

Bowles, S., and Gintis, H. (1976) *Schooling in Capitalist America: Educational Reform and the Contradictions of Economic Life*. Basic Books, New York.

Bowles, S., and Gintis, H. (2000) Does schooling raise earnings by making people smarter? In Arrow, K., Bowles, S., and Durlauf, S. (eds.), *Meritocracy and Economic Inequality*. Princeton University Press, Princeton, chapter 6.

Bowman, C. (1997) BLS projections to 2006: A Summary. *Monthly Labor Review* 120 (11): 3–5.

Boyle, M. (2001) *The New Schoolhouse: Literacy, Managers, and Belief*. Praeger, New York.

Braddock, J.H II, Crain, R.L., McPartland, J.M., and Dawkins, R.L. (1986) Applicant race and job placement decisions: A national survey experiment. *International Journal of Sociology and Social Policy* 6: 3–24.

Bradley, L.J. (1995) Certification and licensure issues. *Journal of Counseling and Development* 74: 185–6.

Bradley (1995) online at: http://www.clearhq.org

Bragg, D.D., Puckett, P.A., Reger, W. IV, Thomas, H.S., and Ortman, J. (1997) *Tech Prep/School-to-Work Partnerships: More Trends and Challenges*. Report MDS-1078. National Center for Research in Vocational Education, University of California-Berkeley.

Braudel, F. (1992) *The Perspective of the World*. University of California Press, Berkeley.

Braverman, H. (1974) *Labor and Monopoly Capital: The Degradation of Work in the Twentieth Century*. Monthly Review Press, New York.

Breen, R., and Goldthorpe J.H. (2001) Class, mobility, and merit: The experience of two British birth cohorts. *European Sociological Review* 17: 81–101.

Breen, R., and Jonsson, J.O. (2000) Analyzing educational careers: A multinomial transition model. *American Sociological Review* 65: 754–72.

Bremer, C.D., and Madzar, S. (1995) Encouraging employer involvement in youth apprenticeship and other work-based learning experiences for high school students. *Journal of Vocational and Technical Education* 12: online at: http://scholar.lib.vt.edu/ejournals/JVTE/v12n1/bremer.html

Brint, S. (1994) *In an Age of Experts: The Changing Role of Professionals in Politics and Public Life*. Princeton University Press, Princeton.

Brint, S., and Karabel, J. (1989) *The Diverted Dream*: Oxford University Press, New York.

Brody, N. (1997) Intelligence, schooling, and society. *American Psychologist* 52: 1046–50.

Brookings Institute message, online at: http://www.brookings.edu/press/books/clientpr/priority/nation_at_risk.htm

Brown, C. (1990) Empirical evidence on private training. *Research in Labor Economics* 11: 97–113.

Brown, C., and Campbell, B.A. (2002) The impact of technological change on work and wages. *Industrial Relations* 41: 1–33.

Brown, D.K. (1995) *Degrees of Control: A Sociology of Educational Expansion and Occupational Credentialism*. Teachers College Press, New York.

Brown, D.K. (2001) The social sources of educational credentialism: Status cultures, labor markets, and organizations. *Sociology of Education* extra issue: 19–34.

Brown, P. (1995) Cultural capital and social exclusion: Some observations on recent trends in education, employment, and the labour market. *Work, Employment and Society* 9: 29–51.

Bruno, R. (1995) *What's It Worth? Field of Training and Economic Status, 1993*. Current Population Report, P70-51. United States Census Bureau, Washington, DC.

Brynin, M. (2002) Overeducation in employment. *Work, Employment and Society* 16: 637–54.

Buchel, F. (2002) The effect of overeducation on productivity in Germany: The firm's viewpoint. *Economics of Education Review* 21: 263–75.

Buchmann, M (1989) *The Script of Life in Modern Society: Entry into Adulthood in a Changing World*. Chicago: University of Chicago Press.

Buchmann, C., and Hannum, E. (2001) Education and stratification in developing countries: A review of theories and research. *Annual Review of Sociology* 27: 77–102.

Buhlmahn, G., and Krakel, M. (2000) Overeducated workers as an insurance device. *Labour* 16: 383–402.

Bureau of Labor Statistics (1998) *New Occupations Emerging Across Industry Lines*. Issues in Labor Statistics 98–11. US Department of Labor, Washington, DC.

Bureau of Labor Statistics (2001) *College Enrollment and Work Activity of Year 2000 High School Graduates*. Technical Report USDL 01-94. US Department of Labor, Washington, DC.

Callahan, R.E. (1962) *Education and the Cult of Efficiency: A Study of the Social Forces that Have Shaped the Administration of the Public Schools*. University of Chicago Press, Chicago.

Cameron, S.V., and Heckman, J.J. (1993) The nonequivalence of high school equivalents. *Journal of Labor Economics* 11: 1–47.

Campanella, T. (1982) *The City of the Sun: A Poetical Dialogue*. Translated by D.J. Donno (with introduction and notes). University of California Press, Berkeley.

Cappelli, P., Bassi, L., Katz, H., Knoke, D., Osterman, P., and Useem, M. (1997) *Change at Work*. Oxford University Press, New York.

Carbonaro, W. (2001) *Explaining Cross-national Differences in the Skills–Earnings Relationship: Contextual Effects of Occupations*. Paper presented at the Summer Meetings of the RC28, Berkeley, CA.

Carnevale, A.P., and Desrochers D.M. (1997) The role of community colleges in the new economy. *Community College Journal* (April/May): 28–9.

Carnevale, A.P., and Desrochers, D.M. (2001) *Help Wanted Credentials Required: Community Colleges in the Knowledge Economy*. Educational Testing Service, Princeton.

Carnoy, M., and Castells, M. (1997) *Sustainable Flexibility: A Prospective Study on Work, Family, and Society in the Information Age*. Organization for Economic Co-operation and Development, Paris.

Carp, F.M. (1949) High school boys are realistic about occupations. *Occupations* 28: 97–9.

Carr, D. (1996) Two paths to self–employment? Women's and men's self-employment in the United States, 1980. *Work and Occupations* 23: 26–53.

Chabbott, C., and Ramirez, F.O. (2000) Development and education. In Hallinan, M.T. (ed.). *Handbook of the Sociology of Education*. Kluwer, New York, pp. 163–87.

Chajewski, L., and Newman, A.E. (1998) *Class and Status in Industry: Linking Global Transformations in Conceptions of Citizenship and Workplace Relations*. Paper presented at the Annual Meetings of the American Sociological Association, San Francisco.

Cicourel, A.V., and Kitsuse, J.I. (1963) *The Educational Decision-Makers*. Bobbs-Merrill, New York.

Coffield, F. (ed.) (1998) *Learning at Work*. Policy Press, Bristol.

Coleman, J.S. (1984) The transition from school to work. *Research in Social Stratification and Mobility* 3: 27–59.

Collins, R. (1971) Functional and conflict theories of educational stratification. *American Sociological Review* 36: 1002–19.

Collins, R. (1974) Where are educational requirements for employment highest? *Sociology of Education* 47: 419–42.

Collins, R. (1979) *The Credential Society: An Historical Sociology of Education and Stratification.* Academic Press, New York.

Collins, R. (2000) Comparative and historical patterns of education. In Hallinan, M.T. (ed.). *Handbook of the Sociology of Education.* Kluwer, New York, pp. 213–39.

Commission on the Skills of the American Workforce (1990) *America's Choice: High Skills or Low Wages.* National Center on Education and the Economy, Rochester, NY.

Cooksey, E.C., and Rindfuss, R.R. (2001) Patterns of work and schooling in young adulthood. *Sociological Forum* 16: 731–55.

Cope, M. (1998) Home–work links, labor markets, and the construction of place in Lawrence, Massachusetts, 1920–1939. *Professional Geographer* 50: 126–40.

Cortada, J.W. (ed.) (1998) *Rise of the Knowledge Worker.* Boston: Butterworth-Heinemann.

Council of Economic Advisers and the United States Department of Labor (1995) *Educating America: An Investment for Our Future.* Washington, DC.

Coverdill, J.E. (1998) Personal contacts and post-hire job outcomes: Theoretical and empirical notes on the significance of matching methods. *Research in Social Stratification and Mobility* 16: 247–69.

Creighton, S., and Hudson, L. (2002) Participation trends and patterns in adult education: 1991 to 1999. National Center for Education Statistics, Statistical Analysis Report. US Department of Education. NCES 2002-119.

Crouch, C. (1997). Skills-based full employment: The latest philosopher's stone. *British Journal of Industrial Relations* 35: 367–91.

Crouch, C., Finegold, D., and Sako, M. (1998) *Are Skills the Answer?* Oxford University Press, Oxford.

Daniels, A.K. (1987) Invisible Work. *Social Problems* 34: 403–15.

Darkenwald, G., Kim, K., and Stowe, P. (1998) Adults' participation in work-related courses: 1994–95. National Center for Education Statistics "Statistics in Brief" Report 98–309.

Davis, K., and Moore, W.E. (1945) Some principles of stratification. *American Sociological Review* 10: 242–9.

Dawson, A. (1999) The workshop and the classroom: Philadelphia engineering, the decline of apprenticeship, and the rise of industrial training, 1878–1900. *History of Education Quarterly* 39: 143–60.

DeFillippo, P. (2001) *Strange Trades.* Golden Gryphon Press, Urbana, IL.

DeFleur, L.B., and Menke, B.A. (1975) Learning about the labor force: Occupational knowledge among high school males. *Sociology of Education* 48: 324–45.

DeLuca, S., and Rosenbaum, J.E. (2001) Individual agency and the life-course: Do low-SES students get less long-term payoff for their school efforts? *Sociological Focus* 34: 357–76.

Denison, E. (1962) *The Sources of Economic Growth in the United States and the Alternatives Before Us.* Committee for Economic Development, New York.

DeYoung, A.J. (1989) *Economics and American Education: A Historical and Critical Overview of the Impact of Economic Theories on Schooling in the United States.* Longman, New York.

Diprete, T.A. (1988) The upgrading and downgrading of occupations: Status redefinition vs. deskilling as alternative theories of change. *Social Forces* 66: 725–46.

Doeringer, P.B., and Piore, M.J. (1971) *Internal Labor Markets and Manpower Analysis.* Lexington, MA: D.C. Heath.

Dore, R.P. (1976a) *The Diploma Disease.* Allen & Unwin, London.

Dore, R.P. (1976b) Human capital theory, the diversity of societies, and the problem of quality in education. *Higher Education* 5: 79–102.

Dore, R.P. (1997) Reflections on the diploma disease twenty years later. *Assessment in Education: Principles, Policy, and Practice* 4: 189–218.

Dougherty, K. (1994) *The Contradictory College: The Conflicting Origins, Impacts, and Futures of the Community College.* State University of New York Press, Albany.

Dougherty, K.J. (1997) Mass higher education: What is its impetus? What is its impact? *Teachers College Record* 99: 66–71.

Dougherty, K.J., and Bakia, M.F. (1998) *The New Economic Role of the Community College: Origins and Prospects.* Community College Research Center Occasional Paper 1. Teachers College, New York.

Dougherty, K.J., and Bakia, M.F. (2000) Community colleges and contract training: Content, origins and impact. *Teachers College Record* 102: 197–243.

Dreeben, R. (1968) *On What Is Learned in School.* Percheron Press: Clinton Corners, NY.

Dubin, R. (1965) *The World of Work.* Prentice Hall, Englewood Cliffs, NJ.

Duncan, G.J., and Hoffman, S.D. (1981) The incidence and wage effects of overeducation. *Economics of Education Review* 1: 75–86.

Durkheim, E. (1977) *The Evolution of Educational Thought: Lectures on the Formation and Development of Secondary Education in France.* London: Routledge & Kegan Paul.

Elbaum, B. (1989) Why apprenticeship persisted in Britain but not in the United States. *Journal of Economic History* 49: 337–49.

Enchautegui, M.E. (1998) Low-skilled immigrants and the changing American labor market. *Population and Development Review* 24: 811–24.

Entwisle, D.R., Alexander, K.L., and Olson, L.S. (2000) Early work histories of urban youth. *American Sociological Review* 65: 279–97.

Eriksson, T. (2001) *The Effects of New Work Practices: Evidence from Employer–Employee Data.* Paper presented at International Conference on

Organisational Design, Management Styles and Firm Performance at the University of Bergamo, June 22–23.

Esping-Andersen, G. (1999) *Social Foundations of Post-industrial Economies.* Oxford University Press, Oxford.

Evanciew, C.E.P., and Rojewski, J.W. (1999) Skill and knowledge acquisition in the workplace: A case study of mentor–apprentice relationships in youth apprenticeship programs. *Journal of Industrial Teacher Education* 36: 24–54.

Farley, R. (1996) *The New American Reality: Who We Are, How We Got Here, Where We Are Going (Volumes 1 and 2).* Russell Sage Foundation, New York.

Featherman, D.L., and Hauser, R.M. (1978) *Opportunity and Change.* Academic Press, New York.

Felstead, A. (1994) *The Gender Implications of Creating a Training Market: Alleviating or Reinforcing Inequality of Access?* Working Paper 5. Centre for Labour Market Studies, Leicester.

Ferrer, A.M., and Riddell, W.C. (2000) *The Role of Credentials in the Canadian Labour Market.* Paper presented at the Western Research Network on Education and Training Conference: Policy and Practice in Education and Training, University of British Columbia.

Finkelstein, B. (1991) Dollars and dreams: Classrooms as fictitious message systems, 1790–1930. *History of Education Quarterly* 31: 463–87.

Fitzgerald, R.A. (2000) *College Quality and the Earnings of Recent College Graduates.* Research and Development Report 2000-43. National Center for Education Statistics, Washington, DC.

Foster, A.L. (2003) On the Web, it's easy to earn straight A's. *Chronicle of Higher Education.* February 7.

Fougere, D., Kramarz, F., and Magnac, T. (2000) Youth employment policies in France. *European Economic Review* 44: 928–42.

Fountain, J.E. (2000) Constructing the information society: Women, information technology, and design. *Technology in Society* 22: 45–62.

Frances, C. (1998) More college students, more faculty? *Population Today* 26 (7/8): 4–5.

Francesconi, M., Orszag, J.M., Phelps, E.S., and Zoega, G. (1999) *Education and the Natural Rate of Unemployment.* Research Working Paper 9902. Institute for Social and Economic Research, University of Essex.

Frazis, H., Gittleman, M., Horrigan, M., and Joyce, M. (1997) Formal and informal training: Evidence from a matched employee–employer survey. In Libecap, G.D. (ed.), *Advances in the Study of Entrepreneurship, Innovation, and Economic Growth.* JAI Press, Greenwich, 47–82.

Freeman, R.B. (1976) *The Overeducated American.* Academic Press, New York.

Frenkel, S., Korczynski, M., Shire, K., and Tam, M. (1999) *On the Front Line: Organization of Work in the Information Economy.* Cornell University Press, Ithaca.

Frey, W.H., and DeVol, R.C. (2000) *America's Demography in the New Century: Aging Baby Boomers and New Immigrants as Major Players.* Policy Brief 9. Milken Institute, Santa Monica, CA.

Fullerton, H. (1997) Labor force 2006: Slowing down and changing composition. *Monthly Labor Review* 120 (11): 23–38.

Fullerton, H.N. Jr. (1999) Labor force participation: 75 years of change, 1950–98 and 1998–2025. *Monthly Labor Review* 122 (December): 3–12.

Furstenberg, F.F. Jr., and Cherlin, A.J. (1991) *Divided Families: What Happens to Children When Parents Part*. Harvard University Press, Cambridge, MA.

Gale, H.F. Jr., Wojan, T.R., and Olmsted, J.C. (2002) Skills, flexible manufacturing technology, and work organization. *Industrial Relations* 41: 48–79.

Gamoran, A. (1989) Measuring curriculum differentiation. *American Journal of Education* 97: 129–43.

Gamoran, A., and Kelly, S. (2001) *Classroom Instruction and Unequal Literacy in Contemporary American Secondary Schools*. Paper presented at the meetings of the Research Committee on Social Stratification and Mobility (RC28) of the International Sociological Association, Madison, WI.

Gangl, M. (2002) Changing labour markets and early career outcomes: Labour market entry in Europe over the past decade. *Work, Employment and Society* 16: 67–90.

Gaskell, J. (1992) *Gender Matters from School to Work*. Open University Press, Philadelphia.

Genda, Y., and Kurosawa, M. (2000) *Transition from School to Work in Japan*. National Bureau of Economic Research 13th Annual NBER-CEPR-TCER Conference, Tokyo.

Gittleman, M., Horrigan, M., and Joyce, M. (1998) Flexible workplace practices: Evidence from a nationally representative survey. *Industrial and Labor Relations Review* 52: 99–115.

Goldin, C. (1998a) America's graduation from high school: The evolution and spread of secondary schooling in the twentieth century. *Journal of Economic History* 58: 345–74.

Goldin, C. (1998b) Labor markets in the twentieth century. Unpublished manuscript. National Bureau of Economic Research, Cambridge, MA.

Goldin, C. (2001) The human capital century and American leadership: Virtues of the past. *Journal of Economic History* 61: 263–91.

Goldin, C., and Katz, L.F. (2001) The legacy of US educational leadership: Notes on distribution and economic growth in the 20th century. *American Economic Review* 91: 18–23.

Goldthorpe, J.H. (1996) The quantitative analysis of large-scale data-sets and rational action theory: For a sociological alliance. *European Sociological Review* 12: 109–26.

Gorard, S., Rees, G., Fevre, R., and Furlong, J. (1998) Society is not built by education alone: Alternative routes to a learning society. *Research in Post-Compulsory Education* 3: 25–37.

Gould, S.J. (1996) *The Mismeasure of Man*. Norton, New York.

Gouldner, A.W. (1979) *The Future of Intellectuals and the Rise of the New Class*. Seabury Press, New York.

Granovetter, M. (1992) Economic institutions as social constructions: A framework for analysis. *Acta Sociologica* 35: 3–11.

Green, F., McIntosh, S., and Vignoles, A. (1999) "Overeducation" and skills: Clarifying the concepts. Unpublished paper, Center for Economic Performance.

Greenberger, E., and Steinberg, L. (1986) *When Teenagers Work: The Psychological and Social Costs of Adolescent Employment.* Basic Books, New York.

Grimshaw, D., Ward, K.G., Rubery, J., and Beynon, H. (2001) Organisations and the transformation of the internal labour market. *Work, Employment and Society* 15: 25–54.

Groot, W., and van den Brink, H.M. (2000) Overeducation in the labor market: A meta-analysis. *Economics of Education Review* 19: 149–58.

Grubb, W.N. (1993) The varied economic returns to postsecondary education: New evidence from the class of 1972. *Journal of Human Resources* 28: 365–82.

Grubb, W.N. (1996) *Working in the Middle: Strengthening Education and Training for the Mid-skilled Labor Force.* Jossey-Bass, San Francisco.

Grubb, W.N. (1999a) The subbaccalaureate labor market in the United States: Challenges for the school-to-work transition. In Heinz, W. (ed.), *From Education to Work: Cross-national Perspectives.* Cambridge University Press, Cambridge, pp. 171–93.

Grubb, W.N. (1999b) *Honored but Invisible: An Inside Look at Teaching in Community Colleges.* New York: Routledge.

Grubb, W.N., and Kalman, J. (1994) Relearning to earn: The role of remediation in vocational education and job training. *American Journal of Education* 103: 54–93.

Grusky, D.B., and Diprete, T.A. (1990) Recent trends in the process of stratification. *Demography* 27: 617–37.

Hage, J., and Powers, C.H. (1992) *Post-industrial Lives: Roles and Relationships in the 21st Century.* Sage, Newbury Park.

Halaby, C.N. (1994) Overeducation and skill mismatch. *Sociology of Education* 67: 47–59.

Hamilton, S.F. (1990) *Apprenticeship for Adulthood: Preparing Youth for the Future.* Free Press, New York.

Hamilton, S.F. (1993) Prospects for an American-style youth apprenticeship system. *Educational Researcher* 22 (3): 11–16.

Handel, M. (2000) *Trends in Direct Measures of Job Skills Requirements.* Working Paper 301. The Jerome Levy Economics Institute of Bard College.

Hanson, S. (1994) Lost talent: Unrealized educational expectations and aspirations among US youth. *Sociology of Education* 67: 159–83.

Hartog, J. (2000) Overeducation and earnings: Where are we, where should we go? *Economics of Education Review* 19: 131–47.

Hauser, R.M., and Warren, J.R. (2001) Socioeconomic indexes for occupations: A review, update, and critique. In Grusky, D.B. (ed.), *Social Stratification: Class, Race, and Gender in Sociological Perspective, 2nd edition.* Westview Press, Boulder, pp. 281–6.

Hauser, R.M., Warren, J.R., Huang, M-H., and Carter, W.Y. (2000) Occupational status, education, and social mobility in the meritocracy. In Arrow, K.,

Bowles, S., and Durlauf, S. (eds.), *Meritocracy and Economic Inequality*. Princeton University Press, Princeton, chapter 8.

Hecker, D. (2001) Occupational employment projections to 2010. *Monthly Labor Review* 124 (11): 57–84.

Heckman, J. (1994) Is job training oversold? *The Public Interest* 115: 91–115.

Heckman, J., and Rubenstein, Y. (2001) The importance of noncognitive skills: Lessons from the GED testing program. *American Economic Review Papers and Proceedings* 91: 145–9.

Heinz, W. (ed.) (1999) *From Education to Work: Cross–national Perspectives*. Cambridge University Press, Cambridge.

Herzenberg, S.A., Alic, J.A., and Wial, H. (1998) *New Rules for a New Economy: Employment and Opportunity in Post-industrial America*. Cornell University Press, Ithaca.

Hillage, J., Uden, T., Aldridge, F., and Eccles, J. (2000) *Adult Learning in England: A Review*. Report 369. The Institute for Employment Studies, Brighton, England.

Hogan, D. (1996) "To better our condition": educational credentialing and "the silent compulsion of economic relations" in the United States, 1830 to the present. *History of Education Quarterly* 36: 243–70.

Holland, S. (2001) How human resource managers and supervisors value the change that skills assessment testing is making in hiring and training practices in the workplace. Doctoral Dissertation, University of Iowa.

Hollenbeck, K.M. (1993) *Classrooms in the Workplace: Workplace Literacy Programs in Small and Medium-sized Firms*. W.E. Upjohn Institute for Employment Research, Kalamazoo, MI.

Hollenbeck, K.M. (1996) *Employer Motives for Investing in Training*. Paper prepared for ILR-Cornell Institute for Labor Market Policies Conference *New Empirical Research on Employer Training: Who Pays? Who Benefits?* Cornell University, November 15–17.

Holzer, H.J. (2001) Racial differences in labor market outcomes among men. In Smelser, N.J., Wilson, W.J., and Mitchell, F. (eds.), *America Becoming: Racial Trends and Their Consequences, Volume 2*. National Academy Press, Washington, DC, chapter 5.

Horn, L.J., and Zahn, L. (2001) From Bachelor's degree to work: Major field of study and employment outcomes of 1992–93 Bachelor's degree recipients who did not enroll in graduate education by 1997. *Education Statistics Quarterly* 3: 64–71. Washington, DC, National Center for Education Statistics.

Hout, M. (2001) *Educational Progress for African Americans and Latinos in the United States from the 1950s to the 1990s: The Interaction of Ancestry and Class*. Paper presented at the Meetings of the International Sociological Association Research Committee on Social Stratification and Mobility. Mannheim, Germany, April.

Howe, H. (1988) *The Forgotten Half*. William T. Grant Foundation, New York.

Huang, L-H. (2001) Was higher education a quasi-fixed factor for firms in the 1980s? *Economics of Education Review* 20: 495–501.

Hughes, K. (1999) *Supermarket Employment: Good Jobs at Good Wages?* Working Paper 11. Institute for Education and the Economy, Columbia University.

Hughes, K.L., Bailey, T.R., and Mechur, M.J. (2001) *School-to-Work: Making a Difference in Education, A Research Report to America.* Institute on Education and the Economy, Teachers College, Columbia University.

Hungerford, T., and Solon, G. (1987) Sheepskin effects in the return to education. *Review of Economics and Statistics* 69: 733–40.

Hunnicut, B.K. (1999) *The Historical Origins of the Time Famine.* Paper presented at the American Psychological Association/National Institute of Health Interdisciplinary Conference on Work, Stress and Health in Baltimore, March 11–13.

Hurst, D., and Hudson, L. (2001) Changes in high school vocational course-taking in a larger perspective. *Education Statistics Quarterly* 3: 21–25.

Iannelli, C., and Soro-Bonmati, A. (2001) *The Transition from School to Work in Southern Europe: A Comparison of the Spanish and Italian Cases.* Paper presented at the Meeting of the International Sociological Association Research Committee on Social Stratification (RC28) on "Inequality Global and Local Perspectives," Berkeley, August 4–16.

Ingram, B.F., and Neumann, G.R. (1999) An analysis of the evolution of the skill premium. Unpublished manuscript, University of Iowa.

Inkeles, A. (1969) Making men modern: On the causes and consequences of individual change in six developing countries. *American Journal of Sociology* 75: 208–26.

Inozemtsev, V. (2001) "Class of Intellectuals" in post-industrial society. *Social Sciences* 32: 125–38.

Ishida, H., Spilerman, S., and Su, K-H. (1997) Educational credentials and promotion chances in Japanese and American organizations. *American Sociological Review* 62: 866–82.

Jackson, M. (2001) *Meritocracy, Education and Occupational Attainment: What Do Employers Really See As Merit?* Sociology Working Papers 2001–003. Nuffield College.

Jackson, P.W. (1968) *Life in Classrooms.* Holt, Rinehart, and Winston, New York.

Jencks, C., Bartlett, S., Corcoran, M., Crouse, J., Eaglesfield, D., Jackson, G., McClelland, R., Meuser, P., Olneck, M., Schwartz, J., Ward, S., and Williams, J. (1979) *Who Gets Ahead?* Basic Books, New York.

Johnson, R.L. (2001) "Dancing Mothers": The Chautauqua movement in twentieth century American popular culture. *American Studies International* 39: 53–70.

Jones, L. (1980) *Great Expectations: America and the Baby Boom Generation.* Coward McCann, New York.

Kalleberg, A.L. (2001) Organizing flexibility: The flexible firm in a new century. *British Journal of Industrial Relations* 39: 479–504.

Kalleberg, A.L., and Berg, I. (1987) *Work and Industry: Structures, Markets, and Processes.* New York: Plenum.

Kane, T., and Rouse, C. (1995) Labor market returns to two- and four-year colleges. *American Economic Review* 85: 600–14.

Kantor, H. (1994) Managing the transition from school to work: The false promise of youth apprenticeship. *Teachers College Record* 96: 442–61.

Karabel, J., and Halsey, A.H. (eds.) (1977) *Power and Ideology in Education.* Oxford University Press, Oxford.

Kariya, T., and Rosenbaum, J.E. (1987) Self-selection in Japanese junior high schools: A longitudinal study of students' educational plans. *Sociology of Education* 60: 168–80.

Karlsson, J.C. (1995) The concept of work on the rack: Critique and suggestions. *Research in the Sociology of Work* 5: 1–14.

Katznelson, I., and Weir, M. (1985) *Schooling for All: Class, Race, and the Decline of the Democratic Ideal.* Basic Books, New York.

Kaufman, R.L., and Spilerman, S. (1982) The age structures of occupations and jobs. *American Journal of Sociology* 87: 827–51.

Keller, G. (2001) The new demographics of higher education. *Review of Higher Education* 24: 219–35.

Kemple, J.K., and Snipes, J.C. (2000) *Career Academies: Impacts on Students' Engagement and Performance in High School.* Manpower Demonstration Research Corporation, New York.

Kerckhoff, A.C. (1996) Building conceptual and empirical bridges between studies of educational and labor force careers. In Kerckhoff, A.C. (ed.), *Generating Social Stratification: Toward a New Research Agenda.* Westview Press, Boulder, pp. 37–56.

Kerckhoff, A.C. (2000) Transition from school to work in comparative perspective. In Hallinan, M.T. (ed.), *Handbook of the Sociology of Education.* Kluwer, New York, pp. 453–74.

Kerckhoff, A.C., and Bell, L. (1998) Hidden capital: Vocational credentials and attainment in the United States. *Sociology of Education* 71: 152–74.

Kerckhoff, A.C., Raudenbush, S.W., and Glennie, E. (2001) Education, cognitive skill, and labor force outcomes. *Sociology of Education* 74: 1–24.

Kett, J.F. (1994) *The Pursuit of Knowledge under Difficulties: From Self-improvement to Adult Education in America, 1750–1990.* Stanford University Press, Stanford.

Kinsella, K., and Velkoff, V.A. (2001) *An Aging World: 2001.* US Census Bureau Series P95-01-1. US Government Printing Office, Washington, DC.

Kleinman, D.L., and Vallas, S.P. (2001) Science, capitalism, and the rise of the "knowledge worker": The changing structure of knowledge production in the United States. *Theory and Society* 30: 451–92.

Klerman, J.A., and Karoly, L.A. (1995) *The Transition to Stable Employment: The Experience of U.S. Youth in Their Early Labor Market Career.* Research Report MDS-764. University of California-Berkeley. National Center for Research in Vocational Education.

Kliebard, H.M. (1999) *Schooled to Work: Vocationalism and the American Curriculum, 1876–1946.* Teachers College Press, New York.

Knoke, D., and Ishio, Y. (1998) The gender gap in company job training. *Work and Occupations* 25: 141–67.

Knoke, D., and Janowiec–Kurle, L. (1999) Make or buy? The externalization of company job training. *Research in the Sociology of Organizations* 16: 85–106.

Kodrzycki, Y.K. (2000) New England's educational advantage: Past successes and future prospects. *New England Economic Review* (Jan/Feb): 25–40.

Koeber, C. (2001) Review of manufacturing advantage: Why high performance work systems pay off. *Contemporary Sociology* 30: 250–1.

Krause, E.A. (1996) *Death of the Guilds: Professions, States, and the Advance of Capitalism, 1930 to the Present.* Yale University Press, New Haven.

Labaree, D.F. (1988) *The Making of an American High School: The Credentials Market and the Central High School of Philadelphia, 1838–1939* Yale University Press, New Haven.

Labaree, D.F. (1997) *How to Succeed in School Without Really Learning: The Credentials Race in American Education.* New Haven: Yale University Press.

Ladd, H.F., and Murray, S.E. (2001) Intergenerational conflict reconsidered: County demographic structure and the demand for public education. *Economics of Education Review* 20: 343–57.

L'ain, B.G. de (1981) Certifying effect and consumer effect: Some remarks on strategies employed by higher education institutions. *Higher Education* 10: 55–73.

LaLonde, R. (2001) The returns of going back to school for displaced workers. *Poverty Research News* 5: 14–15.

Lave, J., and Wenger, E. (1991) *Situated Learning: Legitimate Peripheral Participation.* Cambridge: Cambridge University Press.

Lazaridis, G., and Koumandraki, M. (2001) Youth citizenship and unemployment: The case of passive and active labour market policies towards the young unemployed in Greece. *Sociological Research Online* 5 (4): online at: http://www.socresonline.org.uk/5/4/lazaridis.html

Lazear, E. (1977) Academic achievement and job performance: a note. *American Economic Review* 67: 252–4.

Leigh, D.E., and Gill, A.M. (1997) Labor market returns to community colleges: Evidence for returning adults. *The Journal of Human Resources* 32: 334–53.

Lemann, N. (2000) *The Big Test: The Secret History of the American Meritocracy.* Farrar, Straus, and Giroux, New York.

Lenn, M.P. (2002) The right way to export higher education. *Chronicle of Higher Education* (March 1).

Lerman, R.I. (1996) *Helping Disconnected Youth by Improving Linkages Between High Schools and Careers.* Presentation at the American Enterprise Institute Forum on America's Disconnected Youth: Toward a Preventive Strategy, Washington, DC.

Lerman, R.I. (1997) *Meritocracy Without Rising Inequality.* The Urban Institute, Washington, DC.

Lerman, R.I., and Schmidt, S.R. (1999) *An Overview of Economic, Social, and Demographic Trends Affecting the U.S. Labor Market.* The Urban Institute, Washington, DC.

Lerman, R.I., Riegg, S.K., and Salzman, H. (2000) *The Role of Community Colleges in Expanding the Supply of Information Technology Workers*. The Urban Institute, Washington, DC.

Leventhal, T., Graber, J.A., and Brooks-Gunn, J. (2001) Adolescent transitions to young adulthood: Antecedents, correlates, and consequences of adolescent employment. *Journal of Research on Adolescence* 11: 297–323.

Levesque, K., Doug, L., Teitelbaum, P., Alt, M., and Librera, S. (2000) *Vocational Education in the United States: Toward the Year 2000*. NCES 2000-029. National Center for Education Statistics, Washington, DC.

Levin, H. (1991) Can education do it alone? *Economics of Education Review* (1994): 97–108.

Levine, D. (1994) The School-to-Work Opportunities Act of 1994: A flawed prescription for education reform. *Educational Foundations* 8: 33–51.

Levitan, S.A. (1973) *Work is Here to Stay, Alas*. Olympus Publishing Company, Salt Lake City.

Levitan, S.A., Gallo, F., and Belous, R.S. (1988) *What's Happening to the American Family?: Tensions, Hopes, Realities*. Johns Hopkins University Press, Baltimore, MD.

Lewis, L., Farris, E., and Greene, B. (2003) *Programs for Adults in Public Library Outlets*. NCES 2000-010. National Center for Education Statistics, Washington, DC.

Lewis, D.R., Hearn, J.C., and Zilbert, E.E. (1993) Efficiency and equity effects of vocationally focused postsecondary education. *Sociology of Education* 66: 188–205.

Lewis, L., Snow, K., Farris, E., and Levin, D. (2000) *Distance Education at Postsecondary Education Institutions: 1997–1998*. Statistical analysis report NCES 2000-013. National Center for Education Statistics, Washington, DC.

Li, B., and Walder, A.G. (2001) Career advancement as party patronage: Sponsored mobility into the Chinese administrative elite, 1949–1996. *American Journal of Sociology* 106: 1371–408.

Li, J.H., Konig, M., Buchmann, M., and Sacchi, S. (2000) The influence of further education on occupational mobility in Switzerland. *European Sociological Review* 16: 43–65.

Licht, W. (1988) How the workplace has changed in 75 years. *Monthly Labor Review* 111 (2): 19–25.

Liker, J.K., Haddad, C.J., and Karlin, J. (1999) Perspectives on technology and work organization. *Annual Review of Sociology* 25: 575–96.

Lillydahl, J.H. (1990) Academic achievement and part-time employment of high school students. *Journal of Economic Education* 21: 307–16.

Lin, N. (1999) Social networks and status attainment. *Annual Review of Sociology* 25: 467–87.

Linnehan, F. (1998) Measuring the effectiveness of a career academy program from an employer's perspective. *Educational Evaluation and Policy Analysis* 18: 73–89.

Lipartito, K.J., and Miranti, P.J. (1998) Professions and organizations in twentieth-century America. *Social Science Quarterly* 79: 301–20.

Lippman, L. (2001) *Cross-national Variation in Educational Preparation for Adulthood: From Early Adolescence to Young Adulthood.* Working Paper 2001–01. US Department of Education, National Center for Education Statistics, Washington, DC.

Little, A. (1997) The diploma disease twenty years on: An introduction. *Assessment in Education: Principles, Policy, and Practice* 4: 5–22.

Livingstone, D.W. (1998) *The Education–Jobs Gap: Underemployment or Economic Democracy.* Westview Press, Boulder.

Lowe, J. (2000) International examinations: The new credentialism and reproduction of advantage in a globalising world. *Assessment in Education* 3: 363–77.

Lucas, S.R. (1999) *Tracking Inequality: Stratification and Mobility in American High Schools.* Teachers College Press, New York.

Lucas, S.R. (2001) Effectively maintained inequality: Education transitions, track mobility, and social background effects. *American Journal of Sociology* 106: 1642–90.

Lucas, S.R., and Good, A.D. (2001) Race, class, and tournament track mobility. *Sociology of Education* 74: 139–56.

Lundgren, L., and Rankin, B. (1998) What matters more: The job training program or the background of the participant? An HLM analysis of the influence of program and client characteristics on the wages of inner-city youth who have completed JTPA job training. *Evaluation and Program Planning* 21: 111–20.

Lynch, L. (1998) Do investments in education and training matter? *Perspectives on Work* 1 (3): 43–7.

Lynch, L., and Black, S.E. (1998) Beyond the incidence of employer-provided training. *Industrial and Labor Relations Review* 52: 64–81.

Mane, F. (1999) Trends in the payoff to academic and occupation-specific skills: The short- and medium-run returns to academic and vocational high school courses for non-college-bound students. *Economics of Education Review* 18: 417–37.

Mann, H. online at: http://www.tncrimlaw.com/civil_bible/horace_mann.htm

Mare, R.D. (1995) Changes in educational attainment and school enrollment. In Farley, R. (ed.), *State of the Union: America in the 1990s: Volume I Economic Trends.* Russell Sage Foundation, New York.

Mare, R.D. (2001) Observations on the study of social mobility and inequality. In Grusky, D.B. (ed.), *Social Stratification: Class, Race, and Gender in Sociological Perspective, 2nd edition.* Westview Press, Boulder, pp. 477–88.

Mariani, M. (1999) High earning workers who don't have a Bachelor's degree. *Occupational Outlook Quarterly* Fall: 8–15.

Marquardt, M.J., Nissley, N., Ozag, R., and Taylor, T.L. (2000) Training and development in the United States. *International Journal of Training and Development* 4: 138–49.

Marsh, H. (1991) Employment during high school: Character building or a subversion of academic goals. *Sociology of Education* 64: 172–89.

Massey, D. (1995) The new immigrants and ethnicity in the United States. *Population and Development Review* 21: 631–52.

Maxwell, N., and Rubin, V. (2000) *High School Career Academies: Pathways to Educational Reform in Urban School Districts*. Upjohn Institute for Employment Research, Kalamazoo, MI.

Mayer, K.U. (1991) Life courses in the welfare state. In Heinz, W.R. (ed.), *Theoretical Advances in Life Course Research: Status Passages and the Life Course*. Deutscher Studien Verlag, Weinheim, pp. 171–86.

McDonald, P., and Kippen, R. (2001) Labor supply prospects in 16 developed countries, 2000–2050. *Population and Development Review* 27: 1–32.

McEneaney, E.H., and Meyer, J.W. (2000) The content of the curriculum: An institutionalist perspective. In Hallinan, M.T. (ed.), *Handbook of the Sociology of Education*. Kluwer, New York, chapter 8, pp. 189–211.

Medrick, E., Merola, L., and Ramer, C. (2000) *School to Work Progress Measures: A Report to the National School-to-Work Office*. MPR Associates, Inc., Berkeley.

Meister, J.C. (2001) The brave new world of corporate education. *The Chronicle Review* online at: http://chronicle.com/weekly/v47/i22/22b01001.htm. Issue dated February 9, 2001.

Meredith, J. (2001) Firms give hard lesson on false degree claims. *Chicago Tribune* August 27.

Merton, R.K. (1963) *Social Theory and Social Structure*. Free Press, Glencoe.

Meyer, J.W. (1970) The charter: Conditions of diffuse socialization in schools. In Scott, W.R. (ed.), *Social Processes and Social Structures*. Holt, Rhinehart, and Winston, New York.

Meyer, J.W. (1977) The effects of education as an institution. *American Journal of Sociology* 83: 55–77.

Meyer, J., Tyack, D., Nagel, J., and Gordon, A. (1979) Public education as nation-building in America: Enrollments and bureaucratization in the American states, 1870–1930. *American Journal of Sociology* 85: 591–613.

Meyer, S. (1995) Technology and work: a social and historical overview of US industrialization. In Bills, D.B. (ed.), *The New Modern Times: Factors Reshaping the World of Work*. SUNY Press: Albany NY, pp. 29–50.

Miller, S.M. (2001) My meritocratic rise. *Tikkun* 16: 63–4.

Miller, S.R. (1998) Shortcut: High school grades as a signal of human capital. *Educational Evaluation and Policy Analysis* 20: 299–311.

Miller, S.R., and Rosenbaum, J.E. (1997) Hiring in a Hobbesian world: Social infrastructure and employers' use of information. *Work and Occupations* 24: 498–523.

Mincer, J. (1958) Investment in human capital and personal income distribution. *Journal of Political Economy* 66: 282–302.

Mincer, J. (1974) *Schooling, Experience, and Earnings*. National Bureau of Economic Research, New York.

Mincer, J. (1989) Human capital and the labor market: A review of current research. *Educational Researcher* 18 (4): 27–34.

Miozzo, M., and Ramirez, M. (2000) *Technological and Organisational Changes in the Telcommunications Industry and the Changing Pattern of Skills and Work Organisation.* Paper prepared for the Eighth International Joseph Schumpeter Society Meetings, Manchester, England.

Mjelde, L., and Daly, R. (2000) *Learning at the Point of Production: New Challenges in the Social Division of Knowledge.* Paper presented at the Western Research Network on Education and Training Conference: Policy and Practice in Education and Training. University of British Columbia.

Moen, P. (2001) *PRB Reports on America: The Career Quandary.* Population Reference Bureau.

Morgan, S.L. (1996) Trends in Black–White differences in educational expectations, 1980–1992. *Sociology of Education* 69: 308–19.

Morgan, S.L. (1998) Adolescent educational expectations: Rationalized, fantasized, or both? *Rationality and Society* 10: 131–62.

Morrill, R.L. (1990) Regional demographic structure of the United States. *Population Geographer* 42: 38–53.

Mortimer, J.T., and Kruger, H. (2000) Pathways from school to work in Germany and the United States. In Hallinan, M.T. (ed.), *Handbook of the Sociology of Education.* Kluwer, New York, chapter 21, pp. 475–97.

Moss, P., and Tilly, C. (2001) *Stories Employers Tell: Race, Skill, and Hiring in America.* Russell Sage, New York.

Muller, W., and Shavit, Y. (1998) The institutional embeddedness of the stratification process: A comparative study of qualifications and occupations in thirteen countries. In Shavit, Y., and Muller, W. (eds.), *From School to Work: A Comparative Study of Educational Qualifications and Occupational Destinations.* Clarendon Press, Oxford, pp. 1–48.

Murnane, R.J., Willett, J.B., and Boudett, K.P. (1999) Do male dropouts benefit from obtaining a GED, postsecondary education, and training? *Evaluation Review* 23: 475–503.

Murnane, R.J., Willett, J.B., and Tyler J.H. (2000) Who benefits from obtaining a GED? Evidence from high school and beyond. *Review of Economics and Statistics* 82: 23–37.

Murphy, R. (1988) *Social Closure: The Theory of Monopolization and Exclusion.* Oxford University Press, Oxford.

Namboordiri, K. (1987) The floundering phase of the life course. *Research in the Sociology of Education and Socialization*: 59–86.

National Center for Education Statistics (1998) *State Comparisons of Education Statistics: 1969–70 to 1996–97.* Compendium 98-018. United States Office of Education Office of Educational Research and Improvement, Washington, DC.

National Commission on Excellence in Education (1983) *A Nation at Risk: The Imperative for Educational Reform.* United States Department of Education, Washington, DC.

National Research Council (1999) *The Changing Nature of Work: Implications for Occupational Analysis.* National Academy Press, Washington, DC.

National Skills Task Force (2001) *Opportunity and Skills in the Knowledge-driven Economy*. Report from the Secretary of State for Education and Employment. England.

Neckerman, K.M., and Kirschenman, H. (1991) Hiring strategies, racial bias, and inner-city workers. *Social Problems* 38: 433–47.

Nelson-Rowe, S. (1991) Corporation schooling and the labor market at General Electric. *History of Education Quarterly* 31: 27–46.

Nock, S.L. (1993) *The Costs of Privacy: Surveillance and Reputation in America*. Aldine de Gruyter, New York.

Norman, D.A. (1993) *Things That Make Us Smart: Defending Human Attributes in the Age of the Machine*. Addison-Wesley, Reading.

Olneck, M.R., and Bills, D.B. (1979) What makes Sammy run? An empirical assessment of the Bowles-Gintis Correspondence Thesis. *American Journal of Education* 89: 27–61.

Olneck, M.R., and Crouse, J. (1979) The IQ meritocracy reconsidered. *American Journal of Education* 88: 1–31.

Organization for Economic Co-operation and Development (1994) *OECD Jobs Study: Facts, Analysis, Strategies*. Paris, OECD.

Organization for Economic Co-operation and Development (1996) *Lifelong Learning for All*. Meeting of the Education Committee at Ministerial Level, Paris, OECD.

Orlikowski, W.J. (1992) The duality of technology: Rethinking the concept of technology in organizations. *Organization Science* 3: 398–427.

Orr, J.E. (1996) *Talking About Machines: An Ethnography of a Modern Job*. ILR Press, Ithaca.

Osterman, P. (1993) Why don't they work? Employment patterns in a high pressure economy. *Social Science Research* 22: 115–30.

Osterman, P. (1994a) Supervision, discretion, and work organization. *American Economic Review* 84: 380–4.

Osterman, P. (1994b) How common is workplace transformation and who adopts it? *Industrial and Labor Relations Review* 47: 173–88.

Osterman, P. (1995) Skill, training, and work organization in American establishments. *Industrial Relations* 34: 125–46.

Osterman, P., and Iannozzi, M. (1993) *Youth Apprenticeship and School-to-Work Transitions: Current Knowledge and Legislative Strategy*. Working Paper 14. National Center on the Educational Quality of the Workforce, University of Pennsylvania.

Pallas, A.M. (2000) The effects of schooling on individual lives. In Hallinan, M.T. (ed.), *Handbook of the Sociology of Education*. Kluwer, New York, chapter 22, pp. 499–525.

Pantazis, C. (2000) The new workforce investment act. *Public Policy*. American Society for Training and Development, online at: http://www.astd.org/virtual_community/public_policy/new_wia_99_article.htm

Park, J.H. (1999) Estimation of sheepskin effects using the old and the new measures of educational attainment in the current population survey. *Economics Letters* 62: 237–40.

Parkin, F. (1971) *Class Inequality and Political Order: Social Stratification in Capitalist and Communist Societies*. Praeger, New York.

Parnell, D. (1985) *The Neglected Majority*. Community College Press, Washington, DC.

Parsons T. (1959) The school class as a social system. *Harvard Educational Review* 29: 297–318.

Parsons, T. (1967) *The Structure of Social Action*. Free Press, New York.

Pascarella, E.T., and Terenzini. P.T. (forthcoming) *How College Affects Students: Findings and Insights from Twenty Years of Research (2nd edition)*. Jossey–Bass, San Francisco.

Pastor, M., Jr. (2001) Geography and opportunity. In Smelser, N.J., Wilson, W.J., and Mitchell, F. (eds.), *America Becoming: Racial Trends and Their Consequences, Volume 1*. National Academy Press, Washington, DC.

Perez, S.M., and Salazar, D. De La Rose. (1993) Economic, labor force, and social implications of Latino educational and population trends. *Hispanic Journal of Behavioral Sciences* 15: 188–229.

Perin, D. (2001) Academic–occupational integration as a reform strategy for the community college: Classroom perspectives. *Teachers College Record* 103: 303–35.

Perkinson, H.J. (1991) *The Imperfect Panacea: American Faith in Education 1865–1990*. McGraw-Hill, New York.

Petersen, T., Saporta, I., and Seidel, M-D.L. (2001) Offering a job: Meritocracy and social networks. *American Journal of Sociology* 106: 763–816.

Petroski, H. (1992) *The Pencil: A History of Design and Circumstance*. Knopf, New York.

Phillips, B.S. (1971) *Social Research: Strategy and Tactics*. Macmillan, New York.

Piore, M.J., and Sabel, C.F. (1984) *The Second Industrial Divide: Possibilities for Prosperity*. Basic Books, New York.

Pittman, V.V. (1998) Low-key leadership: Collegiate correspondence study and "campus equivalence." *American Journal of Distance Education* 12: 36–45.

Pollard, K.M., and O'Hare, W.P. (1999) America's racial and ethnic minorities. *Population Bulletin* 54 (3).

Pollert, A. (1988) The "flexible firm": Fixation or fact? *Work, Employment and Society* 2: 281–316.

Portes, A., and Rumbaut, R.G. (1990) *Immigrant America: A Portrait*. University of California Press, Berkeley.

Potter, W. (2003) Fake diplomas are easy to purchase on the Internet, federal investigators find. *Chronicle of Higher Education*, January 23.

Poulos, S. (1997) The aging baby boom: Implications for employment and training programs. The Urban Institute, Washington, DC.

Powell, A.G., Farrar, E., and Cohen, D.K. (1985) *The Shopping Mall High School: Winners and Losers in the Educational Marketplace*. Houghton Mifflin, New York.

Preston, S. (1996) Children will pay. *New York Times Magazine* September 29: 96–7.

Pryor, F.L., and Schaffer, D.L. (1999) *Who's Not Working and Why: Employment, Cognitive Skills, Wages, and the Changing U.S. Labor Market*. Cambridge University Press, Cambridge.

Pucel, D.J., and Sundre, S.K. (1999) Tech prep articulation: Is it working? *Journal of Industrial Teacher Education* 37: 26–37.

Recesso, A.M. (1999) First year implementation of the School to Work Opportunities Act Policy: An effort at backward mapping. *Education Policy Analysis Archives* 7.

Regini, M. (1997) Different responses to common demands: Firms, institutions, and training in Europe. *European Sociological Review* 13: 267–82.

Resnick, L.B. (1987) Learning in school and out. *Educational Researcher* 16: 13–20.

Reynolds, J., and Pemberton, J. (2000) *Rising College Expectations Among Youth in the U.S.: A Comparison of the 1979 and 1997 NLSY*. Unpublished paper. Florida State University.

Riley, J.G. (1979) Testing the educational screening hypothesis. *Journal of Political Economy* 87: S227–S252.

Rindfuss, R.R. (1991) The young adult years: Diversity, structural change, and fertility. *Demography* 28: 493–512.

Rindfuss, R.R., Cooksey, E.C., and Sutterlin, R.L. (1999) Young adult occupational achievement: Early expectations versus behavioral reality. *Work and Occupations* 26: 220–63.

Ringer, F.K. (1991) *The Decline of the German Mandarins: The German Academic Community, 1890–1933*. Wesleyan University Press, Middletown, CT.

Rogers, D.L., Toder, E., and Jones, L. (1999) *Future Demographic Changes and the Economic Environment Surrounding Pensions*. Unpublished paper. The Urban Institute, Washington, DC.

Rogers, D.L., Toder, E., and Jones, L. (2000) *Economic Consequences of an Aging Population*. Retirement Project Occasional Paper 6. The Urban Institute, Washington, DC.

Romer, P.M. (1990) Endogenous technological change. *Journal of Political Economy* 98: S71–S102.

Rosenbaum, J.E. (1976) *Making Inequality: The Hidden Curriculum of High School Tracking*. John Wiley, New York.

Rosenbaum, J.E. (2001) *Beyond College For All: Career Paths for the Forgotten Half*. New York: Russell Sage Foundation.

Rosenbaum, J.E., and Binder, A. (1997) Do employers really need more educated youth? *Sociology of Education* 70: 68–85.

Rosenbaum, J.E., and Jones, S.A. (2000) Interactions between high schools and labor markets. In Hallinan, M.T. (ed.), *Handbook of the Sociology of Education*. Kluwer, New York, chapter 18, pp. 411–36.

Rosenbaum, J.E., DeLuca, S., Miller, S.R., and Roy, K. (1999) Pathways into work: Short- and long-term effects of personal and institutional ties. *Sociology of Education* 72: 179–96.

Rosenbloom, J.L. (2002) *Looking for Work, Searching for Workers: American Labor Markets during Industrialization*. Cambridge Univesity Press, Cambridge.

Rothschild, J. (2000) Creating a just and democratic workplace: More engagement, less hierarchy. *Contemporary Sociology* 29: 195–213.

Rubinson, R., and Hurst, D. (1997) A college education for any and all. *Teachers College Record* 99: 62–5.

Ruhm, C.J. (1997) Is high school employment consumption or investment? *Journal of Labor Economics* 15: 735–76.

Rumberger, R.W. (1981) *Overeducation in the U.S. Labor Market.* Praeger. New York.

Rumberger, R.W. (1987) The impact of surplus schooling on productivity and earnings. *Journal of Human Resources* 22: 24–50.

Ruppert, S.S. (2001) *Where We Go from Here: State Legislative Views on Higher Education in the New Millennium.* Educational Systems Research, Littleton, CO.

Russell, H., and O'Connell, P.J. (2001) Getting a job in Europe: The transition from unemployment to work among young people in nine European countries. *Work, Employment and Society* 15: 1–24.

Ryan, P. (1988) Is apprenticeship better? A review of the economic evidence. *Journal of Vocational Education and Training* 50: 289–325.

Sabel, C.F. (1984) *Work and Politics.* Cambridge University Press, Cambridge.

Salzman, H., Moss, P., and Tilly, C. (1998) *New Corporate Landscape and Workforce Skills.* National Center for Postsecondary Improvement, Stanford University, Stanford.

Samuelson, P.A., Koopmans, T.C., and Stone, J.R.N. (1954) Report of the Evaluative Committee for *Econometrica*. *Econometrica* 22: 141–6.

Sayer, A., and Walker, R. (1992) *The New Social Economy: Reworking the Division of Labor.* Blackwell, Oxford.

Scherer, S. (2001) Early career patterns: A comparison of Great Britain and West Germany. *European Sociological Review* 17: 119–44.

Schill, W., McCartin, R., and Meyer, K. (1985) Youth employment: Its relationship to academic and family variables. *Journal of Vocational Behavior* 26: 155–63.

Schneider, B., and Stevenson, D. (1999) *The Ambitious Generation: America's Teenagers, Motivated but Directionless.* Yale University Press, New Haven.

Schultz, T.W. (1962) Investment in human beings. *Journal of Political Economy* 70: 1–8.

Schuman, H., Walsh, E., Olson, C., and Etheridge, B. (1985) Effort and reward: The assumption that college grades are affected by quantity of study. *Social Forces* 63: 945–66.

Scott, W.R. (1995) *Institutions and Organizations.* Sage, Thousand Oaks.

Secretary's Commission on Achieving Necessary Skills (1991) *What Work Requires of Schools.* United States Department of Labor, Washington, DC.

Secretary's Commission on Achieving Necessary Skills (1992a) *Learning a Living: A Blueprint for High Performance.* United States Department of Labor, Washington, DC.

Secretary's Commission on Achieving Necessary Skills (1992b). *Skills and Tasks for Jobs.* United States Department of Labor, Washington, DC.

234REFERENCES

3FERENCES

REFERENCES

Sewell, W.H., and Hauser, R.M. (1975) *Education, Occupation, and Earnings.* Academic Press, New York.

Shanahan, M.J., Elder, G.H. Jr., and Miech, R.A. (1997) History and agency in men's lives: Pathways to achievement in cohort perspective. *Sociology of Education* 70: 54–67.

Shanahan, M.J., Miech, R.A., and Elder, G.H. Jr. (1998) Changing pathways to attainment in men's lives: Historical patterns of school, work, and social class. *Social Forces* 77: 231–56.

Shavit, Y., and Blossfeld, H.-P. (eds.) (1993) *Persistent Inequality: Changing Educational Attainment in Thirteen Countries.* Westview Press, Boulder.

Shavit, Y., and Yuchtman-Yaar, E. (2001) Ethnicity, education, and other determinants of self-employment in Israel. *International Journal of Sociology* 31: 59–91.

Siegel, J.S. (2001) *Applied Demography Applications to Business, Government, Law, and Public Policy.* Academic Press, New York.

Sloane, P.J. (2002) *Much Ado about Nothing? What Does the Over-education Literature Really Tell Us?* Keynote Address at International Conference on Overeducation in Europe: What Do We Know? Berlin, Germany.

Smelser, N.J., Wilson, W.J., and Mitchell, F. (eds.) (2001) *America Becoming: Racial Trends and Their Consequences (Volumes 1 and 2).* National Academy Press, Washington, DC.

Smith, C.L., and Rowjewski, J.W. (1993) School-to-work transition: Alternative for educational reform. *Youth & Society* 25: 222–50.

Smith, J.P. (2001) Race and ethnicity in the labor market: Trends over the short and long term. In Smelser, N.J., Wilson, W.J., and Mitchell, F. (eds.), *America Becoming: Racial Trends and Their Conseuences, vol. 2.* National Academy Press, Washington, DC, chapter 4.

Smith, J.P., and Welch, F. (1981) No time to be young. *Population and Development Review* 7: 71–84.

Sommestad, L. (2000) *Education and Research in Times of Population Ageing.* Paper presented at the Informal Meeting of Ministers of Education and Research, Uppsala, March 2000.

Sorokin, P. (1927) *Social and Cultural Mobility.* Free Press, Glencoe, IL.

Spenner, K.I. (1983) Deciphering Prometheus: Temporal change in the skill level of work. *American Sociological Review* 48: 824–37.

Spenner, K.I. (1985) The upgrading and downgrading of occupations: Issues, evidence, and implications for education. *Review of Educational Research* 55: 125–54.

Spilerman, S., and Lunde, T. (1991) Features of educational attainment and job promotion prospects. *American Journal of Sociology* 97: 689–720.

Spilerman, S., and Petersen, T. (1999) Organizational structure, determinants of promotion, and gender differences in attainment. *Social Science Research* 28: 203–27.

Steel, L. (1991) Early work experience among white and non-white youths: Implications for subsequent enrollment and employment. *Youth and Society* 22: 419–47.

Steinberg, L., and Dornbusch, S.M. (1991) Negative correlates of part-time employment during adolescence: Replication and elaboration. *Developmental Psychology* 27: 304–13.

Stern, D., Finkelstein, N., Urquiola, M., and Cagampang, H. (1997) What difference does it make if school and work are connected? Evidence on co-operative education in the United States. *Economics of Education Review* 16: 213–29.

Stinchcombe, A.L. (1990) *Information and Organizations*. University of California Press, Berkeley.

Strathlee, R. (2001) Changes in social capital and school-to-work transitions. *Work, Employment and Society* 15: 311–26.

Streeck, W. (1989) Skills and the limits of neo-liberalism: The enterprise of the future as a place of learning. *Work, Employment and Society* 3: 90–104.

Suen, W., and Tam, M. (2000) Labor market crisis at mid-life: A report of the employment prospects of people aged 40–49. Unpublished manuscript, Hong Kong Institute of Economics and Business Strategy.

Szafran, R.F. (1996) The effect of occupational growth on labor force task characteristics. *Work and Occupations* 23: 54–86.

Tausky, C. (1984) *Work and Society: An Introduction to Industrial Sociology*. Peacock, Itasca, IL.

Terkel, S. (1997) *Working: People Talk About What They Do All Day and How They Feel About What They Do*. New Press, New York.

Theodore, N., and Weber, R. (2001) Changing work organization in small manufacturers: Challenges for economic development. *Economic Development Quarterly* 15: 367–79.

Thurow, L. (1975) *Generating Inequality*. Basic Books, New York.

Tilly, C. (1998) *Durable Inequality*. University of California Press, Berkeley.

Tilly, C. and Tilly, C. (1998) *Work Under Capitalism*. Westview Press, Boulder, CO.

Toder, E., and Solanski, S. (1999) *Effects of Demographic Trends on Labor Supply and Living Standards*. Retirement Project Occasional Paper 2. The Urban Institute, Washington, DC.

Trow, M. (1961) The second transformation of American secondary education. *International Journal of Comparative Sociology* 2: 144–66.

Turner, R.H. (1960) Sponsored and contest mobility and the school system. *American Sociological Review* 25: 855–67.

Twentieth Century Fund (1996) *No One Left Behind: The Report of the Twentieth Century Fund Task Force on Retraining America's Workforce*. Twentieth Century Fund, New York.

Tyack, D., and Cuban, L. (1995) *Tinkering Toward Utopia: A Century of Public School Reform*. Harvard University Press, Cambridge.

Tyler, J.H., Murnane, R.J., and Willette, J.B. (2000) Estimating the labor market signaling value of the GED. *Quarterly Journal of Economics* 65: 431–68.

United States Bureau of the Census (2001) *Population Change and Distribution*. Census brief, United States Bureau of the Census, Washington, DC.

United States Department of Labor (1999) *Report on the American Workforce.* United States Department of Labor, Washington, DC.

United States Department of Labor (2000) *Report on the Youth Labor Force.* US Department of Labor, Washington, DC.

United States Department of Labor (2001) Economic change and structures of classification. In *Report on the American Workforce.* US Department of Labor, Washington, DC, chapter 3.

United States Immigration and Naturalization Service (2003) *2001 Statistical Yearbook of the Immigration and Naturalization Service,* US Immigration and Naturalization Service, Washington, DC.

Urquiola, M., Stern, D., Horn, I., Dornsife, C., Chi, B., Williams, L., Merritt, E., Hughes, K., and Bailey, T. (1997) *School To Work, College and Career: A Review of Policy, Practice, and Results 1993–1997.* MDS-1144. National Center for Research in Vocational Education, University of California–Berkeley, Berkeley.

Useem, M. (1989) *Liberal Education and the Corporation: The Hiring and Advancement of College Graduates.* Aldine de Gruyter, New York.

Vallance, E. (1973) Hiding the hidden curriculum: An interpretation of the language of justification in nineteenth-century educational reform. *Curriculum Theory Network* 4: 5–21.

Vallas, S.P. (1990) The concept of skill: A critical review. *Work and Occupations* 17: 379–98.

Vallas, S.P. (1999) Rethinking Post-Fordism: The meaning of workplace flexibility. *Sociological Theory* 17: 68–101.

Van Ours, J.C., and Ridder, G. (1995) Job matching and job competition: Are lower educated workers at the back of job queues? *European Economic Review* 39: 1717–31.

Veum, J.R., and Weiss, A.B. (1993) Education and the work histories of young adults. *Monthly Labor Review* 116 (4): 11–20.

Vignoles, A., Green, R., and McIntosh, S. (2002) Overeducation: A tough nut to crack. *CentrePiece,* London School of Economics.

Vonnegut, K. (1961) Harrison Bergeron. *Fantasy and Science Fiction Magazine* 21, (reprinted in 1998 in *Welcome to the Monkeyhouse,* Delta Publishing, Addlestone, Surrey, UK).

Walters, P.B. (2000) The limits of growth: School expansion and school reform in historical perspective. In Hallinan, M.T. (ed.), *Handbook of the Sociology of Education.* Kluwer, New York, chapter 10, pp. 241–61.

Walters, P.B., and Rubinson, R. (1983) Educational expansion and economic output in the United States, 1890–1969. *American Sociological Review* 48: 480–93.

Warren, J.R. (2001) Changes with age in the process of occupational stratification. *Social Science Research* 30: 264–88.

Warren, J.R., and Forrest, E. (2001) *Trends in the Selectivity and Consequences of Adolescent Employment, 1966–1997.* Paper presented at the meetings of the International Sociological Association Research Committee on Social Stratification and Mobility, Berkeley, CA, August.

Webster, F. (1994) *Theories of the Information Society*. Routledge, London.

Weeden, K. (1998) *From Borders to Barriers: Strategies of Occupational Closure and the Structure of Occupational Rewards*. Paper presented at the Annual Meetings of the American Sociological Association, San Francisco. Weiner online at: http://www.backgroundbriefing.com/mcguffee.html

Wentling, R.M., and Waight, C.L. (2000) School and workplace initiatives and other factors that assist and support the successful school-to-work transition of minority youth. *Journal of Industrial Teacher Education* 37: 5–30.

Whitfield, K. (2000) High-performance workplaces, training, and the distribution of skills. *Industrial Relations* 39: 1–25.

Wieler, S.S., and Bailey, T.R. (1997) Going to scale: Employer participation in school-to-work programs at LaGuardia Community College. *Educational Evaluation and Policy Analysis* 19: 123–40.

Wilson, K. (2001) The determinants of educational attainment: Modeling and estimating the human capital model and education production functions. *Southern Economic Journal* 67: 518–51.

Wolniak, G. (2002) Defining and testing sorting hypotheses of schooling. Paper presented at the Annual Meetings of the American Sociological Association, Chicago, IL, August.

Wolpin, K.I. (1977) Education and screening. *American Economic Review* 67: 949–58.

Wright, R., and Jacobs, J. (1994) Male flight from computer work: A new look at occupational resegregation and ghettoization. *American Sociological Review* 59: 511–36.

Young, M. (1994 [originally published 1958]) *The Rise of the Meritocracy*. Transaction Publishers, Somerset.

Zemsky, R. (1998) Labor markets and educational restructuring. *Annals of the American Academy of Political and Social Sciences* 559: 77–90.

Zemsky, R., Shapiro, D., Iannozzi, M., Cappelli, P., and Bailey, T. (1998) *The Transition from Initial Education to Working Life in the United States of America*. NCPI Project Paper 1. A Report to the Organization for Economic Co-operation and Development (OECD) as part of a comparative study of transitions from initial education to working life in 14 member countries.) National Center for Postsecondary Improvement, Stanford University.

Zhou, M. (2001) Contemporary immigration and the dynamics of race and ethnicity. In Smelser, N.J., Wilson, W.J., and Mitchell, F. (eds.), *America Becoming: Racial Trends and Their Consequences, Volume 1*. National Academy Press, Washington, DC, chapter 7, pp. 200–42.

Zuboff, S. (1984) *In the Age of the Smart Machine: The Future of Work and Power*. Basic Books, New York.

Zuboff, S. (1996) Work in the United States in the Twentieth Century. In *Encyclopedia of the United States in the Twentieth Century*. Charles Scribner's Sons, New York, pp. 1091–127.

Name Index

Note: "n" after a page number indicates a note on that page.

Subject Index